I,
The Christ

I,
THE CHRIST

Dolores Pevehouse

for the evolving human spirit

HAMPTON ROADS
PUBLISHING COMPANY, INC.

Cover design by Grace Pedalino
Cover art by PhotoDisc

For information write:
Hampton Roads Publishing Company, Inc.
1125 Stoney Point Road
Charlottesville, VA 22902

Or call: 804-296-2772
FAX: 804-296-5096
e-mail: hrpc@hrpub.com
Web site: www.hrpub.com

If you are unable to order this book from your local bookseller, you may order directly from the publisher. Quantity discounts for organizations are available.
Call 1-800-766-8009, toll-free.
Library of Congress Catalog Card Number: 99-91423
ISBN 1-57174-177-1
10 9 8 7 6 5 4 3 2 1
Printed on acid-free paper in the United States

Dedication

To my dearest earthly Father, D. F. Pevehouse, who joined my Heavenly Father in 1985. He prayed daily for the publication of this material as he watched me every day, day after day, writing it; even though he had no idea what it was all about. And neither did I.

Acknowledgements

John Van Auken, who referred me to Hampton Roads as a possible publisher. John and I started discussing this work when he had a company that helped authors self-publish and has encouraged me over the years. He finally sent me a letter in February of 1997 suggesting Hampton Roads. It took me two years to see his suggestion as a positive one, rather than just another rejection.

Charlie Dungan, who insisted I query publishers the moment he discovered I had written a book. He is my beloved friend, an author in his own right, and a sculptor in clay. Best of all, he nurtures me in my darkest moments of doubt and anxiety.

My editor, Richard Leviton, whose suggestions were so superb that I knew I was working with a true genius of our time.

Frank DeMarco, who said "yes."

Priscilla and Gerardo who permitted me to observe their fifteen-year-old son to get an idea of how teenage Jewish boys behave when they are born brilliantly gifted.

Persons who first read the manuscript or parts of it: Billie Manck, Carmen Carroll, Susan Nickonic, Diane Fix, Charlie Dungan, John Van Auken, Jeanie Wall Collins, Lindsay Wagner, Dr. Gladys McGarey and members of her staff, Lyn Costaldo, Eileen Brown Eifred, Judith Stevens, Ken Skidmore, Ray Cooper, Holly and Lisa Blythe, Ten Speed Press, Hugh Lynn Cayce, who encouraged me to write it, and others, all of whom gave me feedback or encouragement.

William Fix, who encouraged me not to self-publish, but to wait.

Table of Contents

Chapter 1

The Journal

In my twenty-eighth year at the School for Initiates in Giza, I, Yeshua the Nazarene, have received my final task. I am assigned, as were all other Initiates before me, to write a journal about my life. My instructions are to begin with an event that stands out boldly in my memory, write extensively about it, then cover all that I can remember of events, people, feelings, places, thoughts, philosophies, everything large and small that has influenced me as I have grown into manhood. It is an overwhelming task, but required before I can take my final initiation into my chosen mission for my life on Earth.

As I sit here totally isolated in a cell that contains only a small table, a chair, a large jar filled with writing fluid, many sharpened quills, and an urn of empty papyrus scrolls, I ponder just how and where to begin. The assignment is awesome, for it is to be read by the high priest of Osiris, made available to all my masters, and used to determine if I am to be allowed the final rite of passage.

So I begin this journal with much fear and trembling. I hope I do not completely undo myself for being full of truth and honesty, characteristics instilled in me from my earliest days by both my father and mother.

What stands out most boldly in my remembrances is my twelfth year when I went to Jerusalem with my parents and became separated from them. That single event seems to divide my life from the years of my childhood and those of my manhood, signaling that henceforth nothing would ever again be the same.

As was the custom every year, my parents went to Jerusalem for the feast of the Passover. In my twelfth year, they included my bar mitzvah, a passing from childhood to manhood, according to the interpretations by the doctors of the law of the commands of Moses, our lawgiver. It was a most solemn event, for no longer would I be treated as a child or speak as a child, but henceforth would be expected to take on the responsibilities as well as the rights of a man. I could not imagine a greater event and so had looked forward eagerly to that day of reckoning.

However, as solemn as this anticipated rite was, it failed to match the event that stands out so boldly in my memory–the one that lifted me out of the physical into the spiritual.

Becoming entranced with the many contradictions of the priests, rabbis, and doctors of the law who stood arguing in the area of the Temple grounds reserved for men only, I failed to notice that my family had left without me. In fact, it was nightfall before I noticed. The blowing of the ram's horn alerted me to the closing of the Gate Beautiful. Then I realized I was probably trapped inside the Temple walls for the night.

The old rabbi who was explaining things to me was of the Essene sect, as were my parents, and I was immersed in his great teachings when I heard the horn blow. Rabbi Jochanim was my cousin Yochanan's uncle on his mother's side of the family. He was in great mourning over the recent death of his sister, Elisheva, Yochanan's mother. Jochanim was the one who helped Elisheva and Yochanan escape into the desert after Yochanan's father, Zekharyah, was murdered while holding onto the Horns of Refuge in the holy of holies almost thirteen years before.

Yochanan, my cousin three times removed, and his mother had lived in the wilderness all those years to escape being murdered also, for soon after I was born, King Herod had ordered all babies under the age of two to be killed for some reason or other.

Although my mother, Miryam, was quite good about answering most of my questions, both she and my father, Yosef, seemed to grow mysteriously silent when I asked about certain things. The rabbi in our village of Nazareth was also very good about answering my most probing questions and had even gone into some interesting information about my private parts shortly before we came to Jerusalem that year. I was fascinated to learn that creation, justification, and elimination could be centered in such a small part of me. So when the rabbi suggested I take particularly good care of that part, I could certainly see why.

I determined that just to be safe, I would keep that crucial part of me hidden from prying eyes of all sorts at all times. When I mentioned it to Yochanan, he was just as eager as I to be extra careful. The cutting at the rite of passage almost did us in, however. I will never forget it.

It was a continuation of the explanation of this particular part of me with Jochanim that had so fascinated me that I lost track of time and our caravan left without me. He had been explaining to me that the Essene sect as a group had reached the same conclusion that I had about this mysterious private part and therefore never married, whose joining ritual included a necessary exposure.

Most of the Essenes put that kind of energy into other areas of creation. Even so, some did marry in order to have children when required, such as my parents. Most of the Essenes, however, were dedicated to healing, growing plants one could eat, and other productive activities such as copying ancient writings or building things of wood, as my father, Yosef, did. Yochanan's father, Zekharyah, had followed the tradition of at least one Essene following the line of work of the Levites, becoming a priest and remaining in the Temple in Jerusalem. This was a very courageous thing to do.

Essenes remained content to have "converts" for children, except for cases like Yochanan and me. So, I became interested in the school they had created at Mt. Carmel for not only the children of the Essenes who did marry, but also those that were sent to them by God, which is how they looked upon all unfortunates such as orphans, strays, and runaways. According to Jochanim, the school had become famous and even the wealthy sent their children to school there in order to better prepare them for schooling in faraway places such as Egypt, where all the best advanced schools were located.

My mother had even talked about sending me to that school at Mt. Carmel and Yosef had agreed with her, claiming they both had gone to school there years before and that was where they had met and were married. I was a little surprised to learn they met and were married at a place where the members never married.

Therefore, I was fascinated to find someone who knew so much about the things that interested me so much and was willing to explain it all to one so young as I. I had been about to ask Jochanim for more details on the murdering of all the young children of Judea when I heard the blowing of the ram's horn that signaled the closing of the gates. I jumped up and ran as fast as I could, hoping to get through them before they closed tight, but alas, I was too late.

The great doors slammed shut and all of my weeping and wailing did not move the guards one bit. They laughed hard at me, pointed their fingers at me, and shouted words that haunt me to this day, "Look, look at the boy so soon a man only to crash back into childhood the moment he finds his hopes dashed."

I was completely undone. I realized how foolish I must look to them, so I cleared my eyes, managed a smile, and declared that it was really unimportant because I had a relative I could visit until the new dawn. Believing I had managed to retrieve some of my dignity as a newly designated man, I stalked away from their continued mirth that was so full of derision.

Nevertheless, I was appalled that I had allowed myself to be trapped inside the Temple walls, and worry my parents as to my whereabouts. I knew they would not realize I was missing until they made camp for the night, a full day's journey from Jerusalem. That was small comfort, since there was no way I could get out of the Temple grounds and catch up with them until the new dawn.

I rushed back to find Jochanim in hopes he could help me out, but he was gone. He probably assumed I had made it through the gates in time and retreated to his usual place somewhere on the Temple grounds, quite unknown to me.

What to do, I pondered, as I sat down on a Temple bench and watched the last rays of the sun as they danced along the golden archways of the fast-shut gates. In my childhood mind I wondered how I had gotten into such a predicament and started to search for solutions. Whereas problems had always been worth a thought or two, solutions were what I worked on most of the time. It is still my great desire.

I considered finding the holy women who stayed inside the Temple grounds day and night praying and waiting for the Mashiyah to appear. Even as they believed that long-prophesied messenger from YHWH would appear on the Temple grounds, they also accepted that a lost boy hungry for food could be the Hallowed One. They always helped lost boys with kind words and bites of food, knowing that boys are always hungry, even a young Mashiyah.

I dismissed that solution to my problem, however, since I had just recently achieved my manhood and did not want to revert so soon to childish things. Especially since I had made such a fool of myself at the Temple gates. But, it did tempt me greatly to seek the safety and security of those holy women as darkness descended on the glow of a magically sunlit sky.

Even now, at the end of my studies in my twenty-eighth year, I can still remember how alone and fearful I felt as I sat there wondering what to do, where to go for the night, and how worried my parents would be.

I wandered about the Temple, which was much like a small city. It had recently been rebuilt by King Herod the Great and boasted sixteen Corinthian columns, the tallest of which was 100 feet high. The Temple stood within a series of courts and was built of great stones, massively grand.

The men of Israel have always believed themselves to be special and the Temple reflected that specialness. The court of the men of Israel, which I had so lately entered for the first time in my life, was separate from the court of the women. And the court of the Gentiles was separate from them both.

The long, narrow court of Israel, where only Jewish men gathered to worship, was separated from the court of the priests by a rail atop a row of small columns. Only priests and Levites could enter the court of the priests. In the center of that court was the great horned altar of sacrifices, where Zekharyah had been murdered.

Dominating the entire complex was the majestic sanctuary itself, which stood at the rear of the court of priests. The sanctuary was built of perfectly fitted white marble stones covered with plates of gold. The separateness of Israel from all others, as commanded by YHWH to our father, Abraham, was clearly built into the great Temple complex.

As the rays of the setting sun struck the golden dome of the sanctuary, the light was blinding. Just as I shielded my eyes from the flashing brilliance, I heard a voice cry out. "Yeshua, thou son of God, why stand you here gaping and hiding when there is great work to be done?"

Quickly I looked around and saw Yochanan, standing aloof in all the glory only a thirteen-year-old can create. My blessed, beloved Yochanan was with me. I almost fell at his feet and kissed them I was so glad to see him. Yet, with great restraint I managed to resist and respond, "I gape at the marvelousness of you Levites who can copy the splendor of Solomon without the blessings of his wisdom," I grinned.

Of course my cousin was not fooled by my play at casualness. He knew I was beginning to panic at my plight, but he graciously ignored the crack in my voice, the squeak in my vocal cords, and the knock in my knees.

"What a banquet I have for the Star of Bethlehem," he exclaimed as he twitted me concerning my birth in a manger in Bethlehem and brought out fresh figs and bread from his basket.

Since my father was from the ancient house of Judah, my family had been required to travel to Bethlehem for the taking of the census about the time of my birth. No one was excused. My birth and a comet that regularly made an appearance every few thousand years had coincided at the city of David, and gave my arrival an air of mystery. I learned about the comet while pursuing my studies of the stars in Persia, or perhaps it was while studying in Tibet. I am not sure. But it was years later. At the time in the Temple grounds, however, I was the hapless victim of Yochanan's teasing, which came from a special significance attached to my birth and discussed among the Essenes. He had told me about it at first in his twitting way. Seeing my consternation at such things, Yochanan continues to this day with his slippery comments, claiming to know more about me than I know about myself.

Yet, I loved him with all my heart. He was a fearless boy of the wilderness and made the most of it, while I was often hesitant and sought to seek solitude as a place of refuge from people, places, and things.

As boys will do, we hungrily devoured every bite of food before I thought to ask him how he had gotten back into the Temple grounds with the gates closed. Ever true to himself, this strange boy of the desert just gave me a knowing look as if only an idiot could be stopped by high walls, ironbound gates, or guards.

"Yochanan," I pled, "I must get out of here and catch up with my parents' caravan. You must help me and come with me, also."

"Getting in is no problem," he replied. "Getting out is impossible." He ducked his head to prevent me from seeing the gleam in his eye.

I glanced at my cousin as he sat munching. I can still see his rough clothes made from the skins of animals he trapped in the desert. Most Essenes refused to wear anything but cloth because they ate only vegetables or fruit or other growing things. They ate nothing that had life, nothing that they would have to kill to eat.

Yochanan maintained that YHWH had given all the Earth for man to subdue and use and explained that if he were to sleep in the desert on the cold ground of sand and rocks, he must be clad in the skins of animals who did so comfortably. "They gladly give me the coats off their backs," he would say slyly, staring at me to see if I accepted his explanations.

To this day I am not sure who is right, Yochanan or the other Essenes. But all I could say then was "Hmmmm, maybe you are right."

Yochanan was always the practical one. He had gone for food when he saw I was engrossed with his Uncle Jochanim's stories. My cousin accused me of being a dreamer.

"You are a novice about life, an innocent about evil, and a bit of a boor on religion," he declared, direct as always. Never one to circle a problem, he, too, cared more for solutions.

"Stop talking about it all and do something," he demanded without ever a hesitation that I might not know what to do.

Suddenly, I realized Yochanan had a plan. He wanted me to talk to someone well known who had been a friend of his father's. According to Yochanan, he only came to the Temple once in a great while those days and was due at dawn the very next morning.

"You will never regret having heard him, Yeshua, I promise," Yochanan urged. "He speaks as no man ever has or ever will. It is thought that he might be the Teacher of Righteousness, who founded the Essenes over two hundred years ago to save the Jerusalem priests from their many sins."

I knew I was lost. My secretive cousin was about to educate me while I merely talked about education. My heart sank. What would my parents think of me? I worried. And well that I worried, for as time would show, they not only worried, they became frantic with fear. They asked each other over and over the question all parents do: Why had they been so careless as not to check and see if their boy was with them? They quite forgot that on that very day, I became a man, according to Jewish law.

But, for that moment, I just followed Yochanan meekly into a corner of the court of women that no one ever bothered with because the court was for women, who mattered not at all to God, or so they believed. Women were only a little above Gentiles, who were less than human. Because the court was for women and children only it was unimportant to the priests and rabbis and high officials.

The corner Yochanan chose was a snug place, just right for two teenagers to curl up into the night out of everyone's way. It was in a giant old terebinth tree gnarled with age. A long ago strike by lightning, followed by insects, had carved a perfectly sheltered spot into the base of the tree. As we wrapped ourselves with our robes and breathed the faint scent of leaves and grasses, we fell asleep, slumbering deeply until dawn.

About half an hour before the new day filled with light, the birds began a furious chorus that awakened both Yochanan and me. The terebinth tree that seemed to lean against the wall was crowded with the two of us, so I moved out of the nest and gazed up into the branches. It was loaded with birds: they had slept peacefully through the night above us, but now had suddenly become an anthill of activity and chatter.

"Quick!" I shouted, as the first bird dropping hit my head and I yanked Yochanan out of the way. Too late, he too caught a dropping on his woolly mane of hair. We had a good laugh over our early anointing, snatched his remaining parcels and hungrily searched for scraps of food we might have left the night before. Finding only a hunk of bread, we devoured it and searched for the basins of water set out for dusty travelers to purify themselves before approaching the altars of sacrifice. A drink of water, while not as satisfying as food, was better than nothing.

Slapping the cold water on our faces and hands, we both were filled with the joysprings of youth, a kind of excitement over life in general and new experiences in particular. I had grown anxious about hearing this Hillel that Yochanan had talked about so fervently. The venerable rabbi was a patriarch after the old ways of

Israel who counted each disciple as a child not only of his, but also of YHWH. Yochanan said he referred to himself only as a light shining in the darkness of man, but talked about one who was yet to come who would be the Light of the World. My excitement grew.

Gone from my head were my worryings about my parents. Hearing so famous a teacher must take precedence. It was as though my parents had never existed and I was on a path they could not share. Little did I know how much my mother already shared my path. But at that moment she was far from my thoughts.

"Where did you say he would be?" I asked Yochanan for about the third time.

He was as excited as I, so he carefully repeated that the great Hillel sat in the court of the Gentiles because he wanted anyone that YHWH might send, whether Hebrew or not, to be able to see the coming Light. In fact, Yochanan said that Hillel had many "converts" among his followers who had never known about YHWH at all. These "little ones," as he called them, were given extra teachings lest they fall away in a time of trial.

I was trembling with excitement as Yochanan and I worked our way toward the court of the Gentiles. I heard the blowing of the ram's horn that opened the great gates just as the sun tipped over the edge of night. I shivered from the chill of the morning air. It was a glorious dawn fit for drinking fully from the waters of knowledge that flowed from the throne of YHWH. And I, Yeshua of Nazareth, planned to drink deeply.

I can still see Yochanan as he marched along just a step ahead of me, his fierce mane of hair flowing down his back like many snakes snarled in loops and rounds. Early worshippers stepped aside for him as though he were a prince instead of a semiwild boy fresh from the southern desert of Judea. Even at thirteen years he had the steady eye of purpose and the stride of a man of mission.

"I will be the harbinger," he would say to me, "for there is one coming after me whose very shoes I am unfit to latch."

I always scoffed at this show of humbleness from my otherwise brash cousin who thought it nothing to raid a nest of bees, steal their honey, jeer at the Temple priests, or criticize the king. Nevertheless, it gave me pause for him to be so circumspect in an otherwise howling storm. The early stirrings of prophecy already surrounded him like a mist rising from the desert floor. His pale blue eyes seemed to sparkle like the sunlit waters of the Great Sea when he would wonder aloud at his mission.

"Wild eyes," the scribes murmured behind his back as they whispered one to another concerning Yochanan's right to be a Levite priest as his father before him had been. But they need not have worried. Temple ritual was form without substance to my glorious cousin who clearly thought priestly robes would wrap worse than chains around his hard, lean body.

His animal skins that hung like loosely woven threads from his broad but bony shoulders were his only raiment, and he wore them with a kind of magnificence.

"They were my friends, and they gladly gave me the coats off their backs," he would declare over and over in mock humility as he shifted the skins into a more comfortable drape and winked at me, almost running just to keep a few steps behind him.

Again, his humbleness when he talked about his mission always threw me off guard only to be snagged upon his cutting wit. Like all Essenes, Yochanan was expecting the Mashiyah. But Yochanan's expectancy had a sense of urgency that seemed to announce the blessed event was just around the next corner and he was hurrying to be on time. He believed that the Holy One would never appear at Herod's Temple built to glorify Herod, but would rise out of the wilderness, stark and alone like a juniper tree. He would shine like a daystar in a cloudless sky, like the sun at high noon or the full moon of harvest, so bright would be his light.

"Adon Mashich Cumi," he would shout across the hills. "Come, Mashiyah, arise. Lord Mashiyah arise," he would chant, willing the Anointed One to come in our time. . . .

The Essenes had set themselves apart as a holy people for this very purpose. The belief that YHWH sent blessings only to those who prepared and stayed awake expectantly for them was strong in the Essene sect, but mighty in my cousin. Whereas each one constantly purified himself and renewed daily his willingness to be a perfect channel, Yochanan emptied himself of all that was not divine. My own mother and father were accepting and had the air of expectancy about them as devoted, loyal Essenes. Yet, Yochanan seemed above them all. I cannot recall a time when it was not so.

This morning I eagerly followed my beloved cousin to the spot where the great Hillel had announced he would be on this day.

"What will he be talking about?" I asked Yochanan.

"My favorite subject," he replied, and I could not resist the opportunity to twit him a bit.

"You?" I feigned surprise.

Yochanan stopped dead in his tracks. It was so sudden that I fell headlong into his array of skins and hair and body. As I quickly pulled myself back and stared into his eyes, those glaring pools of cerulean water that now were like daggers of smoking ice, I could feel the wrath rising with his seething temper.

"Yeshua," he spoke very slowly, "do not ever tease a man about the thing dearest to his heart."

I begged for his forgiveness and promised never to twit him again. I said I just had not realized that Yochanan had already put his hand to the plow and would never again look back. My remorse would have overcome me, I am sure, if the great Hillel had not suddenly appeared.

My mouth dropped open as I saw that stunning figure silvery from his shining head to his delicate toes. He moved like the wind blowing gently through a field of ripened wheat. His silver hair was wispy as it framed a face of pure light. His robe and mantle were like the shimmering snows of Tibet. For a moment I thought the fabled Saoshyant of Persia had found his way to Jerusalem. I felt Yochanan's hand under my chin, closing my gaping mouth.

"He's beautiful," I whispered.

"You are seeing his soul, Yeshua," replied my cousin and best friend, matter-of-factly.

I blinked several times, but there was no escaping the vision before me. I knew that I was about to hear the holy words of YHWH in an audible voice from a live man, a rabbi of great report, who was revered by everyone without question. I could not believe my good fortune, but here it was right in front of me. Thanks to YHWH, I could clearly see this truth.

"They say," began the blessed rabbi, as he took his accustomed place among the gathered students and disciples, "that Adonai is hidden away in a holy mountain, hiding in the holy of holies behind a veil, unseen in a cloud and inaccessible to man. But, I tell you it is not so. Adonai stands at the gate of your heart and knocks for admittance, refusing to come in uninvited. And if you will but open your heartstrings, Adonai will come in to you and sup with you, and you with Adonai."

"When will this be?" queried a disciple. "In an afterlife?"

"If not now, then when?" answered the sage. "It is written that 'Today is the Day of Adon.' Now is the time to see the face of YHWH," he barely whispered the sacred letters.

"But is it not also written that if we look on the face of God, we shall surely die?" pursued the young disciple, puzzlement written all over his face at this seeming contradiction.

"The pure in heart shall see God, and live," responded Hillel.

I could not help but marvel at his words. I could feel the Temple priests screaming over this usurpation of their place among the people as intercessors to YHWH. It became clear why the great rabbi taught in the court of the Gentiles. No wonder Yochanan, a rebel himself, loved him so. The simplicity was that of Socrates of Greece, the purity of Zoroaster of Persia, the enlightenment of Gautama Buddha of India. Who would ever have believed that such a learned rabbi would even permit such a question, much less give such an answer, so obviously in direct conflict with all we Jews had ever been taught?

But I did not know about all those other messengers from God in those days. I had no idea they had been appearing to man for centuries in many places. And it is only now, as I complete my initiation in this land of Egypt that I can see the same message coming down through the centuries, clear and shining and unchanging, falling like sparkling waters from the lips of perfect channels sent by YHWH, the All of the Universe, to man, His most perfect creation.

This truth has always been denied by man by substituting rituals, intercessors, and vain words for self pleasures, only to rise again from eon to eon in the person of a simple man completing the promises of YHWH to the creations of the All.

Like a blazing light full of sound for the seeing eye and the hungry ear, a precious jewel for the treasure chest of the hunter, the truth survives. Yet, there have been many dark days in the lives of men in which this marvelous light dimmed, seeming to flicker and be lost forever. Yet, it survives and grows, waiting for another willing servant to take up the challenge.

This event, this moment of truth, this revelation from an ancient but honored Jewish teacher, already perched on the edge of eternity, was the most staggering moment of my life. It was then and there that I realized beyond any doubt what my mission must be about, even as it had been that of Gautama Buddha five hundred years before me, Zoroaster six hundred years before me, Moses twelve hundred years before me and last but not least, Abraham, who arose from his safe place and honored position in Ur of the Chaldees to do the perfect will of God.

Although years ago I probably was not so completely aware of the path I must travel as I am now, I felt intensely what I must be about during that singular moment experienced in the courtyard of the Gentiles in the Temple at Jerusalem in Judea, Palestine, when I was only a boy of twelve. And I still feel so, just as intensely.

Recalling that crispy morning with Yochanan, which was so powerful in my life, brings back floods of recollections. Many of them remain vividly woven into the fabric of my being. Thus, I begin my story about my life, which never again was normal, safe, secure, or even precious to me.

Yochanan and I sat all day long at the feet of this wondrous teacher. Even when we grew hungry as boys always do, we somehow felt nourished and full the moment Rabbi Hillel gave us a new idea. At the end of the day, he finally closed the class amidst many protests. Although he was obviously weary, he did one more astonishing thing.

He moved slowly toward my cousin and me, never once taking his eyes off me. "Who is this young man you have brought with you today, Yochanan?" he asked.

Suddenly, I perceived that Hillel and Yochanan were much closer than I had realized, and that I must have been under discussion at some prior time. Bold, brash Yochanan seemed to wilt into a nearby tree with overwhelming humbleness. He spoke just above a whisper, as though he were in the presence of YHWH.

"This is my cousin from Nazareth, Master, the one born in Bethlehem."

I half expected him to add "the Star," but he did not. He merely stood quietly waiting for the venerable teacher to respond, which Hillel did after a few minutes of thought.

"Ahh, yes, that is who I thought he must be," mused the rabbi, half to himself as he looked at me from the top of my head to my sandal-clad feet, from my raw worsted tunic to my orange-colored hair. I stared openly at my own dusty feet, not daring to lift my eyes to his lest I fall face down and commit the unpardonable sin of worshipping a man. I shifted uncomfortably.

Suddenly, I could hear every sound in the courtyard, the bleating of sheep, the cooing of doves, the songbirds in the trees, even the rough-talking men from faraway places. Everything needed for sacrifice was moving about, as well as the moneychangers calling out the value of their Temple coins to the visitors, newly arrived from faraway places. The barter going on between the moneychangers and their hapless victims rose above the clamor, and I began to tremble with something akin to rage. How dare they do this in the House of Adonai?

Yet, I calmed myself as I realized that Yochanan and Hillel had discussed my place of birth. Even though I had been trained since birth never to ask a question of my elders without permission, I desperately wanted to ask, "Why me?" I stayed my tongue and focused on the discussion going on about me between Yochanan and Hillel, as though I were not there. It seemed hours went by before the great rabbi turned those marvelous eyes back to me and spoke to me for the first time.

"So, you are Yeshua of Nazareth?" he stated more than asked.

"He even knows my name, shortened by my mother from Yeheshua while I was yet in the cradle," I gasped to myself as I spoke softly, "I am, Great Rabbi," whispering in my awe that he spoke to me at all.

"You are to dine with me at my house; you two young men must be faint with hunger," said Hillel.

I almost swooned. I did feel faint, but not from hunger. I was taken aback to have such a grand invitation from so famous a teacher. Out of my mind flew any thoughts about my dear parents, who were surely frantically looking for me by now.

We went quickly and gladly to the home of this man who honored us so, feasting us in body and soul for the next two days and nights. It was only on the third morning that Hillel asked me quite gently, "Do you have a mother and father, Yeshua?"

My guilt at having forgotten the dearest people in my whole life flowed through my body, bringing the blood rushing to my face. How could they have slipped from my mind? I was aghast at such a grievous omission of manners and turned my anxious face to Hillel. He was moved by my obvious pain and quickly soothed me. "You must be about your work, Yeshua. Your life is no longer your own. It has never belonged to your parents. It belongs to YHWH."

Those simple words put my soul at rest as we walked from Hillel's home back to the Temple. As students and disciples ran to greet the master teacher, I saw my mother and Yosef running toward me. Their faces were filled with fear and anxiety and even anger. I could read all those emotions clearly and my heart sank.

"Yeshua," cried my mother. "We have searched for you the past three days. Where have you been? Did you not know we would be anxious about you? How could you be so thoughtless? Have we taught you nothing?" Later I realized her heart was clutched in fear for my safety. Her tears showed this even as she tried to be stern with me.

I steadied myself and repeated Hillel's words to them about me, "Know you not that I must be about my Father's business?" I turned to introduce my parents to Hillel, but he was gone. I looked about for Yochanan, anxious to have someone back up my story. He, too, had disappeared, leaving me alone with my gentle but anxious parents.

Yosef, angry at my having been so cool to my mother, said, "Are you unaware that my business is in Nazareth, Yeshua?" He spoke through tight lips in a voice I had seldom ever heard. It was gruff and strained and even a little haughty. His long dark hair and shaggy eyebrows seemed to enlarge over his squinting deep brown eyes. He must have added an extra foot to his height somewhere, for he seemed much taller, and heavier. I shrank into what I hoped was a tiny ball, but steadfastly responded, "Not your work, Yosef," hoping it sounded man to man. "My Father in Heaven's work, the great All to whom I have been committed since before my birth. That is the Father of whom I speak."

My mother visibly sagged as she leaned against Yosef. Her sweet mouth let out a soft moan as her eyes filled with tears once more. She seemed to grow even smaller than her normal diminutive size as she pulled her mantle closer about her raven hair and closed her gray eyes. "Oh, oh, oh," was all she could murmur.

Clearly, Yosef was not about to permit this fuzz of a boy to devastate his beloved. He slapped my face and told me to hold my tongue. "Can you not see that your mother is on the verge of death?" he raged.

I didn't feel the slap, for I could clearly see into her soul and knew she shared my life enough to know the time she had always feared had arrived. She must let me go, and even be glad the prayers of her youth had been answered, although it was the same prayer every other young girl of Judah always prayed. She put her hand on Yosef's arm and softly chided him for his great love for her. "Our son was lost, but now he is found. Let us go home to Nazareth."

Yosef softened and apologized to me for the slap, explaining he had lost his reason. I understood and denied it had been anything at all if not deserved by so unthinking and inconsiderate a boy. The usual protestations went back and forth between this beloved man and I until all seemed right and we moved toward the gates of the Temple grounds on our way home, arm in arm across my mother, enclosing her between the two men who loved her best.

Chapter 2

Hillel

I went with my parents, heading back to Nazareth to ponder all that I had learned from Hillel. I wanted to savor his every word, for not an idle one had fallen from his lips the three days we spent with him. I was not worried about what happened to Yochanan, for I knew that if he sat at the feet of the great Hillel, he was now feasting at the banquet table of YHWH.

The three of us threaded our way out of the Temple courtyard into the streets of Jerusalem. We walked along silently for a while. I could almost hear my mother turning my abrupt words over and over in her mind. I glanced over at her and saw her brow knitting in a most perplexed frown, unlike her usual serene countenance. Yosef, as always, was accepting the events as God's will in our lives. Steady as a rock, he had the look of a father whose son had asserted his manhood for the first time and been found acceptable by all who knew him. Except my mother, of course, who failed to understand men at all.

Yosef was a true Essene who believed there were no accidents or coincidences in life, that everything was in accordance with a divine plan created by the great All. He indulged my mother, however, as he always did, even when she worried, even though Essenes considered worry a lack of faith. Yosef had perfect faith, an example I wanted to follow in all things. Of all my teachers through the years, he probably was the finest, for he said little but set examples I could hardly miss. I had walked in his footsteps all of my twelve years, or at least had tried.

I gazed at my mother as she trudged across the rolling hills. Her long hair was graying even at her relatively young age of twenty-seven.

She brushed the hair out of her face as a light westerly wind kept blowing it across her finely sculpted nose. Her sandals kept picking up sand and small rocks, and she absent-mindedly shuffled to drain them from under her feet. The grit that blew across her face seemed to set her teeth on edge as she concentrated on her thoughts in an effort not to show how uneasy she was with me.

My heart went out to her and I felt guilty at all the trouble I had caused both my parents. They were not young anymore, especially Yosef, who was almost twenty years older than my mother. He had been more father than husband to both my mother and me, it seemed. A protector of us as though some vague evil were about and could harm us should he ever let down his guard.

Yosef was a fine figure of a man in his own rough-hewn way, like a block of granite carved from a mountain of stone. His constant happiness at being married to my mother always brought such warmth to my heart, as though nothing in the world could penetrate the safety he had built into our lives. Like the presence of the great All, Yosef was always there for us.

His large, rough hands made the finest pieces of wooden implements for households all over Galilee; some were even sent all the way to Judea and beyond. Some of his pieces were intricately carved works of art that often could be found in faraway marketplaces, while others were simple. Ever practical, he took pride in working intricacies into usable items. He had lovingly taught me the value of working with my hands, and it had been assumed that I would follow him in his busy carpenter's shop. My announcement to my parents must have broken his heart, but he said not a word again about it, ever.

I searched my mind for a way to make them happy with me. Perhaps, I thought, I could tell them about my three days in Jerusalem. My mother was not allowed into the inner courts of the Temple because she was a woman. And Yosef refused to go anywhere she could not. Because of this, I decided early in life that my career as a rabbi would be spent in the court of the Gentiles or on a hillside or by the sea, away from all rigid separations of people. Like Hillel, I wanted everyone who chose to hear me to be able to do so without interferences of any kind, especially separations.

It seemed to me even then that a message from YHWH was surely for all creatures, not just a select few. God comes to man and woman alike, I believed; it is the spirit that hears, or is deaf. And spirit is neither male nor female. This fact, while vague in my early years, grew much more pronounced as I traveled the world during my studies. Yet, it never was anything any of my teachers actually said, except maybe for Hillel.

"I met this most wonderful rabbi while I was in the Temple," I began, tentatively lest either parent frown on my speaking at all after such a stunning rejection of their plans for my life.

My mother turned her clear gray eyes from the distant Ascent of Lebonah and rested them on me. Noticing my anxious look, her face softened and a quick little smile flashed across her full mouth.

"Did you?" she responded.

"Oh, yes," I continued enthusiastically, knowing that I had been forgiven. "His name was Hillel and he is quite famous. He invited Yochanan and me to his house."

Miryam and Yosef gasped. Everyone knew of Hillel, for his fame spread beyond Judea into all of Palestine and beyond. He was reported to be the greatest rabbi in all the world and headed a school of thought that often was at odds with the officials of the Temple. His students were the best trained, the most thoroughly indoctrinated in the ancient writings, and the ones most sought after for their wisdom in the traditions. My parents looked at me as though I had lost my mind and were sailing somewhere on another sea.

My astonished mother inquired, "You mean he actually spoke to you, personally?"

"For all three days past," I replied, proud now that I had said something to get their complete attention, even if not in a most friendly way.

"Yochanan seems to know him very well, and it was he who brought me to this great rabbi's circle. Listening to such a famous rabbi caused me to forget my obedience to you; he was so awe inspiring, full of wisdom and truth." Whereas I hardly ever blamed anyone else for my lack of judgment, I was anxious to give an explanation that would satisfy their worries.

I rushed on to explain why I had not come running the moment the Temple gates had opened the next morning at dawn.

"You mean he talked to you in a lesson as he does to all his circle of students and disciples?" questioned Yosef.

"Yes, that too, but also for the whole three days alone with Yochanan while you were searching for me," I hastened to assure them.

Their look at me in utter disbelief stabbed me in my heart and I felt undone. The fame of Hillel was such that everyone knew he counted his time as precious and never, ever gave unlimited time to anyone, not even the high priest. He had stopped taking private students long ago and therefore my claims must simply be an outrageous lie.

However, my parents were gentle people. Yosef began in a kindly voice, one reserved for idiots and imbeciles.

"Yeshua, the great Hillel would not waste his time on a mere boy, especially one from Galilee. Please do not tease your mother with such a fine story. We forgive your one lapse of obedience to our wishes for the first time in your entire life and know it will not happen again."

As usual, my dear father would never call me a scheming, lying boy that ought to have a thrashing. It was not his way to harm a living thing with even a harsh word, and I fear his loss of control that caused the slap would probably haunt him all of his days. However, the one thing in all the world that could cause such a lapse was my mother's feelings. No one, not even her beloved first son, was allowed to torment her gentle, sensitive soul.

Yosef's balance between protecting my mother and urging me to speak only truth was a harmony of balance that has guided me all of my young life, even up to this very day. And only now can I appreciate it to its fullest.

"B-b-but it is all true," I stammered. "I would not say it, if it were not so."

That was enough for my mother. She put her hand lovingly on the sleeve of Yosef's coat. Let the mountains move to the sea, the deserts flood with water, or the stars fall on Israel, a touch from my mother soothed even the tempest of a stormy night. And so it did my blessed father.

"Let him tell us about it," she murmured softly.

I began my story by telling about a meeting Yochanan and I had with a Sadducee. A look of shock crossed my mother's face, because that sect was thought to be the furthest from YHWH of any group.

They did not believe in eternal life. Whereas Essenes never questioned that a just and merciful God constantly renews the life of the created, the Sadducees claimed only YHWH has life everlasting.

Essenes believe that YHWH created man and gave him every chance at gaining perfection lifetime after lifetime. Salvation is viewed as gaining at-one-ment with God, referred to as atonement. It was unacceptable that God would give man only one chance at achieving perfection; therefore they worked long and hard at purifying the soul through many washings of the body and fasting and prayer. They teach in their school that the soul never dies; only the body that holds the soul dies. Resurrection of the soul into many lifetimes on its way to perfecting it in God seemed an appropriate idea to me.

Sadducees argue that if the soul had more than one life, it would remember at least one of the prior lives. They had no idea that the rejection of life after life guaranteed no memory of any other lifetime. Rejection throws up a wall that only acceptance can tear down.

On the other hand, Pharisees believe in the eternal life of man, but claim it is all a mystery and man is not supposed to know about such things as the mysterious ways of YHWH.

The Teacher of Righteousness, founder of the Essenes, taught that seeking after the truth is the only path to YHWH. Each one is therefore the way, the truth, and the light to eternal life. It is the seeking that brings about the finding, he taught. And so it has been taught by every master in all of my studies, as Hillel taught, also.

Hillel harangued both Sadducees and Pharisees for believing they already had all of the truth and therefore were not open to any other information. They had plunged into the well of ignorance and argued over minutiae in their separate belief systems while missing the grander truths and their grandeur. Often they wanted to kill each other over a single word in the ancient writings.

Hillel taught that there had been many changes in mere words over the years of the ancient writings and one must lift one's eyes to the higher meanings enveloped by the many words, lest an entire truth be missed. He constantly encouraged his pupils to took for the higher meaning, the one that spoke to the soul of man, his spirit, his being. That was the path to righteousness.

"Oh, mother, I was so happy to be in the presence of such a rabbi. Yochanan, too, was such a part of it all." I knew I would never have to doubt my cousin, his ideal was so plain. "Just being in the presence of such a man as Hillel was almost a guarantee of righteousness," I enthused.

"'What does YHWH require of thee, oh man, but to do justly, to love mercy, and to walk humbly with thy God?' Hillel would whisper, loudly, holding us all in a trance with his intensity. He would gather our souls up and lift us to the seventh heaven followed by a dash down to the depths of Gehenna as he roamed the entire saga of man's sojourn on the face of the Earth. He spared nothing, least of all himself.

"'Know the truth about yourselves,' he cried out to the early-morning sun, 'and it shall set you free. Know the truth about God and you shall have life eternal. Know you not that you are all gods in the making?' demanded Hillel."

I looked at my parents and exclaimed, "What a truth; how can I not teach it to everyone? What is my life if I continue the practice but hide it away from those who have such a great need to know? Shall I answer God's call to come out from among them and follow his truth? I must, for anything less will cast me out of life eternal.

"Hillel said that the Creator and the created must be reconciled, that we have all flung ourselves away from the divine and taken upon ourselves the body of destruction in our continued seeking of carnal pleasures.

"He said that we must seek first the All, the Creator, the Lord of the Universe and that then all our needs will be met, added to the fullness of our lives. He insisted we not argue among ourselves or with others over the name of God. Whether God be named YHWH or Osiris or Pan or Zeus, it is all the same God. There is only one God and Israel must become one with God. Believe that God is, because YOU are and I am and we are all one. The God of Israel is one and we must all become one.

"'If you can see me, then you can see God,' shouted Hillel and his voice thundered all over the Temple grounds.

"Everyone had gathered around to hear him. Surely the Temple priests would come for him; I trembled, but they did not. They did seem to fear him somehow, but I could find nothing in him to fear, except perhaps that I might miss some of his words should I look away from him or some interruption come. I wanted to know all his truth, every jot and tittle.

"I thrilled at his words, for they stirred memories within my soul that although I could not quite recall them, I knew I was remembering some long-forgotten glory.

"In the manner of a Socratic dialogue, Hillel allowed questions for discussion. Often he answered a question with a question and even allowed pagans to give their views. After what seemed simple questions of him that he did not scorn in the least, I finally gathered enough courage to query him. 'Can I compare YHWH, who is spirit, to my father, who is a man?'

"'Of course,' he quickly responded. 'And, how appropriate that you should make that comparison. Men miss the essence of God simply because we rabbis have made it unfathomable to the average man. Even the elite of Israel miss it, for who among us can think comfortably in the abstract?'

"He seemed pleased at my question. He said the great masses of the Hebrews were left with signs and symbols they often did not understand and which had long since lost all meaning. It had made for divisions among a people that YHWH had meant to remain undivided as Israel.

"'Who can miss the essence of YHWH when it is as simple as one's own father?' Hillel simplified the concept for me.

"'Can I compare Adonai with my mother?' I pursued.

"He seemed puzzled, as if the idea had never occurred to him. Could YHWH be a woman in some characteristics? He pondered deeply, closed his eyes, and went into a state of some sort, perhaps asking for an answer of the great All. Time passed slowly and some grew restless. He slowly opened those great old eyes, stared even deeper into the sky, and finally turned back to us.

"'Surely you must be right, Yeshua,' the great Hillel mused. 'But I will have to think deeply on this idea, for it is alien to Oriental mystics who have long thought of women as more servant than God. Yet, God serves as well as creates, nurtures as well as demands. It is a heady thought, and I will spend much time in meditation and prayer before I can answer with truth and surety.'"

Later, on my own, I recollected more of my conversation with Hillel. It was not a problem to me. Every time I looked upon the face of the kindred soul I called mother, I fancied I saw God. Her very touch was healing and all wounds stopped aching just from my listening to her soothing voice. Her love was boundless and was all-giving and all-forgiving and surrounded me like a great web of safety, security, and above all, with feelings of warmth and light. That said, I could not begin to truly describe it, even as I found it difficult to describe YHWH to someone who had no idea or even where to begin. Yet, I knew I must. A rabbi is nothing if he is not clear.

I spoke: "My mother cannot be a mere servant. No woman since the beginning of time has blessings all around her more. Her presence in my life is second only to YHWH, whose presence is all I know of God."

Hillel smiled at my love for my mother. But, I think it gave him pause for thought. He seemed to be remembering his own mother, for his eyes once more rolled over and he seemed to stare into a dim, distant past and leave us for another time and place.

As I finished telling my parents about the great rabbi, they seemed pleased that I had been singled out for special instruction by the greatest master of all time.

"Perhaps we do not need to send him to Mt. Carmel now?" she asked Yosef.

"Oh, yes," I answered for him, again forgetting my place and manners in my anxiety not to let that idea get a foothold in my parents' minds.

"He told both Yochanan and me that disciplined schooling was very important for rabbis in the realm of Roman rule, that we could not just sit on a mountaintop or stand in the desert and expect YHWH to drop all the knowledge of the Earth on our heads. I think that was directed more at Yochanan than me, but I cannot say for sure, for he said it to us both."

"Did he say especially that you should go to Mt. Carmel to the Essene brotherhood's School for Prophets?" she anxiously inquired of me.

"Well, not exactly," I hesitated. "He said that the greatest teachers went to Egypt and even beyond to study. But that if one wanted to be the greatest teacher of all time, then he should go to as many schools as he could. He said we both had a lot of time, because no man was truly adult until he was at least thirty years, claiming we were still wet behind our ears. I do not know exactly what that meant because I am always careful to dry behind mine. He said the

Elder at Mt. Carmel would know how to direct us, so to go there first."

My mother and father laughed greatly at that. Even now, I blush at how very much I did not know. I marvel at how kind Hillel was as he gently encouraged us to study, to travel, to live among all kinds of people, and above all to see the world with clear eyes and open minds, especially open minds.

"God cannot pour knowledge into a mind that is closed," he told us. "All knowledge comes from God, but you must seek truth to find it; you must knock at doors for them to open. It is not easy to learn all that is there for you or anyone else."

It seemed settled as we reached the Ascent of Lebonah that I should go to Mt. Carmel for at least a year. We were all so excited that we decided not to camp for the night, but to walk on. We could stop at Sychar, near the ancient ruins of Shechem just below the towering rugged crags of Mt. Gerizim, if we needed to rest, stated Yosef, who always made the final decision in family matters.

Since we were not bothered with feelings of animosity toward the Samaritans, crossing their land was always our path to and from Jerusalem. Yosef said the Samaritans often followed the spirit of the law much more closely than the Essenes and certainly more than the Pharisees. He never hesitated to talk to the men, or even the women, and he taught me to do the same, for all were God's created ones.

"They are seekers of Adonai just like us, Yeshua," he would say, "and because a lamb has strayed or lost its way, there is no reason to hate it. Rather, it is even more reason to go looking for it and show it the way home."

This highly unusual attitude for a devout Jew went far beyond even the Essene teachings. I am sure it had more to do with his love for my mother, in whom he found no reproach ever, than in any secret teaching of any religious sect.

Because Samaria had been settled by Romans and other soldiers of fortune during the conquest of Palestine, Samaritan women were suspect more so than the women in Judea or even Galilee. Many of them had failed to kill themselves when threatened with rape of their bodies. Many had even married the invaders and produced large families with the many conquerors who came sweeping through over the years. Devout Jews viewed all Samaritans as pariahs and contaminated; this was especially so with the Pharisees.

Also, Samaritans refused to accept the many explanations carefully worked out by the lawyers and doctors of the law who interpreted the Torah for the people. The Samaritans only accepted the first five books of Moses as being divinely inspired of YHWH. All other ancient writings were merely the vain prattle of mere men, they claimed, not necessarily even ones inspired by God.

The insistence of the Samaritans that the true Temple was not in Jerusalem, but rather was located where YHWH had commanded Abraham to establish a place of worship on a mountain in Samaria, was a special point of conflict.

The view of the doctors of the law in Jerusalem was that all this had come through the women, because it was they who bore children to the invaders. Thus, even talking to a woman of Samaria was not permitted for a devout Jew.

Yosef taught me differently. He said that God wanted worshippers and cared not for the place of worship nor even who they were. He taught me that God had sent the invaders, who were also created ones, like us; that women were victims and the greatest sin of man was to blame the victim for the crime. It was a denial of God, he pointed out, to call some of God's created ones impure or unclean for refusing to kill themselves, a right reserved to God only.

"The one who gives life is the only one with the right to take it away," said Yosef, ever so gently, for he believed in life, not death, and certainly in not killing anyone for anything. The will of God was always paramount in Yosef's mind and anyone presupposing a woman even had the means with which to kill herself was presumptuous to him. I quite agreed.

My father practiced daily what he preached, always seeking the will of YHWH in his life, regardless of what his personal opinion may have been. No one ever knew whether it was ever different. He did what he had to do or was bidden to do; so did my mother. So do I.

We did not tire as we walked on throughout the night. I entertained my parents with lengthy descriptions of the ornate inner court of the Temple with its tapestries of spun gold and walls of lapis lazuli. I told them of the court of the priests and the Temple itself that King Herod had built and was even still building in such a manner that the business of the Temple could go on without interruption.

I continued to tell them of the words of Hillel, for I could recall each and every one of them then and can recall them all this very day. They became a part of me and my mind ever dwells on them. Between the teachings of my father and Hillel I could have skipped the rest of my many travels and studies and probably arrived at the same place I am this day.

Soon I got the impression from my parents as I talked about the great opportunity I had at the Temple, that they were in agreement with my decision when I was forced to choose.

"There will be many choices for you to make in life, Yeshua," my mother cautioned, "and many times it will seem to you that either one is fair and just and therefore right. But you must always be aware that only one will be correct for the development of your soul and the pursuit of your life's mission, whatever that may be."

I thought about this advice from my mother as we trudged along the caravan trail toward the mountains of Gilboa. It had not occurred to me that I had made a choice between obedience to my parents' will and obedience to the will of God. I had not realized that in seeking truth and knowledge I had chosen to get caught within the Temple walls at sundown.

Rather, I had reasoned that it was carelessness on my part, rather than an active choosing. After all, I was deep into a favorite subject and enjoying myself immensely–how could that be the will of God? Surely it was, however.

Whereas my mother understood I had made a choice, I could not see it then. Now I can see clearly she was right. I had made a choice, and it was the best one for me. To follow after truth and enlightenment was a course I chose to follow for the next sixteen years and I feel that I am only now ready to pursue my mission on Earth.

Chapter 3

Yochanan

But, I digress. The outstanding event of my remembrances is meeting the great teacher, Hillel, when I was only twelve. However, becoming a man according to law was also most eventful and many would think it the greatest of all. But I did not feel like a real man, although I had no idea how real men felt. I felt more like a boy who had passed by ritual from childhood into an in-between stage, sort of an indeterminate land of flashing back and forth between the childhood of my past days and the coming manhood of my future, but never really stabilizing anywhere. Sometimes I would feel like I wanted to crawl back onto my mother's knee and hold on to her fast. Yet, other times I felt like I could go out and conquer the world. So when I was thirteen, I finally had to choose, going out into the world, and leaving my safe childhood behind forever.

For the next fifteen years I traveled from school to school, first to the School of Prophets at Mt. Carmel on the western edge of Judea, near the Great Sea, then to Egypt, where I became an initiate at the School for Initiates in Heliopolis. From there I traveled to India, Tibet, and Persia, where Jews had been captive for many years. I shall do my best to focus on the schools first and the land and people second; a bit of organization is surely in order, even for a journal about my life thus far. I have omitted my very young years, for they were much like all other children who have dear and wonderful parents living in a small community.

This task is already pulling up my innermost thoughts, ideas, feelings, and remembrances that I thought were gone out of my mind entirely. Not so. They are all with me still. And, in my twenty-eighth year, I discover that I can revert to twelve in a blink.

As my parents and I headed up the path toward our summer cottage in the tiny community called Nazareth, I heard a familiar voice crying after us.

"Ho, wait up there, and I will walk with you," called Yochanan in that matter-of-fact voice that seemed to assume he would be welcome. And he was right.

My heart leapt as I turned and saw his scraggly form running toward us. Realizing that he must have decided to go to school with me at Mt. Carmel, as Hillel had suggested we both do, I ran down the path toward him with open arms. We grabbed each other, laughing and crying and patting each other's back in the ancient Essene greeting, expressing great joy at being together again.

My parents stood and watched us with smiles, joyous that Yochanan had forsaken his wild ways for a formal education. I cannot describe how happy I was over his decision to join me, which had been in doubt even with so great a teacher as Hillel making the suggestion. Yochanan was not exactly one to follow directions from anyone, for he was the most inner-directed soul I had ever known, even at thirteen.

Knowing Yochanan was like having a twin brother who walks in tandem with me, a companion of equal merit with whom I could share life at its best or worst. My boyish heart became a wellspring of effusiveness, even at the risk of a good teasing.

"Oh, Yochanan," I exclaimed, "we'll have such a wonderful summer together chasing sheep, fishing the lake, threading streams, and following my father through his daily chores." I hoped that adding this last part to my list of great things to do would not discourage my cousin.

However, Yochanan turned a stern eye on me and feigned exasperation all over a face that so recently had begun sprouting fuzz.

"Did I come all this way to trivialize away the summer?" he mocked. "Better I should have stayed in Jerusalem with the Pharisees than rob the lake of innocent fish."

I laughed uproariously, for I knew Yochanan's opinion of the Pharisees of Jerusalem was only a little better than his opinion of dead rats rotting behind the barn. He considered them all hypocrites, calling them "whitewashed coffins" that should be committed to the city of the dead. But I was happy that he was planning to take seriously the study necessary for entering the School of Prophets and was not fooled by my efforts to outline an idle summer of boyhood fun.

"So serious you are," I returned with mock surprise. "Have you decided to forsake the life of a wild man of the desert for the cultured role of a rabbi?"

"Not so," he quickly pointed out, getting into our favorite game at once. "I intend to be a prophet of God, a wild one in the desert where wind and sand will make my words sound holy." He grinned, as I shrank back in mock alarm at his mock blasphemy.

We both fell down laughing at the idea of Yochanan striding across the desert floor, wrapped in animal skins, shouting warnings from YHWH to cringing Pharisees. They always skulked about finding fault with everyone and everything, whereas the Essenes had tolerated Yochanan's eccentricities from his birth. Such a break with tradition would cause the Pharisees to shriek in alarm, or so we thought.

We laughed even harder at the prospect of shocking those kindly old Essene gentlemen in their long, flowing, white robes and beards–they held the name of YHWH so sacred they never even whispered aloud the letters that stood for the Lord of the Universe.

They, who washed so many times a day to be pure and clean and humble, would surely be in a constant state of apoplexy. Yochanan would be like an ox in their chamber of pottery, crashing about, breaking their many traditions.

On the other hand, he would be like a fresh wind from Mt. Hermon, like spiritual water into their wilting religious gardens. Such was their need to break out of the rigid cast of traditions that now encrusted the school that bold Elijah had been the first to establish and which was followed years later by the ancient school reestablished by the Teacher of Righteousness. From these mighty souls before him and now embodied in Yochanan would spring a new Jerusalem. I saw it all in my mind's eye, suddenly and from whence I knew not, but there it all was laid out before me.

I could not contain my happiness. It flowed like geysers over everyone. What a day it was when Yochanan joined my precious family in body as well as spirit. Even my younger brother welcomed him like a long-lost friend and immediately became a devoted follower. Y'cov doted on Yochanan, calling him his "wild desert man." Yochanan loved it, too, never lucky enough to have brothers of his own. The warm love and attention we gave him made this newly orphaned boy of the wilderness blossom like a wild desert flower after a spring rain.

Yochanan and I spent the summer and early fall getting him ready for the school at Mt. Carmel. He was an apt pupil for one rumored to be so undisciplined. He had learned to read and write from the Qumran Essenes, but he functioned mostly in Aramaic, the language spoken over most of the known world. Therefore we concentrated on the Hebrew language, which was almost extinct, but is the language of our ancient writings. I had heard there was a translation of some texts in Greek in Alexandria at their great library, but at the time it was out of our reach; in any case, Yochanan was even less familiar with that language than his own Hebrew.

Seeking to encourage Yochanan, I said, "There is nothing quite like reading a prophet in his original language. The subtle meanings are often lost in translation."

My cousin, who had developed his own sense of devotion to YHWH, responded that God did not allow important messages to get lost in translation. Such a simple faith he had, so clear and undiluted. Even at twelve years, I did not want to shatter it in any way. Again, I had to make a choice: I could leave Yochanan to continue in his simple faith that divided everything into white or black; or I could carefully move him into the more powerful realms of totality where the grays far exceed the blacks and whites. What to do, I pondered. First I discussed it with my father, Yosef. As always, he was fairly noncommittal.

"I am a simple man, my son, following a simple task," he explained to me. "The education of Yochanan is not mine to do but apparently is yours. I can offer him a warm bed, a good roof over his head, good food, and love. I can send him to school with you at Mt. Carmel. More than that is beyond me."

"But you have taught me everything I know," I protested.

"You have been a different case entirely," my gentle father replied. "Filling the mind of a little boy with the simpler lessons of life is a task assigned to all fathers. But Yochanan is now thirteen. He is not a little boy anymore who needs to know his right hand from his left, the difference between a chisel and an axe, or why milk turns to butter. You are asking a very deep and difficult question for which I have no answer. Yet, it is for you to choose for your chosen pupil on your path toward becoming a great rabbi."

How well my father taught me. He could have told me the answer to that knotty problem. But he was not a rabbi and I claimed I wanted to be one. Practice at discerning what my students needed was there before me. Who was teaching me? My father, of course. But I failed to realize it at that moment.

So I went to my mother for an answer. The purity of her soul, the simplicity of her faith, and the clarity of her thought always enchanted me. Her wisdom was boundless. She seemed to me never to be unsure about anything; perhaps that is how all boys see their mothers, but I knew mine was perfect.

She had given me a surety in my own life that flowed from hers. But she refused to give me the answer I sought, either with a yes or a clear no.

Instead she told me a story.

"Elisheva, Yochanan's mother, took him into the wilderness of the southern desert for many reasons to raise him," she began. "She reasoned that in the starkness of the desert where mere survival was a major study, Yochanan could learn the necessities of life without interference from others seeking to turn his mind away from YHWH. She refrained from exposing him to the scholars of Jerusalem, even after it was safe for her to return and assume her rightful place as the widow of an honored priest and mother of a son who was heir to life as a priest. She preferred that Yochanan not follow the teachings of those who clearly were the murderers of Zekharyah. She never really had enjoyed that life of presumption that was so alien to Essene thought. She reasoned that Yochanan could make his own choices when he was of age, but she would make them for him until he could make his own decisions. Survival in touch with YHWH was the best kind, she believed, and that is what she taught him. The Essene brotherhood quite agreed with her and sought never again to send one of their own into that lion's den of priestly power, so corrupting to the soul.

"Does he not have his life goal, his mission, already in hand?" she asked, looking deep into my inquiring mind with a knowing look.

I felt humbled by her story and especially her question that was more a statement than a query. I instantly knew I wanted Yochanan to share my mission with me, rather than follow his own. It is a mistake often made by men. He had told me many times that he was preparing a way for the Promised One who was yet to come, that he was to be the harbinger, a simple announcer, a voice crying in the wilderness, "Make way. Make way."

I was seeking to have him cry out in at least four languages if that were to be his mission. Clearly it was his decision, not mine, as to how he prepared and which faith he would hold on to.

"Should he not go to Mt. Carmel to school with me, then?" I asked, trembling with fear she might encourage me to send him away.

But such was not my mother. She said softly, "Yeshua, Yeshua, he came with us of his own free will and in his own time. The master Hillel suggested a year of it. I would suggest only that if he chooses not to follow you into the labyrinths for which you have chosen to prepare yourself, be not disappointed at his choice. His is a simple way that is right for our simple people, but yours, well, who knows what or where or how yours will resolve?"

Over the years I have thought of her words many times. My thirst for knowledge led me all over the world to study every school of thought, every discipline, every creed that ever existed, although my mission was to be first to my own people, the Hebrews. A simple people, former slaves in Egypt and even now not free in our own land, they are mostly shepherds on the sides of hills in Judea, fishermen on the Sea of Galilee, or like my own father, simple carpenters. All that I have studied and learned must now be simplified to reach those Yochanan can reach without effort, because he is one with them while not of them. And like my mother's example, simple stories seemed the best teaching tool.

Because of that long-ago conversation with my parents, I have done a lot of my task already. The greater the message, the simpler it must be, in order that even a child may understand. It is not for those who claim to already know. It is for those who hunger and thirst for what they know not.

So I quit urging Yochanan to expand his mind. It was already outside the usual. He would reach out and take whatever he needed and cast off all that was chaff. He would winnow the grain and feed the sheep in preparation for the One to come. He held fast to the Essene's belief that if one truly wants a blessing to come, he must live a life of expectation, for nothing comes to a man that he is not expecting, at least at some level of his being. Even my masters in Tibet knew that. They probably invented the concept.

Yochanan kept himself pure to be able to recognize the Mashiyah when he appeared. He didn't need to be constantly washing, however, because he instinctively knew it was not the body, but rather the mind, that sees clearly, or not. Keeping his belief system clear and uncluttered was how he kept pure, part of his mission.

Like all those who search, I examined carefully Yochanan's position and considered that perhaps I, too, should follow the path he had chosen. But my thirst for knowledge was much too strong. The simple path was not mine. The best I could hope for was that our paths would cross along the way, more often than not.

When I suggested that the messenger from YHWH might come early, then what would Yochanan do with the rest of his years, he stared at me for a little while. Then he murmured that when his assigned task was over, he would take leave of this world and cross over into the next. I marveled at his self-assurance, his single-mindedness, his single-purposed life, his steadfastness in his mission, and I learned from him.

That summer flew by, with Yochanan teaching me the beauty of wildness, the bounty of the wilderness, and how full of life a desert really is. He taught me where to find water where everyone said none could be found, food when the land seemed barren and desolate. Food, in fact, that was so nutritious only a small amount was needed for life. I learned how to keep warm when everyone else was cold and how to keep cool in a swelter of heat. This is a real feat in the desert, where frying an egg on a rock is an art form. I learned survival under the most difficult of conditions, and this saved my life many times before I studied in Tibet and added to Yochanan's simple store of practical knowledge.

Yochanan's simple teaching was that YHWH has provided abundantly for all creatures of the Earth, including man. Just as the lily in the field is dressed beautifully and hungers not, so can a man benefit from such blessings.

"Look about you, Yeshua," he would urge. "Be calm, walk carefully, seek only what you actually need. It is in the seeking that you find. All things come to those who wait with patience."

My cousin, who had no patience with hypocrites, had the patience of Job for locating a tasty morsel hidden away from prying eyes or a spring just under a large rock. From Yochanan I got my first taste of patience sitting by a bees' nest and grabbing a handful of honey the moment it was safe to do so. Had I grabbed it one minute sooner, I would have gotten a great red welt for my failure to wait.

I was humbled by Yochanan's wealth of knowledge, a thing sorely needed by one who chose to travel about the world. All I could teach him was a dead language, no longer spoken by our people. It was a great exchange, he insisted, for who else would bother? I looked upon him with tender eyes, for I could only guess how I would feel without my wonderful and growing family of parents, brothers, and perhaps even a sister later on. A family was the greatest of blessings to a young boy trying to become a man. I was happy to share mine with my beloved Yochanan.

* * * * * * * * *

We left for Mt. Carmel soon after the harvest. Although my family was not in the farming business, we boys assisted other farmers "to learn the joy of helping others," as Yosef put it, who worked alongside us. He was always the example of good. My mother readied clothes for us, having put away Yochanan's camel skins after a good washing. He wept and wailed and exclaimed they were his friends, but she turned a deaf ear and soothed his ruffled feelings, saying even the best of friends need a good cleaning and rest. She loaded packages of food into our packs for the trip. Mt. Carmel, which could take several days even if we ran most of the way, didn't seem that far considering we were young and probably foolhardy.

Yosef wanted to come with us at least as far as the foot of the Carmel mountains, but Yochanan would have none of it. "Am I a baby that I must have a mother waiting on me and a father walking me to school? Is Yeshua? If so, then we are not yet old enough to go away to school and should wait here until we are."

He plopped himself down on a bench beside our well, folded his arms, and stared straight ahead, looking neither to the right or left to see who might be watching. My mother laughed with great glee and Y'cov danced around yelling that we had to stay because we were still little kids like him. The point was not lost on my father, so we soon set off at a long lope, turning west, then southwest toward the Great Sea and the mountains of Carmel. Yochanan actually wanted to give the food away to beggars along the way, insisting they were keeping us from making good time and he could feed us better anyhow. However, I managed to persuade him to let us keep to the plan we had and to not improvise so soon into our journey. He laughed at that, and I knew we were on a journey that would never end until death parted us.

It was not a very long trip, as trips go. We spent only a few nights on the road, and I marveled at Yochanan's way of finding safe, secure places to sleep. We would not waken until the sun shone full in our faces each morning, reminding me of our first adventure on the Temple grounds in the courtyard of the women, only this time without birds.

Fully refreshed, we would eat some fruit and be on our way, running with the wind from the western sea blowing full upon our faces. It was always a glorious way to start a new day and was fully as educational as any school I ever attended. Our eyes were watchful for everything from small furry things to bandits who might want to steal from us. Meadowlarks sang as we went walking by and hawks circled high to see what was moving through their land.

"Watch the trap," Yochanan would call out, and we both would circle a sandpit, perhaps sheltering a viper waiting for its breakfast.

I labeled everything in Hebrew. It became quite a game, one of the many we invented over our years together. Yochanan warned of traps, while I labeled them in Hebrew. Full of joy and health and happiness, we never dreamed our chosen missions held traps in Hebrew that few minds would ever comprehend, but which would always be the will of God.

Reaching Mt. Carmel while the sun was still high, we clambered up the rocky slopes and reached the school for our first meal in a new world, believing with all our hearts the best was yet to come.

Chapter 4

The School of Prophets

When the Essene community at Qumran was destroyed many years before, the brotherhood moved to the mountains of Carmel and fashioned a marvelous network of caves to accommodate everything from living quarters to storage. In the central part they built a meeting place for all their communal activities. Their claim that Elijah had established a school for prophets on that very spot in his day was something no one could prove, but it became tradition and was followed nevertheless. We stood on hallowed ground.

Since we arrived in time for the first meal, which was always eaten after the sun was high in the sky, Yochanan and I quickly washed in a small pool created for mealtime cleansing and purification and entered the communal hall. We both were surprised to find a woman there named Judith. She saw us first and with a silent cry rose up to greet us. She ran up to us, throwing her arms around us and kissing us fervently. Her warmth enveloped us like the warm springs that emerge from the center of dormant lava beds near quiet volcanoes. She pulled us outside of the hall to remind us that Essenes take their meals in silence.

Judith had been to my home many, many times. For years I thought she was a relative. When she came to visit us, she always brought small gifts from the farms at Qumran or handicrafts from Carmel, depending on which place she most recently departed. She began as a teacher of girls when they were first allowed at the school, but had become a liaison between the two communities of Essenes when she insisted on the reestablishment of the farms at Qumran. I loved her dearly. She always had some bit of wisdom to impart to give me direction in my life. She would talk with me for hours on end and never treated me like a child, even from my very earliest encounters with her.

We would talk about the most awesome things. At-one-ment with the Adonai was one of the more constant subjects and the one I loved best. Judith was always careful, now that I think about it, to mention that the Essenes had moved from the Temple in Jerusalem to the mountains of Carmel in order to perfect their own ideas about how to approach the Adonai. It had been the misfortune of Zekharyah to inform the Temple priesthood that they were no longer needed to intercede with God for the people, for Israel. Whereas Zekharyah was pure in heart and sought only to tell the truth, the priesthood instantly knew that his news was dangerous to their survival.

Killing him while he held on to the sacred horns of refuge had been a terrible mistake, for it martyred him, but they all agreed among themselves to tell the same story: The priest had lost his mind and they accidentally killed him trying to get him to let go of the sacred horns. What they actually claimed was that he had died of a mysterious stroke, failing to mention it was the stroke of a sword.

Judith always spoke matter-of-factly and only now do I understand that she and Hillel must have had some conversations on the subject of YHWH and the holy of holies. They had agreed to keep silent about it until the Mashiyah came to reveal all things to men. Nevertheless, she was not so silent with me about it.

We talked a lot about selecting a mission for one's life. Judith always impressed on me that point by saying it was very, very important and the earlier one decided, the better. I knew she meant me, of course, and so I am not surprised that Hillel's teachings opened me up to my life-changing experience of understanding that I must always tell the truth and always tell it to everyone. Deciding whom to tell or not tell was not my path.

Judith also told me about the Teacher of Righteousness who had come over two hundred years before and had moved the Essenes from Jerusalem to Carmel. The haggling in the outer courtyards over money by the moneychangers and the bloody sacrifices all became too much violence to please YHWH, he had realized. Judith was good at pointing out reasons for what people did, especially such a major move as the Essenes leaving the Temple to the Pharisees and Sadducees. In the wilderness they could worship in peace and quiet, in spirit and truth.

Judith was beautiful to the eye, also. Her blue black hair cascaded down her back in a rush of tiny ringlets, also framing her oval face, which was perfect in every way. Her flashing brown eyes that turned to mud when she was annoyed seemed also to add ten feet to her small stature. Even when she was making a point that some kept missing, she seemed to tower like Mt. Hermon. However, it was her voice that entranced me. It was like the soft moan of the wind sweeping across the hills just before a torrent of rain floods the plain. It soothed and excited at the same time. From somewhere deep inside her milky throat came marvelous sounds that calmed and lifted me up to mountain peaks. I was hopelessly in love with her, but I also loved her as a friend and teacher and presumed relative.

She was sexless, or so it seemed to me. Judith went to extremes to prevent prompting sexual urges in others, through her demeanor and attitude; in this way, she could add the feminine to a purely male brotherhood. She was not only my ideal, but also a perfect leader of the Essenes, second only to the Teacher of Righteousness. Since men were never permitted to teach women, nor women teach men, she was perfect as a liaison there, for she always seemed one of us.

When I questioned her about comparing YHWH with Yosef, she agreed it was a fine idea. She discussed with me how many earthly fathers were good and wonderful men who dearly loved their children, even their girls. Any good thing an earthly father would do for his children, God would also do, even more so. When Judith and the great Hillel agreed, the subject was closed for me. A fact is a fact. I would never question it again. However, the idea never seemed to arise anywhere else in any other discipline in any of my travels. Everywhere God was portrayed as aloof, unknowable, compared to the vastness of the ocean, and most of all, unforgiving and a truly negative force.

The most fascinating subject that we ever discussed, and I loved to hear about over and over, was how Judith and the Elder, who was the head of the Essenes, worked through the problem of YHWH's

Mashiyah that was to come, the Promised One. It seemed every one of the Essenes had an idea on the subject, and each one was a little different. Judith determined the subject must be decided if they all were going to focus on bringing it about. The very name of the community, Essenes, meant "expectant ones." How could they expect something about which they had no fully developed idea?

I am tired and need a break. It is intense, writing about my life. It may take me as many years as I have lived it to write about it. Already I have been writing for five days, which is torture for me.

Thus Judith and the Elder resorted to the ancient writings to make a decision in the name of unity. For several years they pondered the meaning of every word of every sentence of every prophecy about the Promised One. From the Psalms to the raging prophets of old–the Essenes gathered in groups to discuss it all. Judith and the Elder would draw apart after all others had gone to bed and talk far into the night by a flickering fire under a starry sky, where God seemed ever near. In the coldness of the winters they sat close for warmth and talked of YHWH and the One YHWH was to send. The wispy old mystic and the beautiful young girl breathed life into the mysterious words of those long dead.

"'He will not be beautiful so that men will desire him,'" quoted Judith. "Does that mean he will be awesomely ugly?" she asked.

They got the giggles over that and she said they were not so serious after that moment. They explored every possibility. "'He will be born of a young girl,'" pointed out the Elder.

Judith said she refrained from asking, "What else?" Nor did she mention that another Sarah and Abraham story might be too much. Clearly as a youth she had a lot of wit about her so she made sure the Elder did not get the idea she was not serious. She was even more careful with the Council, because they were not sure she should even be involved. But she had convinced the Elder that a woman's thoughts needed to be considered since the most appropriate vessel from which the Mashiyah could come would be a woman. It was a point well taken and even the elderly men of the Council consented it was probably true, even if the idea did come from a woman. Judith would laugh in the telling of this and wonder just what other ways they would consider had she not been there.

"From wolves, like Rome, probably," she giggled. It was just a hop, skip, and jump for her to move from the sublime to the ridiculous. And in my childhood I moved with her. Now, I realize she kept me entertained so that I would always want to talk about it. I am not sure it was necessary with me, but a teacher must always find common ground to teach anything well, I know now. So, I learned from the best teachers just how to do it. Simple little stories that make the point seem to serve best, I decided then and there, and now I still think so. Even Zoroaster taught his king that way, but that is later on in my life story.

I could see how confused the elderly Essenes must have been with her incisive thought processes. Women ordinarily were not so learned and their ideas wrapped around their family. But the Essenes were Judith's family and she knew more about them than they knew about themselves. She could persuade them of almost anything.

They were called "the pious ones" because they insisted on many rituals of cleansing. They had a cleansing for the hands, a cleansing for the body, a cleansing for the spirit, and a cleansing for the soul. Much of their cleansing rituals involved water, and so they had created many pools in and around their school and living areas.

Carefully, they had connected the pools so that the water was constantly flowing and cleansing itself while seeming to remain still and unmoving. Quietly, the water flowed over the edge of the stones, down the sides, and into the next level. I had to peer closely to see any movement at all and it was exciting to do so the first chance I got after Yochanan and I arrived.

According to Judith, part of the Essene belief system is that silence is where one finds God. The great YHWH flashes across the skies in brilliant displays of lightning, roars across valleys in rumbles of thunder, and moves the Earth with much shaking, but meets those who seek the Presence in the quiet of the evening or the solitude of the morning. Usually on a mountain top or along the shores of the sea, a lakeside, maybe, but always in the silence.

The Essenes were so sure of this concept that they arose before dawn, climbed to the mountaintop and waited for dawn to break. Just as the sun splashed the darkened sky with hues of orange and gold and crimson, they would stretch out their arms to greet the new day. (One must never be caught asleep or lying about when YHWH's day began.) Thus, they waited, silently, searching the horizon for the flash of green that came as the blue of night met the yellow light of day casting away the dark.

Their chant sounded and reverberated among the rocks and hills and valleys, "Aley-aleyooooooo-ya, aley-aley-looooo-yah." Then a deepened chant of "Ommmmm" would grow, slowly from deep within each soul until the sky would fill with that ancient sound that clearly was the sound of creation, of YHWH, the All.

Shortly thereafter, the silence of the hills would break into joyous song as even the birds of the air joined in the symphony of sounds. The echoes of the caverns bounced into cadences that swelled and receded as the sun seemed to rise slowly above the land and to appear on the horizon as a giant flaming ball of color and warmth.

It was the only major sound of the day for the "expectant ones," who always hoped and prayed that the day of YHWH might also be the day of the advent of the Mashiyah. They reasoned that the Promised One had been so long in coming because the people had never made a way for him to come. Thus, in reestablishing the school of Elijah, the School of Prophets, they were making a way. By constant purification, they were making a way. By constant expectancy, they were making a way, the way for the Lord to come.

They must be pure of carnal thoughts, carnal ideas, carnal acts. Thus, they held themselves apart as a perfect channel for this messenger from God. They must not shed blood. Nor should they support anyone else who had killing thoughts. In peace was the way for a Prince of Peace to come.

They had prepared themselves for so many years, they had failed to give any thought to what was coming or how or when, which prompted Judith to suggest it might be a good idea to hold some kind of image of it all as they waited.

His name will be Immanuel, meaning one who comes from God, but was this a description or an actual name? Were they to be part of the actual preparation? The answer seemed to come as Judith contributed the feminine to the Essene way of living. Preparing young girls had been part of her reason for being among the Essenes. The Elder had said that God created perfect souls, but when the souls wanted bodies, God divided them into two, male and female. One without the other could not be perfection nor bring about perfection. Judith's influence became clear, even to those who had waited expectantly so long that they had about given up all hope. The men of the community were astonished by the Elder's idea, but the women were delighted and knew it came from Judith.

No one dared ask openly where such an idea came from. It would be a breach of obedience to God, for the Elder spoke for the Adonai in matters of great importance. Even in the matter of training for the soul that would become the Mashiyah, they all gave deference to directions from the Elder, who gave deference to his teacher, Judith.

"The Mashiyah must be able to raise others from the dead," said the Elder. "Not only that, but also he must be able to raise himself from death."

The Essenes were shocked. How could it be? And, who would train him to do that? They had no idea how to do it, much less teach it. But, the Elder knew there was a ritual taught in the Egyptian school that included such a feat. They concluded that when they brought in the Mashiyah, he would go to school in Egypt, the School for Initiates, where all future princes were sent.

They accepted the Elder's ideas wholeheartedly because he was noted for his abilities to go beyond all others in his grasp of spiritual concepts, even when they seemed beyond belief. Support from Judith gave it even more credence. They had perfected themselves and therefore only perfect ideas could flow from them. Faith required it of them.

"If the Mashiyah is to be even greater than Elijah," the Elder had argued, "how can it be so if he cannot raise himself from the dead? Elijah raised the widow's son from death at Zidon. What act is greater than that? Of course it was to raise oneself."

As each pondered the Elder's words, a great gloom settled over the group. Since none knew how to teach such a thing and they would therefore have to send the Mashiyah to Egypt, would their own Promised One ever come back? They had many worries and doubts as gloom deepened. Even the flickering candles seemed to dim in the council room. The winds that whistled around their mountain also seemed to die down, suddenly, into a low moan. A deafening silence enveloped the room such that mere breathing seemed like blasphemy.

"Let it be so," whispered Judith.

Quietly, they had all filed out of the council room and headed for their solitary cells. The rest of the night would be spent in deep prayer, each one seeking the knowledge and the wisdom they must have to teach the Mashiyah what he must know. The burden of bringing in the messianic age weighed heavily on each soul. They were aware that three thousand years of development and prophecy had brought them to this moment, and their task was to be ready. To lose this moment in history to the forces of evil, or even to the forces of ignorance, was unthinkable. It could easily cost them another ten thousand years of darkness and struggle. The light must come and it must come now. They knew they were close, very close.

The Essenes became one. The great I AM was in their midst. It was a flowing presence. They could almost hear the voice, like the lower notes of a musical instrument moaning through windpipes in the mountains.

"I AM THAT I AM. CALL ME I AM. SAY THAT I AM HAS SENT YOU."

No one slept that night.

While the Essenes were on their knees pleading with YHWH for knowledge, the Elder and Judith sat talking. They sat wrapped in their mantles beside a small fire. Judith spoke after much thought.

"God is a spirit," she said.

"Yes, the great I AM," agreed the Elder.

"Then, the Promised One will insist the new kingdom be a spiritual one, is that not so?" she questioned him, as she brushed her hair back from her face, leaving her sculpted high cheekbones glowing in the firelight. Judith's long straight nose underlined by her full mouth gave her face a look of strength that belied her tiny frame, and gave her steady gaze a look of great authority.

"Perhaps so," he responded gently, "but I believe the kingdom must be like that of King David." The Elder did not want to discourage her from giving her ideas, but he certainly did not want ideas coming from the future teacher of the Mashiyah to stray down idle paths on their way to oblivion. That would not be profitable for anyone, especially a messenger from God.

He sought to correct her: "The Mashiyah is to be a descendant of King David, claim our ancient writings, is that not so? Surely the kingdom must be the same."

"From his house," she corrected him gently.

"There is a difference?" he asked, surprised that she questioned him more intently than usual.

"Yes, I believe there is a difference. King David himself was known for his carnal acts, but it was his spiritual house that YHWH blessed and said his line would produce the Promised One."

"Yes, I see," said the Elder. "But, the kingdom itself was a material one that everyone could see and feel and touch, ruled by a man. It was not spiritual."

"It passed away, did it not? Are we not slaves in our own land, now, where once we were free and even powerful? What do you suppose happened to all of that?"

He knew he was on the spot now. He persisted. "Yes, yes, but the Promised One is coming to reestablish that kingdom for us, just as we have reestablished this school of Elijah. That is our mission. That is what we are all about, is it not?"

"I don't believe so. Isn't our mission to bring in the Mashiyah, who will then tell us what God wants for us? We cannot decide that for him, can we? Isn't the promise that he is to establish an everlasting kingdom? How to do that will be his decision. What kind it will be will be his decision, I think. I am just guessing that it necessarily will be spiritual if it is to be everlasting."

The Elder gave a little. "Well, you have a point there, but if we are to educate him, then our teaching will have to be different for a spiritual kingdom than it would be for a material kingdom."

Judith breathed a deep sigh. Her relief was overwhelming. She had at least moved him off the fatal idea of the Promised One being some kind of general who would kill thousands of Romans and take Palestine by force. What can be taken from one by force can surely be taken by another the same way. There is no Prince of Peace in that concept. She carefully pursued the idea of a spiritual kingdom.

"Our holy writings say God is a spirit and seeks worshippers who will worship in spirit, is that not so?"

"Yes, yes, of course, that is clear," he decided to humor her.

"And, we Essenes moved away from the slaughter of animals as sacrifice to YHWH because we finally realized the Adonai was not really pleased with killing of any kind, in violation of his holy commandments given to our teacher, Moses. Right?"

"Right," he agreed, sensing where she was going and unable to think of a thing to prevent it.

"Are we not committed to spiritual things symbolized by cleansing rituals, rather than actually wearing phylacteries tied to our bodies, praying loud prayers to be heard in the marketplace by men, along with blood streaming all over the Temple floors to show we sacrifice to God?"

"True," he mumbled.

"Did we forsake all the vain trappings of a dead religion just to continue another set in a new location? Are we not falling into the same trap, even to setting up a hierarchy of our own?" She knew she was treading on dangerous waters here.

The Elder looked at her kind, thoughtful face for a long time. There was no guile about her. Judith spoke with the tongue of an angel. She walked daily with God. She knew what she was talking about, and, she was right. He gave another deep sigh, realizing he must agree with her or all was lost. How easy it was to create the same set of rules by different names and fail again and again with them. Of course, it must be a new, startling concept uncomfortable to man. How else could change come? How else could peace be accomplished?

"I had not thought of it just that way," he murmured.

"Because our ancestors sought to change sacrifice to God with innocent little children, Moses said lambs would be the new sacrifice in the new kingdom he was ordered by God to establish. But, even so, were not men sent into the Promised Land to kill every man, woman, and child? When God seemed displeased, they ordered even the animals slaughtered. But after all that killing we are still a people enslaved in our own land. We must be doing something wrong, or so it seems to me," she said.

"Yes, yes, we must be doing something wrong. Our Promised Land is rife with chaos, bloodshedding, and misery. That is all true. When we are not fighting other nations, we turn on each other. There must be another way to peace. We must have gone wrong somewhere."

The Elder almost cried. He had to admit it was much too late in the night to think upon such a complicated idea with his weary mind. He added, "Dear Judith, I must sleep."

"Forgive me, dear Elder," she cried. "I have been thoughtless of your needs."

He waved a hand and encouraged her to continue with her thoughts and ideas on the morrow, when he would be more alert.

She said, "Just consider one point: No one will ever be able to destroy a spiritual kingdom or even take it away from the Mashiyah or the children of Israel. It will be eternal and spread far from the land of Palestine, even all over the world. I believe that is why Israel was created: to do this one thing.

As the Elder walked slowly toward his cell for sleeping, he rolled the idea over and over in his great mind. Surely from the mouths of babes come the truth of God, he thought. He could not argue with her logic. Surely she was right. Judah was split from the northern kingdom. All of Israel was broken. Who could bind such wounds, if not a Prince of Peace? He must rethink his entire position and argue this great new concept. Tomorrow. Tomorrow when he was rested.

He breathed a deep sigh as he realized once more the goodness of God for sending him Judith. She was like the morning star to him, shining, brilliant, and solitary in a limitless sky. And, although he was old, she constantly sought his company and refreshed his spirit. Her clear mind sparkled with wit as well as spiritual freshness. He could believe in heaven with such an angel by his side.

Without a real struggle, the Elder let go of his ancient dream of a Mashiyah who would take Rome by force and set up his capitol in Jerusalem and rule the world. It had been the dream of a hot-blooded young man translating his passions to a dream of conquest. Now with those passions banked and the embers dying, he was happy that for yet a little while, he would be within this utterly peaceful part of the world peopled with saints who had gathered into one soul, each free will merging with the will of YHWH. His happiness welled up in him, and he hugged himself closer with his mantle. But he said nothing of these feelings to Judith. He did not have to, for she divined them all, even implanting them in his ever-fertile mind so precious to her.

Chapter 5

A Spiritual Kingdom

In telling me this story, Judith always talked about herself as if she were talking about someone else. She never made clear to me who Immanuel was, nor did I ask. To this day I do not know if he came before I did to Mt. Carmel, or afterward. But it was so exciting to know that he had been born–and in my own time. I did not tell Yochanan, nor even my mother, that Judith said he had come. I kept the secret to myself, so happy that she had entrusted it to me.

It was from Judith that I first learned about life's missions and the value of finding early in one's life the direction it should go. From my earliest days, I wanted to be a rabbi. Even when I learned that I was descended from the House of David and could make a claim to the throne of Israel, I hardly considered it as my calling. The notion of priest kings had already been tried and failed. Judith was right. A spiritual kingdom was the only way. I planned to teach all my students to listen closely to this Immanuel the moment he made himself known.

Daydreamer that I am, I saw myself as a sort of assistant to Yochanan directing seekers to the Anointed One. Standing off to the side pointing the way was my most frequent vision, an echo to Yochanan's calls from the wilderness.

My days at Mt. Carmel seemed to fly by. Yochanan was engrossed with learning enough Hebrew to study for himself the ancient writings, especially the Psalms, our favorite. He found one that he felt positively identified his selected mission. He had even identified closely with Elijah, the great prophet of YHWH, and studied every word written about this powerful man. We both loved the story of Elijah raising the widow's son from the eternal sleep.

"How did he do that?" Yochanan whispered to me in the scriptorium where we studied the scriptures hours upon hours, memorizing them, copying them onto copper scrolls.

"I do not know," I replied, "but I plan to keep studying until I find out."

"That could take forever, as much as you love to study," he sniffed.

I was never put off by Yochanan's cryptic observations. I loved him, and I thought his straightforward attitude was marvelous, and his observations probably correct. I never had to wonder what was on his mind, as he spat it out of his mouth the moment it entered his head. Even though I often thought that characteristic would surely cause him terrible trouble sooner or later and even told him so, he said he did not care.

"If I think it," he said, "it is the truth, for I am a channel that receives only the truth. I purify myself daily for just that mission."

I believed him. When he got that strange light in his eyes, even his teasing had a ring of truth to it. Idle words did not drip from his mouth. They were all fraught with meaning, some more than others, but all contained a kernel.

Judith told Yochanan his love of Elijah, his feelings of closeness, and his identification was an indication that the soul of Elijah was with him. She said that Elijah would come to us in our dreams, when all our logic and defenses were down, if we willed it. She even hinted that Yochanan and Elijah might be twin souls, or even more. It was the "even more" that Yochanan and I discussed often.

"Is she saying you might be Elijah himself?" I asked Yochanan.

"Well, I cannot think of anything else it could mean," he replied.

"Do you feel like Elijah reincarnated?" I eagerly pursued the subject.

"That is a good question, Yeshua, and I do not yet know the answer."

We would then spend hours on the subject of reincarnation. We had many laughs exploring the ancient writings, trying to decide which ancient son of Israel we might have been, or even how many different ones we could have been. Sometimes we went all the way back to Adam and fancied that one of us might have been the very first man.

"Or woman," Yochanan would twit. "You could have been a woman, Yeshua!"

I would give that a lot of serious thought in our mock game and even feign being a woman, making mincing little steps like my mother, and swishing my shift a bit. Yochanan would scream with laughter and claim I should be an actor going about the countryside entertaining the people instead of educating them.

"You may be missing your calling, Yeshua," he would giggle. And we would both howl.

One cool winter day, as we sat by the quiet pool talking on this favorite subject of ours, I declared, solemnly, "I must have been Joshua!"

"Why so?" he dutifully inquired, not knowing if I were going to be humorous or serious.

"Well," I began, carefully, "Moses argued with YHWH in the desert, and gave all kinds of excuses for not following YHWH's directions. But Joshua just always did what he was told, and I am more like that. And, our names are spelled kind of the same," I threw in for good measure.

"So you are going to be serious this afternoon," he quipped.

"Not so, Lion of the Desert," I responded with the descriptive name I had settled on for him, since he insisted on calling me the Star of Bethlehem. "It is much too chilly to be heavy today. I thought it quite light to give a simple answer rather than an intricate, detailed exposition as you claim I am wont to do."

His eyes sparkled as he looked up at me from his reclining position on the sun-warmed boulders. I could sense that he was going to clobber me with his sharp wit. I braced for the thrust.

It probably will draw blood, I thought helplessly.

"Soooooo, you led an army, did you?" he began. "You circled Jericho, blew the walls down, killed every living soul, and claimed YHWH made you do it. My, my, Yeshua, no wonder you have to keep reincarnating. It will take forever for you to undo such a murderous soul."

I crumbled. He must have been leading me to this point for days. I could see clearly in retrospect how he had baited me. But, still, he was at the core of truth. Our long-running argument that the zealots had chosen the wrong way to bring in the kingdom of God, which was my position, and Yochanan's claim that you had to get people's attention before you could tell them anything, even how to please YHWH, fell like hail on the story of Joshua and the battle of Jericho. Yochanan admired the zealots because they were men of action, always willing to lay down their lives. I always argued that their actions were so violent that these spoke louder than their works.

Yochanan's thrust struck me to the depths of my soul. Had I really once been Joshua and slaughtered thousands in the name of God? It was Joshua's obedience to God through Moses that I identified with, quite forgetting the bloodshed. But the two seemed inextricably entwined. How could I explain away the violence of murdering every man, woman, and child in Jericho, sparing none but Rahab, the harlot, and her family? Even now my soul shrinks from such bloodshed.

Somewhere from deep within me came a tiny light that slowly grew; my soul grasped at the idea that perhaps Joshua had misunderstood the command of YHWH. In the deepest recesses of my soul I knew that my Heavenly Father could not have given such a deadly command. Either the ancient writings misstated the facts, or the leaders misunderstood the command. Or perhaps the obedient Joshua perceived the command "to dedicate" as meaning "to destroy" for God. What really happened? Their beliefs required bloody sacrifice; we Essenes do not so believe. Creation and destruction seem to be opposing terms. How terrible for poor Joshua if he misunderstood YHWH's command, I reasoned. But then, how often do we Hebrews, even today, misunderstand the will of YHWH?

As I sat in stunned silence, I pondered the many answers I could give Yochanan. Shall I say the ancient writings are wrong? What evidence do I have to support such a claim? People, especially Yochanan, believe the writings are directly from YHWH and are therefore sacred. Can we believe that the Lord of Creation is also the Lord of Destruction? Does man believe God makes him strong in order to kill other men? I did not then have the benefit of all my many travels and study, so I conceived an explanation that made sense to me.

"My soul has come a long way since I was Joshua, if, indeed, I was that gallant fellow," I said evenly, trembling only a little.

"And perhaps it has a long way to go even still. It seems to me that knowing about our past lives is helpful only if it aids in soul development. Perhaps long ago I simply misunderstood the command of Adonai and honestly believed I was doing the Infinite's will. Our Father looks on the intent of the heart, not the result, I think. If I were Joshua, I can see how far my soul has progressed. I now know my Heavenly Father does not want we sons of God killing one another. It has never been so.

"You may be right, Yochanan. My mission may now be to rectify those terrible killings. To clarify my misunderstandings, to be even more obedient to the will of the Infinite with a more perfect understanding of what that will is."

Tears were streaming down my face when I finished speaking. Yochanan was ashen. It was a strange moment between two children old beyond our years. I did not know then what possessed me to say such things.

Yochanan sat up and took my hand, "That was unkind of me to cause you such torment, Yeshua."

"No, no, it was good of you," I replied. "It had to be. It clarified my own thinking and shed light on why I am here."

"Perhaps you are right," he soothed. "What has come down from thousands of mouths then finally written centuries after the events might not be altogether correct."

"That is not important to my soul development," I returned.

"The ancient writings are for us to study, not worship," he offered.

"True."

"So if the ancient storytellers added a little something here and a little something there to add a little color to the tale, what does it matter?" He patted my arm.

I was not soothed. If in fact my soul had resided in that body known as Joshua centuries ago, I certainly must atone for the killings done by him, I brooded. What else could I do but lay down my own life? At least I did not misunderstand YHWH now. Again I renewed my vow to serve YHWH all of my life, with my life.

Yochanan saw that I would not be comforted. He made another effort to cheer me, but finally resigned himself to the fact that he had given me more food for thought than I was able to chew. He did what all should do in such a situation and left me alone to work through my problem.

His parting shot, however, was, "You probably were Melchizedek, the high priest who came from nowhere!"

I went apart from the community to wrestle with this new light. What we had been doing in fun suddenly became so serious that I was in shambles. As was my custom, I searched out a mountaintop in order to be as close as I could to my Heavenly Father. What else could a little boy who was newly a man do with such an earth-shattering idea? Now I had to deal more directly with the concept of reincarnation, or resurrection as some called it.

I truly wanted to be the Joshua who obeyed Moses without question. It was he who went into the land of Canaan and came back to assure Moses that the land was beautiful and fertile, the grapes large and juicy, and the cities well built. It was Joshua who discounted the others' claims that the land was full of giants and told the truth, that they were mere men like all of us.

It was Joshua who had said, "I know not what other men may do, but as for me and my house we shall serve the living God." That was the soul I wanted to be. Yet, that very soul was also the one who fought the battle of Jericho. I believe God had told him how to cause the walls to fall down, but I cannot believe that God told him to kill every man, woman, and child. The Lord of Creation is not a God of destruction. It simply cannot be. I wrestled with the idea for hours.

I toyed with the idea that reincarnation was not a fact, but rather just an interesting idea. Who could prove it either way? Then Yochanan's words came back to me in blinding clarity: "You probably were that priest, Melchizedek, who came out of nowhere." I could deal with that much better. It pleased my soul to think that I might have been so illustrious a being as the priest king of Salem who anointed Abraham as a true son of God. There were no known skeletons hiding in that soul's closet, I hoped.

It was there that I saw the trap that ensnares men's souls. What is pleasing is acceptable; what is not pleasing is anathema, never mind the truth. Had I perhaps reached the height of soul development in Melchizedek, only to plunge into an abyss as Joshua? Was I sent back from YHWH to help Moses conquer Canaan with love, only to fail by conquering with destruction? Seemingly, it was successful. We did take over the land and slay its people. But, therein, perhaps I lost my soul to evil. I succumbed to what seemed the logical way to rid the land of idol worshippers. I killed them, and thus, I killed myself.

Moses, with the works of YHWH in hand–"You shall not kill"–was not allowed into the land of Canaan for striking a rock in anger. I failed to learn of it, and struck down the entire populace I was sent to save.

I collapsed in a river of tears, and my soul moaned for forgiveness.

Even now the tears running down my face wet the parchment so that my quill cannot mark the Hebrew characters of this journal. My soul aches with the pain of remembrance.

Then a strange thing happened to me. A light appeared to be shining on me. I looked all around for the sun, but the fine mist was still falling. In my anxiety the tears ceased, and I strained my eyes to see from whence the light came. It seemed to grow brighter until finally I could see a form standing in the midst of it.

"Yochanan?" I called, thinking he had come again to comfort me. But, no, it was not he.

"Judith?" I inquired, knowing that she seemed always to know my emotional extremes, and I could not tell if the form were young or old, male or female, dressed or undressed. Truly strange.

I waited.

As I calmed and dried my tears, a voice, no, more of an impression, seemed to flow from the light.

"Know the truth about yourself, for it shall set you free."

"What is that truth?" I cried.

"I am truth."

"But how can I know what is true, and what is not?" I pleaded.

"Seek the truth, and you will find it, for I am the truth, the light, and the way."

"Who are you?" I whispered.

"I AM," came the answer, and the form and light faded away.

I fell on my face, losing consciousness. When I came to, Yochanan was there rubbing my hand and calling my name.

"Was it you?" I asked.

"What are you talking about, Yeshua, did you fall?" he inquired anxiously.

"Did you see the light?" I asked again.

But he did not seem to know what I was talking about, only interested in wiping away the blood from a gash on my head where I must have hit it when I fell.

"I saw YHWH," I said, whispering the sacred letters.

He stopped fussing over me and sat back on his heels, staring at me.

"You w-what?" he stammered.

"I saw YHWH. Remember when Moses asked the burning bush who was speaking and God said, "I AM that I AM?" I saw a great light and it said it was "I AM."

"Yeshua," he protested, "the cut on your head caused you to see lights."

"No, no," I cried, "I saw it before I fell."

My face felt very hot, and Yochanan's mouth fell open as he stared at it.

"Your face is shining," he cried, "like the sea with the sun shining on it."

We both looked around to see if the sun had come out, but it had not. The fine mist had become a fog and swirled around us like a great dense blanket of gray smoke.

"I saw YHWH," I insisted.

"You saw something," he agreed.

We walked arm in arm back down the mountain together, inching along in the blinding fog lest we fall off a cliff or lose the path. The smell of the Great Sea mingled with the mist and in the distance we could hear the cry of a bird. Our shuffling scattered pebbles that rolled down the mountainside into oblivion for we never quite heard them hit the bottom. I had not realized how far up I had climbed, and wondered how Yochanan had found me, but I felt secure in his nearness. The wet rocks were slippery, so we stopped to take off our sandals. The cold, moist stones sent a chill throughout my body, and my teeth began to chatter.

Yochanan took off his coat and wrapped it around me, but I was still not warmed, and I began to shake. He pulled me into a crevice in the giant boulders and began to rub my hands to bring warmth back into them.

"A kingdom for a skin of wine," he shouted.

Yochanan never touched wine or any other strong drink, for he had been dedicated since birth not to do so, and I remarked about it.

"Not for me Yeshua," he said. "For you, to bring some warmth into your bones."

"Medicinal purposes only," I opined.

"Yes," he agreed.

I was under no such dedication as Yochanan. I could eat meat, or not; drink wine, or not. My parents were liberals among the strict Essenes, and they had put no such restrictions on me. Even so, I admired Yochanan for his devotion to a dedication not of his own making. It was the way he honored his dead father, I supposed. Even more so did I admire him for not trying to impose on others his strict observances. He would die of chilblains before he would take even a sip of wine, but to relieve my chill he would pour a whole skin down me. I did not understand at the time just why Yochanan had been forbidden some kinds of food and drink.

It was years later in the lamaseries of Tibet that I learned about the chemistries of foods and their relationships to the body. Those lamas knew all about vibrations of every living thing and what unhealthy things occur when one tries to mix the wrong ones, especially within the body.

But at that moment as we stumbled down the mountainside, I thought it merely odd that my cousin would call for a cure for me that he would never accept for himself.

Chapter 6

Judith

Judith's classes were marvels of information. Even Yochanan looked forward to them with eager anticipation. I shall never forget the first one.

Judith called on Moishe to read the first verses of the Books of Moses. They concerned creation. As he read, "God created man in the image of a god; male and female, God created them," Judith stopped the reading.

"The word 'adama' means human being, man, or mind. The word 'ieve' means from the beginning. These words have evolved into 'Adam' and 'Eve,' but simply mean all souls were created in the beginning. This is not a specific time, for there is no time with the All. The Great Mind thought of beings and they came into existence. Each soul's mind is part of the great Universal Mind we call Adonai."

Like babies who have been given their first bite of yogurt, some of the class screwed up their faces in startled astonishment. They looked at each other and began to whisper, "Is she saying there were no real people named Adam and Eve? Surely that is not what she means. But, she seems to be saying we were created like gods along with the Adonai." They seemed perplexed, but no one dared say anything.

Judith perceived their anxiousness, but she continued with this, the most important of Mt. Carmel's teachings–about beginnings, the beginnings of all souls, knowledge, power, life.

"You will note," she continued, "that Adonai created male and female and called them 'man.' We have the singular pronoun 'him' followed immediately by the plural 'them.' Thus, 'them,' a plural, modifies 'him,' a singular. So the intent of these verses is to show that God created sexless souls, like the All, then divided them into two equal halves. In order for each soul to become whole again, it must seek after and find its other half. Once a soul becomes whole again, it becomes holy."

Again the group looked at each other in astonishment. Must they marry to become holy? None of the Essenes at Mt. Carmel were married. What is she saying?

And two equal parts? "Everyone knows the female is not equal to the male," whispered Simon. "That is just a crazy Essene teaching so they can have this woman teaching us men." Simon quickly cast his eyes around to see if anyone else knew what he was thinking. He'd already been warned that some students and all rabbis had mystical powers that included mind reading.

Since I was smiling at him, I know he thought I could read his mind. "You're no dummy," he whispered to me. Judith continued, "I am telling you of the first mystery. It is very difficult to explain and even more difficult to understand. Moses spent forty years wandering in the desert of Sinai, finally understanding this mystery of Adonai enough to explain to it Aaron then to Joshua. So give me your complete attention. You may never understand what I am telling you, but at least you will have knowledge of this mystery."

Simon sat up straight and concentrated on Judith's eyes. "No sense in being thought too stupid to pay attention, especially with all these mind readers in the room," he mumbled loudly enough for me to hear.

Judith continued. "Many times the wandering soul finds what is loosely termed a soul mate. Together, they discover, they can accomplish so much more than they ever could have separately. They may marry, or become good friends, or study together, or go into business as partners. Each one furnishes what the other lacks. But the deepest mystery is how two souls who become one acquire the strengths of each other, and gradually drop the weaknesses they formerly had. Dependency is a snare that must be avoided at all costs. Development of the soul into wholeness requires development from weakness to strength. You were created in the image of God. You are working your way back toward becoming one with God, which is perfection."

An audible gasp went around the room. There, she said it again. She is saying we can become gods. Simon almost ran from the room. I could feel his panic, even as I noted that Simon always gets it a little wrong.

"This woman is a blasphemer. Listening to her could get me crucified by the Romans," he moaned. "How could my mother follow this crazy sect? I did not want to come here to school. I wanted to go to Jerusalem with James."

Simon sat very still. I was a little surprised that I could hear what he was saying, or was it thinking? I seemed tuned in to his fear and wanted to comfort him. His brother, Andrew, was not so fearful. Like the others, he sat in stunned silence, his mind a blank.

"The soul has no sex. It is in the image of God, who also has no gender," continued Judith.

"The body is the temple of the soul. It is not the soul. As long as you identify with your body, you cannot develop your soul into perfection. Your mind, which is part of God's mind, must choose whether to develop the material body or the spiritual body then harmonize it into perfection."

Rachel blanched. She was proud of her body; it was just budding into womanhood. While Judith paused for the class to fully take in what she was teaching, Rachel whispered to Martha. "How can I make my body beautiful and get married and have babies if I am not my body?"

Martha shook her head in bewilderment. Only Yochanan seemed unaffected by Judith's teaching. He seemed to pull apart from the group and become aloof. In Yochanan one sensed only spirit. No problems with that body. He clothed it and fed it and used it to move about, but his preoccupation was with God. It was as if he were a bridge between Heaven and Earth and sought only to be a perfect bridge.

I could do no less. My thoughts had not separated my soul from my body. I just never thought about it, so the whole idea fascinated me. My body never hurt nor caused me any discomfort, so I hardly noticed it at all. It seemed temporary to me when I thought about it.

"This is a mystery," continued Judith. "You are a body, a mind, and a soul. Your mind keeps your soul in touch with your body once you tune into the Infinite. But your mind can also block your soul from your conscious life; then there is conflict and chaos and terrible results."

She looked around the room noting how each one of us seemed to be taking what she was saying. Ever sensitive to the least shuffling of feet, rustling of shifts, or folding of arms indicating lack of belief, Judith took into herself the level of each student. It was a magnificent day when I realized the true essence of her talent as a teacher. Until each and every student understood what she was saying, not one of us would be allowed to go to another subject.

"We are all one, just as the God of Israel is one," she pointed out, "and until each one of us has the mystery in hand, none of us have the information."

I wanted to cry it was so precious. I was humbled to be at the feet of so great a teacher, proud to be in her presence at all.

"Look to your self," she whispered, "see who you are; know what you are. Be not confused, for in confusion rests all evil. You are not bodies; you are souls."

Again Judith looked around the room, pausing for a few moments, then she continued. "What is your soul's purpose in this lifetime? Take no thought for the next lifetime nor the last lifetime. Concentrate on this lifetime, which is the only one you truly know about. The question of importance is why are you here?"

"My mother made me come," Simon whispered and snickered.

Judith's eyes turned to mud as she rested them on Simon. The class grew deathly quiet, waiting for the axe to fall on the irreverent one. But it was not Judith's way to humiliate a soul so obviously in need. We could feel her great mind reach right into the mind of Simon, fill it with warmth and love, and draw it out. She said absolutely nothing at all. The class continued.

"To know your soul's purpose in this life while you are so young is a treasure given to you by Adonai. Think upon it, work with it, consider it carefully. It is your life. You will lay your body aside sooner or later, just as you choose. But your soul will go on forever. It is up to you and you alone to develop it to its greatest potential, which is God."

With that she dismissed the class and walked slowly out of the room. The class had lasted perhaps twenty minutes.

But the lesson would last a lifetime, or perhaps throughout eternity. She had not said that the soul could take its learned lessons with it from lifetime to lifetime, but that was the impression I got. One could never get the idea that life was hopeless with such a treasure of information. It was then that I realized life was a diamond that one must keep polishing until it became a diadem in the crown of the Infinite.

As I walked along the path to the baths, where we practiced the godliness we did not as yet have, a loud whisper slowly filtered into my mind, "Yeshua, Yeshua, wait a minute. I want to talk to you."

Turning, I saw Simon. He had stopped just behind the corner of the communal building and was beckoning to me. It was with a slight case of irritation that I realized he was breaking the rule of silence and was urging me to be a party to it. He knew we were not supposed to discuss our lessons among ourselves, lest we get a wrong explanation going and lose sight of where we got it. Everything learned at schools is not always from the teachers, nor is it even valid information. Nevertheless, I went to him.

"What is it?" I whispered in a tone indicating that Simon's constant testing of authority would get him and me both into trouble.

"I know you saw what I was thinking," he whispered, ever mindful that the self he did not yet understand stood blocking his potential growth.

"So?" I answered, trying to say as little as possible, thinking it was less a breaking of the rule, but knowing it was not.

"So what did you think?" Simon urged.

"You have a right to think what you want."

"No, no, I mean what do you think about the lesson?"

"A lot," I whispered.

Simon hated it when I deliberately avoided his meanings. He knew that I was aware of what he wanted to know and was simply evading the question. But he persisted.

"I mean what do you think of this male and female stuff, of them being equal and all that other crazy stuff?"

"Very interesting," again trying to limit my remarks.

In exasperation Simon jerked my sleeve and demanded, "You don't think she is right, do you? I mean about women being equal to us men?"

I stared at Simon long and hard. Was that all he got out of such a powerful lesson, I pondered? What could I possibly say to one so engrossed, so lost at such a level? The beauty of the lesson lifted me beyond myself, but apparently that had not happened to Simon. Suddenly, I sensed another lesson within my soul. Did I see myself as at a higher level than my cousin Simon? Such audacity, a truly damning thought. How could I ever hope to be a good rabbi while believing myself so far above my pupils?

Simon was hurt and upset at my shortness with him. Were we not boyhood friends? Had we not played together as cousins at family gatherings, festivals, and caravan travels to Jerusalem? Did we not sit together behind the synagogue in Capernaum memorizing long verses from the Psalms and Isaiah? I reached out and put my hand on his sleeve, wrapped my fingers around his arm, and pulled him close to me. He melted into my body as his fear dissolved.

"Let us learn together," I whispered, and he seemed satisfied. A passing elder remarked, "Those who break the rules have not learned the law."

Again Simon was startled. "These mind readers will prove a disaster to my life and a curse on my soul," he stated as he hurried to the baths. "I may not be a body, but I better get it bathed or I will miss feeding it."

Even passing remarks by those priestly Essenes were full of meaning. No idle words seemed lodged in their thoughts. The law was beautiful to me. I loved it so much that studying it and following it was like Heaven to me. Although many believed rules were made to be broken, I believed they were made to give one guideposts along paths that were unfamiliar; the law made decisions for me when I might have stumbled and fallen never to rise again. As I was soon to learn, there are universal laws that no man breaks and gets away with. Yet the man who knows and understands them can do all things.

As we slipped into the baths, we could hear the girls on the other side. Rachel splashed quickly into the cold clear springs and squealed, "I may not be a body but mine stings with cold." Again she squealed as she shivered in the water. She loved rules and usually held fast to them. They made life safe for her, like her beauty and good personality.

We could hear Martha whispering. "I don't care if I am a body or not. I could do just as well without this one."

Martha was tall and straight and thin. There was not a curve anywhere on her. She could have passed for a boy were it not for her long hair streaming down her back stained with sunlight. She held her head high and admitted none of Rachel's dreams as she carefully patted the cold water on her arms. Rachel obviously loved being a girl, but Martha cared nothing at all for it.

"Old Judith probably can't remember when she was young and pretty, if she ever was," whispered Rachel loudly.

Rachel was wrong. I knew Judith had been very beautiful at their age. To me she still was. I saw her as my dear and devoted rabbi who spent much time on her knees in prayer to YHWH. She who had studied with the pythoness of Delphi beseeched YHWH to keep her mind on the great mysteries and help her teach them to her pupils.

The Elder had taken her with him to Greece so that she might see another woman devoted to God. For a young Jewish girl to be permitted to study Pythagorean philosophy at the great temple at Delphi was an unheard of gift. It was only at the behest of the spiritual descendant of the ancient Theoclea that she had been permitted to remain.

Judith stayed with Demetrius, an Essene, while at Delphi, but she spent most of her time with Theoclea. Their laughter sounded like music wrung from a heavenly lyre as they studied together, probing the mysteries as they must have originally been. Together Judith and Theoclea had managed to restore the brilliance of the Pythagorean principles and glean priceless pearls from the clouded oysters of the depths.

As they walked beneath the twin crest of Mt. Parnassus, they pondered the inscriptions over the entrance of the temple, "Know thyself" and "Let no one enter with unclean hands." The months Judith spent with Theoclea resulted in obtaining what she called the major key to the great mysteries. It was the secret of secrets, an open secret inscribed on every rock and every tree and every living thing. Yet, no man saw it who did not first search and know himself.

"Truly all of learning is just remembering," declared Judith as she took leave of her friend.

"I shall never forget again," returned the Pythoness Theoclea as she clung to Judith.

They took leave of each other after two years and never again were to meet in this lifetime. Judith returned to Carmel, where she became a peer among peers. Just one conversation with her and all knew without any doubts that here was a mind that transcended any kind of body to which it might be attached. From teacher of the novices she quickly rose to leader of the Essenes. The Elder retained the title, of course, but Judith was the leader in fact.

Although our course of study usually followed a set schedule of class in the morning, baths, breaking the fast, then afternoon discussion, I skipped breaking the fast in order to search out Judith for a private conversation.

"I am much troubled," I approached her.

"Why so?" she searched my face for some indication of the problem.

"I found myself measuring another's level of enlightenment and deciding he was not so enlightened as I. The Pharisees would be proud of me," I concluded shamefacedly.

"Ah, Yeshua," she hastened to encourage me. "To hear yourself and recognize what you are doing is the very first requirement to knowing yourself. Would that all men learned such a lesson as young as you. The whole world would instantly change into paradise."

I had no idea what she meant, but her words soothed me. I stood and waited for her to explain.

She seemed to study me for a moment, then continued.

"You must be able to measure your pupils in order to teach them. If you have no idea where your pupils are in their development, you will find yourself giving meat to babes and milk to adults. Neither will be nourished by that. If you would keep yourself humble in this exercise, find something in your pupil that is a strength and keep that ever before you. It will be even better if it is a strength in which you yourself are lacking. "Have you decided so soon what your mission in this life is to be?"

"Well, not exactly," I replied. "All I know for sure is that I want to be a rabbi, like you."

She smiled broadly at that and confessed that she, too, was subject to flattery, but not confounded by it. I hastened to assure her that flattery was not one of my tools, that I was sincere in longing for such a task. She responded by assuring me that the world is full of would-be teachers like her. We both smiled at that, for not even my humble Judith believed there were a lot of teachers like her. It was just the humble patter of two devoted to searching for God together.

She had given me the answer I needed as well as the assurance. I apologized for seeking her apart from class and departed quickly. She blew a kiss after me.

From her prayers, Judith came to the classroom again. We were already sitting around the room as she entered. The Elder had not yet arrived, but we knew he would soon do so. He was the other half of the soul that was Judith, we thought, and together they formed a perfect, whole, and holy rabbi. Judith took her place on the mat in front of the low stone table in the center of the room. Since there were only seven of us in the class, her back was to no one. Rachel and Martha sat together, as did Yochanan and I, Simon, Andrew, and Moishe behind us.

Judith never turned her back on anyone, believing it to be a rejection of sorts, which was against her accepting nature. Just as the sun's rays reached the level of the window, placing a glorious halo around her head, the Elder arrived. We quieted and even stopped breathing for a moment as the hush deepened. He raised his hand in both a salutation and blessing, then took his place beside Judith. All heads bowed.

"Holy Most High, Father of us all, we beseech thee to come into our midst and teach us all, your children," intoned the ancient one as he seemed to be surrounded by brilliant shimmering lights cast through the window reflecting on his white hair. It was a high solemn moment we never forgot.

"First question," opened Judith.

I stood quickly, lest I lose the train of thought I had managed to maintain all day. "Why has this great truth given us this morning about 'adama' and 'ieve' been hidden from us who have so carefully memorized all the sacred scriptures and oral traditions since we were old enough to speak?"

Simon gasped as he realized I did not question the information itself, only why I was thirteen years old before it was given to me.

Judith looked at the Elder for a moment, not expecting this to be my question. She hesitated for only a moment lest the Elder give the reason all initiates learned and that I would hear again and again throughout Egypt and the Far East.

"Knowledge is power," she began, "and every truth has many layers. The Adam and Eve story on its surface is for those who never go beyond the surface of anything. From ancient times sages all over the world have believed the great mysteries must be hidden away and made available to those who are willing to dedicate themselves to selfless search for selfless purposes. But we believe spending a lifetime searching for the great truths leaves little time to put them into practice. Thus we have established this school so that all who will might come and learn from us from early youth. Prior to now you have learned the words. From this day forward, you will learn their meanings. The world is directed and controlled by words, which form ideas."

Yochanan then stood and asked his question. "I was under the impression that God has no beginning and no end, yet the Book of Moses talks about the beginning."

The Elder took that question. "You are correct, Yochanan. God has no beginning and no end. The verses are not talking about God's beginnings, for there are none. They are talking about the beginnings of the souls' consciousness in understanding the deep matter that God IS.

"Adonai created the souls and truth was known to everyone. Many souls misused their free will and knowledge of the universal truths. They sought to subvert them and twist them to their own purposes. They began to experiment with matter as manifested on Earth. At first they could come and go as they willed, in and out of the bodies of animals, plants, and fish. As time went by, however, they remained too long, due to the carnal pleasures they had while in those bodies. Soon they forgot how to get out of them.

"As some struggled to get out, they were able to get only partially out and such half-creatures as mermaids, centaurs, and other things developed. Seeing the problem, other souls dipped into matter to save them, but instead enslaved them. Coming into deep matter seemed to bring with it all the baser characteristics. As usual, the souls began to blame God for the problem and insisted they needed bodies more in keeping with their separate and individual abilities. They claimed the animal bodies were the problem.

"So, the Great All did as they wished, creating bodies in the image of godly characteristics. For a brief while the souls were happy with the new types of bodies, but after some time the old problems arose again. The souls kept forgetting about God and their own spiritual nature. Soon they lost their knowledge of the great mysteries, and the universal truths and how to activate them. They succeeded only in destroying the great civilization they had built.

"There were a few survivors, but each went his own way to a separate part of the world, remembering only a part of the truth. The brotherhood of which we Essenes are part has gathered all the mysteries together in our schools.

"Abraham was a very devout worshipper of God, who was called Brahm in the Chaldees. He was so devout that he was called A-Brahm. He was called out from the city of Ur to found a nation of priests who would lead the souls back to their former glory with the Adonai. This land was given to him in peace, but his descendants returned from Egypt and took it by war. So our people, Israel, are not following the will of Adonai. We await the Mashiyah who is to come and show us the way."

"Thank you, Rabbi," whispered Yochanan.

Simon looked perplexed. The entire discussion had hardly touched him. His sole concern was his own burning question, and he quickly arose lest some faster body get the floor. Simon was tall and huge for his age. He had great muscles from rowing the boat, throwing the nets, and hauling in great numbers of fish. His family were fishermen, and that was all Simon wanted to do. The smell of fish clung to him and all our baths seemed not to diminish it one bit. His idea of bathing was to plunge into the Sea of Galilee, occasionally.

It was only at the insistence of his mother that he had come away to school with his brother, Andrew. It was clear that Simon believed schools were where one found fish and anything else was just an exercise in futility. So, my face began to burn even before his question was out. I knew it would be a disaster.

"Rabbi," Simon directed his question to the Elder, "are women truly equal to us men as this woman claimed this morning?"

Although we were to remain standing until our question was answered, Simon sat down immediately with a smirk on his face. He cast his eyes around to see who was agreeing with him only to note in dismay that the class was not with him. Each one leaned away from him lest the doom we all foresaw fall on one of us also.

"Why, Simon," the Elder laughed, "What evidence do we have that you are a man? Your question is that of a mere child, a boy with no beard and no mind. I can assure you that you are not the equal of Judith, so do not fret yourself. Be content with your size for it is all you have."

Simon was stunned. He had no idea what he had done. He was aware he had asked the wrong question, but how could one ask the wrong question? Was this class discussion not intended to be free flowing, where any question could be asked? That had been the description. I took pity on him and asked the question for him.

"Rabbi," I addressed Judith, "your first great truth this morning was the division of souls into male and female bodies, and we understood you to say the body of the female was equal to the body of the male. Yet all that we have been taught prior to now and all that our culture seems to indicate through the law and tradition is that females are here solely to serve males. Even our scriptures say that 'If a man commits adultery, he shall answer to God, but if a woman commits adultery, it shall be her husband's fault for failing to provide for her need.' Everywhere we find females subjugated, servile, and oppressed. What is the truth in all of this?"

"I shall defer to the Elder for the answer to your question, Yeshua," responded the rabbi.

Once again the Elder began to speak, repeating the most basic truth of life on Earth. "All souls began in the Mind of God. There were no male and female. When the souls began to manifest into matter, God warned them that being earthbound would cause them to take on the attributes of the material. But the souls insisted it was their right.

"Again God warned the souls that taking up bodies of earth would require that they follow the laws of matter. Still the souls insisted.

"God warned that bodies had built within them passions that would be in conflict with their spiritual nature, but the souls had no concept of conflict, never having experienced it. Finally, God warned that the manifestation in earthly material would cause them to forget the All and lose their great powers.

"The souls paused at this, but never having been in deep matter they could not conceive of forgetting. Never having had problems, they could not see the possibility.

"'So be it' allowed the Adonai as the souls asserted their free will in conflict with the will of God for the first time.

"You heard this morning how the souls took up residence in animals, which resulted in half creatures and brought about a demand for bodies of a higher nature. Our loving Creator prepared the bodies but warned that the laws of earth required a division into male and female for purposes of procreation.

"To ensure that the divided souls would not try to kill each other in a wholesale slaughter, the Adonai made it impossible for one sex to survive without the other.

"Nevertheless, it was only a short time before the males, who were stronger physically, began to enslave or slaughter the half animals, subhumans, and even weaker ones such as females. The weaker ones were mostly enslaved since they were the females and needed by the males. Thus, the fall of souls was complete.

"God gave Moses ten commandments, but the people groaned that they were much too difficult. So Moses modified them, thus turning ten into a hundred with a thousand levels. Again it separated males and females as the priesthood interpreted the many interpretations. But with God it is not so and was never intended. The fall of man is his enslavement of woman, his failure to believe God.

"The School of Prophets is designed to heal the breach between man and God by first healing the breach between man and woman. The power available to whoever understands this mystery is incredible."

Even I stood in awe of this explanation. Simon seemed not to understand it at all, and I am not sure even Yochanan did. The Elder had gone right over our heads, and I knew it would be years before I completely understood his words. I never thought of myself as male or female except when Yochanan and I played our games of remembrances, but I knew that my mother and Judith were powerful women whose teachings had lifted me up to the Most High all of my life.

The year flew by filled with many such weighty lessons and discussions. We explored concepts that not in my wildest moments had I ever dreamed, and always they were somehow connected to the advent of the Mashiyah. I bounced between Simon who hated the studies and Yochanan who loved them but longed to be back in the wilderness pursuing his chosen path.

At the end of the year, in late fall, Judith called me to walk with her. It was early one crisp morning and we climbed to the top of a mountain where the view was clear and expansive. Just being there alone in her presence was exhilarating. We sat for a moment and looked at the panoramic view spreading out at our feet.

"You are fourteen years old now, Yeshua, and we are sending you to Heliopolis in Egypt.

"Why?" I cried out as I jumped up. "Surely I have not learned enough to leave, and Yochanan is still struggling with Hebrew."

She laughed and said Yochanan would go with me. At that I relaxed a little, but was still a little anxious. Knowing Yochanan I was not so sure I could get him past the southern desert he loved so much. She noted my anxiety.

"You and Yochanan have come along very fast. We are sending you to the School for Initiates to begin your study for the Master Rabbi degree. You will not be there long at this time, for you will go on to India soon after you are enrolled and receive orientation. We think your mind is open enough to receive all the teachings of that land without losing what we have taught you."

"What about Yochanan?" I asked. "Will he really come with me?"

"His way is not yours. He will go to Heliopolis with you, but he will not stay. He cannot tolerate Adonai being called Osiris," she explained.

I had to agree that Yochanan was sticky about words. He hated it when he was called John or I was called Jesus. He would refuse to answer at all and get a little peeved at me for not caring what I was called. He especially showed disdain for those Jews who actually took Greek names. It was certainly true he would not stand for YHWH to be called Osiris.

"He will grow out of it, Yeshua," Judith assured me, "but it will take a while. When you go to Giza for your final studies after your travels to the East, perhaps he will go with you and remain. I will encourage that. For now, enjoy him, for he chooses a very difficult way to learn."

"What about the rest of our class?" I asked.

"Surely you can see they are far behind you two?" she responded.

"Well," I hesitated, "they do seem not to follow the lessons with much understanding."

"Measuring with acceptance is not judging, Yeshua. It is measuring with rejection of another's level of development that curses the soul. Your desire is to lift them out of their ignorance, not castigate them for being there."

"Yes, yes, that is certainly true," I eagerly accepted her explanation. Was it false pride that made me so accepting?

"And," she smiled as she continued, "your problem will not be with measuring those inferior to you, but will be with those superior to you."

That humbled me. For she said it as though millions were superior to such a stupid child as I, or so I thought. How wrong I was, I realize now. But then, well, I was just budding into awareness. What else can I say?

Early the next morning Yochanan and I headed south toward Egypt, where I had not been since I was five years old. Since we were walking, I figured it would take about thirty days, more or less. Yochanan was a willing companion since he was so ready to leave Carmel and any excuse was good enough. He was actually jolly. We loped, then ran a while, then slowed to a walk only to rest. I insisted we follow the route that lay along the Great Sea lest Yochanan decide the wilderness around Qumran was calling.

"'I called my son out of Egypt,'" he quoted our ancient writings as we walked along. "I am going to listen for the call, Yeshua, to be sure you hear it."

"We are not even out of Palestine and already you want to leave Egypt," I replied.

Good Yochanan poked me in the ribs to show he was teasing, and I had a good laugh. He was in such a good mood that I decided to relax and just enjoy him, as Judith had suggested.

Chapter 7

The School for Initiates

As Yochanan and I walked into the verdant little village of Heliopolis, I put away the map that Judith had given me. She explained that it had been given to my mother by visiting magi at my birth, a puzzlement to me, but I thought perhaps they had used it on their first trip to Egypt–a keepsake more than anything. Nevertheless, I was glad to have it since good maps are very difficult to find and who wants to wander around the southern deserts forever? Well, perhaps Yochanan would, but not me.

The village had not changed much in the nearly ten years since my childhood stay there, and I felt like I was returning home since all of my earliest memories were of that place and time.

"I hope Micah still lives in the same place, and that I can find it," I confided to Yochanan.

"Didn't you say he lives in the synagogue?"

"That is where he lived years ago," I returned.

"Well, it won't be hard to find among all these pagan temples," he sniffed.

Ahhh, there it was. My worst fears founded. Already Yochanan was looking at Egypt as a land of pagans instead of as a land that had long nurtured our people Israel in time of need. I loved him for his faithfulness and loyalty to Israel and YHWH, a loyalty that admitted nothing else as worthy of thought. Yet all the world was created by God, so somehow, I thought, it must be my mission to bring Yochanan to love it all. This could easily take a lifetime.

"Look, there is the ancient temple of the sun god Ra," I exclaimed, quite forgetting that that was the most immediate sticking point with Yochanan. I continued on, blissfully unaware of his growing distaste, "I spent many happy hours in those temple grounds with Micah and the great librarian, who were always studying ancient scrolls."

I paused to feast on the ornate structure with its many columns and carvings of human bodies with animal heads, and the animal bodies with human heads, which seemed to confirm the Elder's story of creation. The sun shining on the temple gave off a brilliant glow that could not fail to impress even the most idle observer.

"It must compare favorably with King Solomon's temple to God," I mused.

"Nothing rivals Solomon's temple to God," scowled my cousin.

Too late I realized my mistake. I could see that Judith was right. Yochanan would not benefit much from study in Egypt with such resistance. Yet he was different from the closed-minded Pharisees and Sadducees. Yochanan's mind seemed to be full of YHWH with room for nothing else, whereas the Jerusalem priests seemed to believe they already had all the information of value. There was a difference, I thought. I frantically tried to think of some way to get Yochanan's mind off the gods of Egypt.

"I smell the bakery," I cried out.

Yochanan sniffed the air and his eyes widened. "I believe I do, too," he sniffed again.

"There it is," I pointed. Just a few steps down the lush, lined path past the majestic temple stood the squat, square, sun-baked mud brick synagogue of the Hebrews', a combination of synagogue, home, and village bakery. Its very starkness amidst the splendid temples of Egypt gave it an air that was indescribable.

Suddenly, out of the synagogue flew Micah, rotund as ever. He fell all over us with his warmth and hearty chuckles, pulling us close, and pushing us back to look at us. Tears of happiness streamed down his rosy cheeks as he unabashedly kissed first me, then Yochanan.

"I've been hearing of your progress down the coast for days," he cried.

Startled, Yochanan and I looked at each other, for we thought surely we had traveled faster than any of the slowly moving caravans or even the small family groups we had encountered along the way.

Micah laughed with glee at our surprise. "Behold, Yeshua, you forget the Egyptian runners who speed with the wind lest their lives be forfeit and the camel riders who carry precious goods for the kings of the world. They saw you boys asleep in the night while they had to travel on."

It was unsettling to note that we had thought we were cleverly hidden away from spying eyes as we bedded down for the night's rest. We failed to realize those cat-eyed sprinters knew all the secrets of the highway, especially good sleeping places, where they occasionally caught a few winks themselves. We must have done them out of a few of their favorite spots. I realized someone had been about the morning we awoke to a bag of fresh figs. But Yochanan claimed some careless traveler had lost it the day before and we had just failed to see it.

"Not so, Lion of the Desert," I had argued. "It is not my eyes that grow weak with hunger; I would see bread in every stone then."

He laughed it off and claimed my imagination would be the death of me sooner or later. I forgot about it until a few days later, when there was a pouch of bread and cheese laying on a boulder just where we turned west from Sinai into the Egyptian delta.

"Another careless traveler," I opined. "At this rate we need never worry about food. The careless will feed us."

Yochanan merely shrugged and claimed food was not difficult to find; there were locusts everywhere. My stomach turned over at the mention of his favorite food.

"Your food is dead, Yeshua," he had declared. "Dead foods make dead men; mine is still alive when I eat it."

The Essenes believe that they should eat food while it is still living, which usually means fresh fruit from the tree or vegetables from the ground. They do not eat animals or insects of any kind, dead or alive. But it was no use arguing with my cousin about details. He was one who went his own way, right or wrong, answering only to God. So I resisted chiding him for putting me off the scent of strangers, but it was a mighty effort. Keeping him in Egypt was my goal, and I must not forget it, I reasoned.

Micah pulled us into the combination synagogue, home, and bakery. The bread of life was what he was selling, he claimed, and it was but a step away from a piece of warm, freshly baked loaf to the

Staff of Life pouring from the very mouth of God. He never failed to mention these homey observations to his many customers.

"Osiris, Zeus, Adonai–what does it matter what we call the Creator of us all? Bread is bread," he would tell his Greek customers. He varied the names of the gods a little with each shopper, but the message never varied.

Micah was an Essene. The brotherhood in Egypt, however, was called the Theraputae, for most of them were healers. Micah called himself whatever the occasion demanded. Words were just tools to him for getting the message out. It was my earnest hope the concept would wash over on Yochanan.

Micah never stopped talking. As he filled our bellies with the wonders and delights of his stores, he regaled us with stories of ancient Egypt.

"'Ptah' needs to be spat out of the mouth to pronounce it right," he winked at Yochanan in an effort to trivialize the pagan gods into acceptability.

"Who needs to pronounce it at all?" Yochanan murmured.

Micah looked at me, and I just shook my head and cast my eyes down. Try as he would, even my beloved Micah was failing with Yochanan. I began to count the hours until he found just the right words to trigger a dash for Judea. My bones could feel it coming. Even when we finally slept, my dreams pictured Yochanan fleeing this alien land that I called the home of my heart.

Early the next morning we set off for the School for Initiates. Although the registration building was set apart, I knew that many classes would be held on the grounds of the sun god's temple. When I suggested we visit that beautiful work of art, Yochanan declared he would not enter a pagan temple or its grounds.

"But Yochanan," I urged, "that is where the library for the school is located. Scrolls from all over the world are stored there. You will want to see them."

I shall never forget the look on his face nor his words as he asked, "Did we leave YHWH in Palestine?"

"No, no, of course not," I anxiously protested, searching vainly for the right words to soothe his troubled spirit. "As initiates, we must study the religions of the Egyptians as well as all the others of the world."

"I don't care about the other religions of the world," he replied, his words edged with ice. "The Anointed One is coming then there won't be any other religions in the world, so why bother with what is already dead?"

I stared at him hopelessly. Judith was only a little off in her timing. I sensed I was losing Yochanan's companionship right there, yet more words failed me completely. I could not conceive of such a small thing as walking into a pagan temple stopping his studies, yet I knew it was forbidden to devout Jews, like eating pork. He willingly flouted so much tradition, yet here he was using it to question my devotion to God, towering like a black cloud building before a storm. We were brothers in our devotion to YHWH, but suddenly there was a split in our perceptions that threatened to splinter our relationship into a thousand pieces. I chose to worship with a mind open to all of YHWH's creations, while Yochanan chose to fill his mind with YHWH only.

"Did you not know why we came to Egypt?" I asked softly.

He studied me for a while, looked down at his feet, kicked at a pebble, wrinkled his forehead, and sighed, "No, I guess not. I just never thought about it. Judith suggested I would not like it, but I insisted you not make the long trip alone."

Tears ran down my face. How could I love him so much and still be so different from him? Yochanan was an unbending Essene without a liberal bone in his body. Schooling at Mt. Carmel had set in stone the teachings of YHWH, and Yochanan had no intention of chancing challenge from any other source. He seemed to see my willingness to allow other views to challenge my own as a threat to YHWH. I believed faith must be challenged to grow truly strong.

"Oh, Yochanan" I sobbed, "I must follow this course. It is Adonai who directs me."

"And it is Adonai who directs me," he said simply.

It was at that moment that I saw clearly we must go our separate paths for now. For him to come with me on mine would make us both miserable. It might even shake the faith of one of us beyond our ability to hold fast. There were obviously many paths to God and hardly any were exactly the same. So I let go of my firm grip on his soul. At fourteen, the problem was beyond me. I could not solve it.

Tears were streaming down his face as he realized we were parting. "The southern desert of Judea is where I belong. Already I have been away too long."

We flung our arms around each other as a terrible gloom settled over us. How could the brightness of that wonderful Egyptian morning have been chased away by a slight difference of religious views? Where only an hour before the clear light of YHWH's bright sun had illuminated our paths, there were now only dark clouds of doubt casting shadows over us both. As the years went by, I saw men kill each other for slighter differences, entire nations split over lesser hairs.

I could still remember looking at Ra's obelisk with my parents and Micah. There seemed nothing wrong with that. What was Yochanan afraid of? Ah, that was it. It was fear that I sensed in Yochanan. And why not? His life had been vastly different from mine. How could he help but be full of fear reading those fear-filled writings of a vengeful God while remembering the murder of his father? Having to flee for his own life into the safety of the desert, he could not help but carve out a little fear for a god who was pictured by the priests as vengeful, jealous, and angry. No wonder the poor boy feared setting foot in a heathen god's house, he probably feared it would fall in on us both. Even with this illumination, I knew it was useless to talk about it. A later time when we were both older and had the benefit of maturity would be the best time.

"God go with you, Yeshua," he whispered in my ear as he gave me a final hug. "I will await you forever at Qumran and pray for you daily.

"Your prayers will preserve my life," I responded, "and you will never be far from my own."

With those simple words we parted. He turned away leaving me at the entry to the School for Initiates that would dominate my life for the next fourteen years.

Basically, I am a joyous soul and teenage boys have short attention spans, so I did not grieve for Yochanan long. Standing at the threshold of a whole new way of life in the middle of an ancient, mysterious land, I was filled with anticipation and excitement. After such an experience with my cousin I could not help but wonder at the prohibition that had stopped him. Would the world really cave in if I stepped foot in a pagan temple? Surely it was not so. My parents, Hillel, the Elder, Judith–none had admonished me to stay clear. Nevertheless, it gave me pause for consideration.

As I entered the long, low, rambling building that bordered the temple grounds, I looked up anxiously to see if one of the columns might be on the verge of toppling over. The ancient city of On had always been a religious center, and the ben-ben, an early sun symbol composed of a phoenix perching on a pyramidal plinth, could easily topple over on a Jewish youth so brash as to enter the portals of Re. I took no chances and scurried into the registration building.

"I am Yeshua, most recently from the School of Prophets at Mt. Carmel in Palestine, formerly of Nazareth and Capernaum," I announced to the registrar, a scraggly, skinny old priest with snaggled teeth.

He picked up a quill and grinned at me as he cupped his ear and asked me to repeat my name.

"Joshua? Did you say Joshua?" he inquired.

"No, not Joshua," I exclaimed, a little startled. "Yeshua, Yeshua is my name. Yeshua, y-e-s-h-u-a," I spelled out.

"Jeshua," he carefully wrote in the book.

"We have a difficult time with your Hebrew names," a soft voice spoke quietly behind me. Whirling around, I beheld a tall, majestic man clad in purple robes. He was ageless and had a kingly bearing. Ropes of gold hung from his neck, so I supposed he was the high priest of Osiris, whom I was told would guide my life while an initiate.

His warm brown eyes danced as he suppressed a smile and announced that he was the mysterious Amen, my sponsor at the school. His dark curly hair was neatly trimmed at shoulder length while his facial hair was sculpted to his face closely and cleanly. Although twinkling, his eyes were hooded and shrouded with bushy brows.

Stupidly, I mentioned the registrar had my name wrong and instantly realized only a callow youth would whine over such small things.

"It is unimportant," he explained. "You will be called many names during your lifetime and some will not be so pleasant as the one under which you are registered."

I laughed, too, realizing he was probably right and happy that the Egyptian magi at my birth was here to greet me. Yosef had told me many times about that night when Amen had told them about the king's sickness and how the king would soon order all the babies killed. He had urged them to come away to Egypt at that very moment, but my mother would not.

"Come, Yeshua, let us go on tour of the ancient city of On." He pulled on my arm. The Greeks had renamed the religious center Heliopolis, but many Egyptians who traced their line back past time itself still called it On.

Amen pointed out the pleasant-looking building where I would be housed while receiving orientation, then proceeded to the marketplace.

"It is all right for Essenes to dress simply and ply their trade, Yeshua, but Initiates must dress properly lest our school get a bad name."

I looked down at my homemade shift and realized that beside him I must appear a beggar indeed, "Will you help me pick out the proper wardrobe, most honorable rabbi?" I requested.

"But of course. You must look scholarly if nothing else. You are one of the chosen ones, and you must look the part. Our Initiates are known all over the world and are protected in many countries, but we cannot expect anyone to guess who you are. Your dress is your badge announcing you as a special person." With that he wandered into an elegant little clothing stall and ordered me fitted with clothes proper to my new status.

The merchant fawned and made a fuss that embarrassed me greatly. Yosef was quite well off and certainly my paying for the clothes was nothing. But I was content with clothes made by the woman who sewed for all of us. Never before had I been to a men's clothier. As the man taped and measured and hauled out materials of silk and threaded gold, I winced. Amen ignored my despair. He took me next to a silversmith's shop and picked up a silver medallion with an engraved letter I upon it. Carefully, he hung it around my neck.

"If you are beaten, robbed, and disrobed, this medallion will warn that life for them has shortened considerably. Wear it always. It is your protection and will usually save you."

"It sounds awesome," I mumbled.

"You are never to defend yourself," continued Amen. "You are a holy man blessed by the gods. You will sit in the courts of kings, counsel the royal ones, or reign yourself. Whatever course your life takes, you must never allow your physical person to be mauled. Yet you cannot participate in violence. If you are killed, it is God's wish. Even the bandits of the road know deadly consequences await the one who harms a single hair on the head of a holy man."

I pondered his words as he drew me out of the village and down a path heading toward the pyramids. Giza, where the Great Pyramid rests at the edge of eternity, was not far from Heliopolis. Ancient when Moses lived, the Great Pyramid covered over thirteen acres. I was exhilarated by the magnificence of such perfect symmetry in so huge a monument to man's ingenuity. It towered over the lush valley of the Nile, defying the vast desert beyond to encroach on the fertile plain of the river.

As we walked along, Amen began a story that matched the pyramids in its breathtaking scope.

Chapter 8

Amen

"We magi began to see your star rise centuries before you were born, Yeshua. It was faint at first, but the light of it was never in doubt. We taught our students of the stars exactly where it was and how to chart its progress. Every soul has its own star, of course, but yours stood out from the rest, a little more brilliant, a steadier beam. We marveled, for it never dimmed, but grew ever brighter.

"Some of us began to reckon the time of your birth, and a few of us even perceived the general location. I was young when you were born, a newly mantled initiate, so I insisted that I must follow your star to Palestine. Because astrologers all over the world had been charting your star for centuries, the older ones here helped my cause, and I was allowed to go.

"Day and night I urged my camel to hurry as the star stood ever brighter just ahead of me. I feared greatly that the advent might occur before I could arrive. Even in the early dawn, the star's brightness vied with the sun for dominance of the eastern sky; it was a daystar sparkling brilliantly. I slept little, for the excitement coursed through my body, raising it to a fever pitch.

"As I reached the edge of Jerusalem, I met other magi coming from Persia and faraway places I did not know. They, too, had seen the star and were anxious to see its heralded soul. Some of the astrologers I recognized, for they were kings in their own domains and I had sat in their princely courts. We all considered this phenomenon too great to trust uninitiated runners to accurately report the event.

"Three of us were selected to go into Jerusalem and consult the king for permission to visit the newly born princeling. You can imagine our surprise when we discovered King Herod to be a dissipated old man full of fears and sicknesses. It became apparent that he was not the father of the newly born prince. We left the court as quickly as we could, promising the king to advise him of the whereabouts of the babe. But, as we were leaving, a gnarled, wizened old man (obviously a holy man) whispered that the ancient writings of the Hebrews said Bethlehem was the birthplace we sought.

"I thanked him profusely, covered his palm with gold, and began hurriedly to walk away. The holy man caught my sleeve and refused my gold.

"'I have lived all my life for just this moment', he declared. 'Take the babe and flee, for Herod seeks to kill him.'"

Amen continued as we stood in the lengthening shadows of the palms, "For the first time in my life fear filled my heart. Had we waited so long for this moment only to have it snatched from us by that drunken old debaucher masquerading in the guise of a king? My question was answered as I realized that my country was a perfect place of refuge for the blessed family, and I rushed out of the palace thanking Osiris as I happily removed myself from the stench of evil.

"Quickly, I sought out the waiting magi, told them all I had learned and hurried them off to Bethlehem. Rightly enough, there in a stable, we found you wrapped in swaddling clothes. Some poor shepherds were all that were there to attend your long-awaited birth. Nevertheless, none of us were put off by the humble surroundings. In fact, under the circumstances, we marveled at the supreme intelligence of the Great All for hiding you so cleverly in one of the many caves of the area. What would appear to most to be unprincely surroundings appeared to us as godly bounty.

"Seeing that your mother was just a child herself and your father dumbfounded over our sudden appearance, we quickly organized a plan of escape for them. Informing your father of Herod's plan of evil, I carefully drew a map for them to follow to Alexandria with instructions on whom to see. We each gave them gold and frankincense and other valuables so they could bribe their way out of Judea, if necessary. Gold speaks much louder than words with men of evil regardless of the problem.

"Alas, your mother insisted on following all laws of purification even to presenting you for blessing at the Temple of your God in Jerusalem. Hurriedly, we magi counseled and concluded that the sodden brain of the crazy king would be slow in moving without a clear plan of action. We engaged some protectors to watch over you and your family, called on our many powers for aid, and stole away in the night, as silently as we had come.

"The gods were with us, for only a day or so after your parents left Jerusalem for Egypt, your king ordered all the babies under two years of age in Judea slaughtered. The wily old king was able to keep the deed quiet from all but the hapless mothers and their immediate families. Gold saved those children of the rich and silence covered the shame. Not one chronicler mentions it to this day."

Amen's story astounded me, and my heart quietly broke. Not in my wildest imaginings had I even suspected that my birth and the slaughter of innocents were remotely connected. No wonder Elisheva and Yochanan remained in the safety of the southern desert. No wonder so many Judeans wore sad, long faces.

I had supposed the sadness sprang from the sights of roads leading into Jerusalem lined with crosses to which were nailed purported criminals who more often than not were Jews. Although I never knew any of those hapless victims, it brought tears to my eyes to see them hanging there in various stages of agony and death. I often suspected some of them were not guilty of anything at all.

Amen's information was far worse than I could believe. How could anyone murder all the baby boys under two on the off chance they might get rid of one who someday might become a king? It boggled my mind for its sheer insanity. Does anyone, even a king, truly believe he can stop destiny, or even change it one mite, if YHWH wills otherwise? Surely not. How much I had to learn.

Amen continued, "So you were spirited out of Palestine and brought into Egypt, where you remained for a while in the care of some Hebrews in Alexandria. I searched for just the right influence for your first years. When you were beginning to walk and talk, I moved your family to Heliopolis and put you in the care of Micah, who also was young, full of joy, and not so anxious to deprive you of a normal childhood as were the Alexandrians. I felt that God had put you in my care, and I was responsible for your education at least.

The youth of your mother concerned me, so we educated Yosef and your mother as well, broadly rather than narrowly, as the Hebrews tend to do.

"Therefore, you already have the information we give our beginning Initiates. So we are sending you right away to India. The magi present at your birth insisted you be sent while still young enough to teach new ways and ideas that may be foreign to you. If you indeed take the throne of the Hebrews, the world will be a better place if you have the wisdom of your ancestor, King Solomon."

The idea of me ever being king of anything overcame the sad news of why the babies had been killed that had been uppermost in my thoughts. How could I become king? After all, there were many descendants of the House of Judah as well as claimants to descendancy from David, the king. Amen seemed to be talking about a physical kingdom, while Judith and the Elder talked about a spiritual kingdom. Not to mention the fact that Rome appoints our kings based on political reasons that have nothing to do with who descended from whom.

Amen gave me so much to think about with the death of the babies and the prospect of me being a potential king, that I quite forgot to ask about why my star should cause any excitement at all, much less why magi from far away should care. After all, there were kings all over the place appointed by Rome, and even the Bedouins who traveled the desert had kings of each little wadi. It was nothing to get excited about or to travel around the world just for a look.

"I am here to study to be a good rabbi," I declared to Amen. "I don't want to be a king."

He smiled at me, indulgently, I thought. Perhaps he mistook me for Immanuel. Wondering whether I should enlighten him of his mistake, I stumbled in the darkness that comes quickly in the desert and fell on my face. So much for enlightenment. Watching my step was my first call lest I be called clumsy of head as well as foot. I scrambled up and tried to preserve as much dignity as I could.

"Do I leave tomorrow?" I asked as we walked back toward Heliopolis.

"No, of course not, my son," he replied. "'Immediately' in an ancient land like Egypt means in about two months. 'Right away' means about six months."

Amen never laughed out loud, but I got a case of the giggles over that piece of information. He had produced a strange light that cast a glow on the path, and I deemed wonders never ceased in the land of the pharaohs. A light wind rose and blew the fragrances of the night blooms across my face. Inhaling deeply, I felt intoxicated by the heady night air. It was wonderful to be back in the land of my earliest remembrances and it was exciting to be alive. It was even better to be a youth with the first fuzz of manhood struggling for survival along the edge of my chin.

"Tomorrow you will meet the other Initiates of this class and you will all explore the pyramids. We want you to study them before you lose your sense of awe to familiarity. There will be a guided tour in about two weeks," he instructed.

How different the School of Prophets was, where we were put to studying the day we arrived and never ceased until the day we left. The Egyptians certainly did not believe in rushing things. Overjoyed that I would have two weeks to wander through the pyramids, I wanted to shout aloud my thanks to YHWH for bringing me to this enchanted place. To be ordered to study the pyramids was like being ordered to eat almonds encrusted with honey–it was a pure delight.

As I crawled into my bed of sweet-smelling rushes covered with a soft downy quilt, the idea of me being a king again crossed my mind. Snuggling down into the warmth against the chill of the night, I imagined that perhaps Yochanan had been right; perhaps I was Melchizedek, the priest king of Salem, back to continue that work envisioned so long ago when Abraham was called out to found a kingdom of priests. Certainly no one could accuse that work of being completed. It seemed to be another case of misunderstanding. The House of Levi, set up to become a model for priests, became the only priests. Examples have a way of becoming hard-and-fast rules with no room for growth.

It was enticing to contemplate a past life as something one started that could now in another life be brought to fruition. I drifted off to sleep spinning dreams of peace and prosperity and greatness for Israel, never once dreaming of the power that corrupts the soul of man.

The next day was not only the most exciting day I spent in Heliopolis, it was also the most memorable. There were seventy

Initiates from all over the world gathered together that clear, cloudless day. Many were mere boys, like me. Some were striking in their exotic manners and dress, and it was clear many were princelings. As a matter of fact, I decided early I was probably the only one whose plan was to be a simple rabbi. Whatever dreams others had for my life, whatever my star may have seemed to indicate, I was not convinced of my destiny. YHWH had not made that clear to me, and I had no intention of presuming anything that did not knock me down with absolute certainty.

As a group we went to the Great Pyramid then were left to our own desires. As was expected, we quickly dispersed among the tourists, and I found myself with my chin in the air staring up at the incredible height of the most spectacular sight I had ever seen. From where I stood I could not tell if the sides were glass, highly polished stone, or what. The pure white sides impressed me that this was a monument to mind over body from another time and another world. As I puzzled over the ageless wonder, I suddenly felt a movement behind me. I looked quickly around to see who was there.

Chapter 9

Mina

Standing just to one side was a beautiful, fragile girl of about eleven years clad in rags, indescribably dirty. From her bare feet to her tousled head, the sands of Egypt seemed to cover her. A pumice stone would have a time scraping that neck, I thought, as I stepped back away from her.

"What are you doing here alone?" I asked, not quite knowing what else to say.

"I'm earning my keep," she whispered shyly as she giggled nervously.

"Doing what?" I asked, innocently.

She giggled again and moved her foot closer to mine. She turned her luminous brown eyes up to mine and murmured softly, "Anything you in your desire might want."

I know I flushed from the roots of my hair to the tips of my fingers. I felt blistering heat course through my body and finally center in my private parts. My temples pounded, and I knew everyone could surely hear my heart thumping, it pounded so loudly. The suddenness of it all astounded me. I no longer saw a dirty Egyptian girl, but rather a desert nymph come to take me away on a silky cloud. I shook my head in an effort to clear it of those insane feelings. I moved several steps away from her and spoke harshly, the first harsh words I had ever spoken in my life.

"You should be home playing with dolls or mending clothes," I sneered, not realizing I was falling into the same mode men have for centuries when tempted by forbidden fruit.

"There is no money in that," she returned, ignoring my lack of kind words.

"Where is your father who will beat you?" I again maintained harshness in the vain effort of rejecting the thoughts trying to creep into my head.

"I do not have one at all," she began to cry.

My heart melted and I caught myself just before I put comforting arms around that child woman.

"Don't cry," I urged. "It was unkind of me to snap at you. Where is your mother?"

"She is too sick to work, so I must take her place."

Everything became clear in my mind, suddenly. I took her dusty hand in mine and asked to be taken to her home. As we walked along toward her village, I explained that I was not in the market for such wares as she offered, but that I might help her mother get well. She seemed happy at that and told me her name was Mina, after the Roman goddess Minerva. I was glad that those strange stirrings in my body stilled and returned to normal as I busied myself with information gathering.

It was not very far to Mina's village of Busiris. It was nothing more than a small collection of hovels mostly made of clay bricks, scraps of sundry materials, and cloth. The smell almost choked me. Ragged children, mere babes, crawled around in the filth and seemed more dead than alive. Breathing was dangerous since one inhaled flies along with air. Dust settled on me like a fine mist and soon I was covered, like Mina.

"Is it always like this?" I asked while brushing dust and insects off my face.

"Like what?" she asked.

"So, so—well, so full of dust and flies," my voice trailed off helplessly as I realized she was unaware of her surroundings and just accepted them.

"When it rains," she answered, "then it is all mud."

I groaned. Not even in the back alleys of Jerusalem had I ever seen such filth and poverty. The worst was yet to come, however, and we stooped down to enter the lean-to that was Mina's home. As I adjusted my eyes to the semidarkness, the squalor of the room inundated me. Lying on a pile of dirty rags was a woman old before her time. She was covered with open, oozing sores, her dark hair matted to her head with sweat and grime, her eyes staring vacantly, and I thought surely she was dead. But when Mina called to her mother, the pitiful figure closed her eyes and turned her head slightly toward us. She said nothing. A tear rolled down the side of her face, leaving a trail across the dirt. I wanted to cry with her.

Looking around as I grew accustomed to the half-light, I saw there was not much in the room except cast-off, broken pottery, and a pile of rags.

"We had to sell everything when my mother became ill," explained the girl, "in order to buy medicine and food. We sold our house, our furniture, most of our clothes. Now there is only me to sell."

Again I groaned as I squatted down beside the wretched woman, taking her hand in mine. It was like holding a wet, limp rag. The life was ebbing fast, and I knew I must do something quickly or she would be gone. But what? As I held her hand, I began to pray. I asked my Heavenly Father to give me back this one. As I prayed, I could feel an unusual energy coursing through my body and flowing into hers. I opened my eyes and saw color coming into her face. Her eyes opened and stared at me in a kind of amazement, which we certainly shared.

"W-who are you?" she stammered, weakly.

"I am Yeshua of Nazareth, an initiate from the temple of the Sun, the School for Initiates."

"Ohhhhh," she moaned. "My poor little girl did not know you are a holy man. Please forgive her. It was her very first time."

"You are both forgiven. Tell me your story."

She was brief, but her story was chilling. Her parents had been killed when she was Mina's age, and the bandits had sold her into prostitution. She had been forced to work at that ancient trade until she had Mina, that is until it became obvious she was going to have Mina. Then the bandits threw her out into the desert to die. But she had managed to make her way into Memphis, where she bore Mina. She had then been able to pay for her keep as well as take good care of her baby by selling her body with joy, the only profession she knew.

"Until I came down with this sickness, we had a very nice house and fine things," she concluded her sad tale.

I was completely shaken by her story. I had often heard of this kind of woman, but I had assumed they chose their trade. I never once considered they might be engaged against their will on the pain of death, or worse. It was the first time I had been confronted by the plight of women who had no family at all . . . what do others do for money? Is prostitution all there is for them? What happens in Israel, where we have been commanded to take care of the widows and orphans? I resolved to look at this question much closer.

I gave Mina's mother a pouch of coins and instructed her that under no circumstances was Mina to ply the family trade, that I would come again soon and help them. The wonder on their faces was remarkable. Such faith in a mere boy, even an Initiate, was incredible. But I perceived they believed in me with all their being.

As I left their home, I heard Mina's mother telling her they had been saved by the great god Ra because of Mina's innocence and selfless willingness to provide for her mother the only way they both knew how. I thanked YHWH for making clear to me what was the thing to do in such circumstances, how to cope with my unaccustomed feeling of sexual stirrings, and most of all for my discovery that all women are not as blessed as Judith and my mother.

As I murmured my thanks, it suddenly came over me that there were no female Initiates. It occurred to me that for a real balance in the world, females should be able to rise at least as high as they were forced to descend. Certainly, no one could argue that selling one's body for a piece of bread was about as low as one could be forced to sink. Why were there no Initiates who were female? Why no priestesses of Israel? Judith seemed more a grand experiment than the norm. Why? These were weighty questions, and even in my youth I realized they were beyond my grasp at the beginning of my studies, but worthy of study, I perceived even then.

So I hurried to Micah and told him of my experience with Mina and her mother. He seemed not the least surprised that instead of exploring the pyramids I was in the slums of Busiris aiding the needy. He recalled how I had slipped whole loaves of bread to Asmy, the camel driver's son, when I was only three years of age.

"Nothing ever changes with you, Yeshua," he remarked with a twinkle in his eye, "Now you not only want to share my bread with the world, you also want me to heal their bodies, and, I suspect, their souls."

"What was that energy that flowed from my body to hers?" I knew he would know, as I ignored his good-natured chiding.

But the good-hearted little rabbi merely laughed, picked up an armload of bread and honey, and away we went back across the long miles to Busiris and the ailing woman. They were astonished, I am sure, when a Jewish rabbi loaded with food crawled into their tiny hovel. Mina jumped up and ran to us exclaiming over the food. Her mother struggled to get up, but fell back into her rags.

"Theraputae," she whispered loudly.

"You know of us?" Micah asked as he immediately tore all the dirty rags from the entryway to allow the sun and air to invade the darkened room. "Let us air this place out, and scrub it clean."

He bagged up the filthy cloths and sent Mina to the river to wash not only the rags, but also herself. Out of the pouches we were carrying he produced medicated salves, body brushes, and a small skin of purified water. As he gently scrubbed her body, including the sores, clean, he covered them with the balm, instructing her to cleanse her mind of all impure thoughts.

"You must do on the inside exactly what I am doing to your outside," he insisted.

The miraculous change that was accomplished in a few short hours was a lesson that remains with me to this day. Micah let us all know in those brief moments that whatever was going on outside of one's body was an indication of what was going on inside of one's body, particularly the mind. All the pools of purification for body and mind that the gentle Essenes taught instantly made sense to me, as I beheld their effects on a seemingly unsolvable problem. How incredible, I thought, as I reviewed the glowing health of Judith and my mother, whose thoughts were the purest of the pure. Is this the key to all the mysteries? I pondered. Is mind the builder?

We remained for several days as Micah carefully instructed Mina on how to take care of her mother. He clipped all the hair off the ailing woman's head even to her eyebrows. The freshest leafy greens were to be her only food for a while. Not the garlic buds, but only the garlic greens, he instructed.

"Green is the color of healing," he smiled, "so eat a lot of it."

Mina's mother was not a great deal older than she, and they both solemnly promised Micah to do each and every little thing he demanded. They nodded their heads in unison and looked like flowers bobbing in the morning sun. As I looked upon the love that mother and daughter shared, I thought of a poem I had read somewhere.

You came into being from my deepest wishes
From my heart of hearts
And soul of souls.
When I worshipped God,
I worshipped you,
For the idea of God is born
First in thought,
then in body.

You were never far from my thoughts
As I grew from childhood
Into flower.
You were among my dolls that
Nestled in my arms
And snuggled close on a cold winter's night.

From the very beginning
You were there, in everything
That I beheld.
Wherever flowers bloomed
I saw you
In every star that shined
There was the One
My very own
Child.

And when you finally
Arrived
I took you unto me
And breathed a thankfulness
To my holy God
For you were life
The world to me
You belonged to everyone
And, yet, you were
Mine, my very own
Child.

Micah soon satisfied himself that Mina and her mother understood his instructions, had enough funds to cover their needs, and could do without him. He left while I declared I must continue my study of the pyramids. He was not fooled, however; he knew where most of my studies would be spent.

As Mina's mother recovered her strength and could take care of herself, I began to take Mina with me on my tours. The exploring became much more exciting than ever I dreamed possible. She even began to call me master as I explained the life of Initiates, my studies, Palestine, Judith, my family, and a host of other details that she seemed to drink in. She did so with a skill with which females seem instantly to know how to encourage males to continue their stories and dreams. I took advantage of the situation, of course, to tell her about my God, YHWH, and entrusted her with the secret that my God and hers were one and the same, just with different names.

"We have many gods," she dutifully reported.

"That is just an effort to teach you the many faces of the one God," I explained. "There really is only one."

Although I explained that I was only a beginning Initiate and not a master of anything, as yet, she stubbornly insisted that an older man like me was her elder. She declared that she was the first to call me by my rightful title as prophecy of what was to come when I graduated from the school and was fully mantled. When I showed the slightest irritation with her, she would call me Lord and Master. Soon I despaired of getting her to call me Yeshua or even Jeshua, getting her to walk beside me instead of a half step behind, or of her treating me like an equal. She treated me like a very old man, which gave me mixed feelings to say the least.

"I shall follow you always, everywhere, even to the ends of the Earth," she would stoutly declare as she stood just beyond the reach of my eye. "I am your very first disciple." She would shake her mass of dark curls and flash her opal-colored eyes as she stamped her tiny foot, which was all that remained dusty in her efforts to be Essene-clean.

Who could argue with all of that? I convinced myself that having a disciple so willing to sit and listen as I discussed the many things I had already learned certainly gave me some experience in my chosen profession. Who could resist that? I even succumbed to the belief that YHWH had sent us to each other for purposes of which I was not yet aware. Perhaps it was to learn more from her than I would ever be able to teach her.

Soon my days of exploration were over, and I returned to Heliopolis secure in the knowledge that Mina was now part of my life and ever would be. Micah and I spent a lot of time wondering how best to direct our precious charges, so newly turned from certain death into a new life.

"They should not remain in Egypt, counseled Micah. "They would always be known as the harlots."

"Ah, yes," I agreed. "A new life requires at least a chance to be a success."

We thought upon it for days when, seemingly out of nowhere, my cousin Lazarus popped into mind. Bethany was the home of a number of Essenes. The thought passed, however, as I concluded Mina's mother would never consent to go so far from her home. But, still, the idea lingered just at the edge of my mind.

One bright morning Micah sought me out and declared, "Let's send them to Palestine."

Stunned is an understatement of how I greeted his words. "Wh-what did you say?"

"What is the matter, Yeshua," laughed the jolly rabbi, "are you losing your hearing?"

"N-no," I fairly shouted, "I have been wrestling with that same idea and thought it much too wild."

He laughed again and said, "Ideas are all about us and open minds can easily pick them up."

"I would dearly love to send them to my cousins in Bethany."

"Then it is as good as done."

"What if they will not go?" I asked anxiously.

"They will."

"What if my cousins will not take them?" I indulged in the what-ifs that obscure the vision of men's souls.

The little baker who had often stood against the stiff-necked, ceremonially pure Jews of the north looked at me as though I had lost my senses. I could see him struggling with himself as he wavered between scolding me for doubting God's ability to make a way for divine will and teasing me for falling prey to doubt.

Something in between must have won, for he gently pointed out to me: "Do you think the Divine All put this wonderful idea into your head only to make it impossible to follow through? Is our God so impotent that taking these orphans out of their misery into a new life is left solely to our limited hands or upon your cousins' charity?"

He shamed me. One thing I knew about the family of Lazarus was their reputation for taking in every stray for miles around, Hebrew or not. Like my own beloved family, they constantly poured forth love and blessings on all who came their way, or "who God sent," as they put it. They counted everyone in need as their neighbor and gave generously from their abundance. "We are the hands and feet of Adonai," they claimed and proved it with every act.

"You humble me, Rabbi Micah," I mumbled, "with your divine wisdom."

"Leave it to me," he whispered as he hugged me close. "God and I have worked out many things in this alien land."

Mina was the one who did not want to go. Her mother sighed and accepted the will of Osiris, as was her nature. I explained to Mina that I, too, would soon be leaving to travel to faraway places where she could not come.

"I will finish my studies and return to Bethany when you are all grown up."

Weeping bitterly, she demanded, "Promise me I will always be called your very first disciple.

"A teacher needs disciples," I said solemnly, "and I promise you are and always will be my very first one."

I can see her still, with her mass of glistening ebony curls and clean shining face like a rainbow from stormy clouds. Her luminous eyes never flickered or glanced away from me. Her devotion was like a pure white pearl filtering its essence into my soul. Her laughter was gentle and tinkling in the soft summer winds. She lavished me with childlike love, and I wallowed in it.

True to his promise, the persuasive rabbi soon had our charges packed and scheduled to leave Heliopolis on the next caravan heading toward Palestine. Mina's mother was healed and growing healthier by the day.

As Micah and I stood waving to our orphans we had entrusted to the caravan, I called an anguished farewell. I knew even then that best plans sometime go awry, and I might be gazing on those wistful faces for the last time. Mina waved goodbye until I could see her no more. My last call to her were words for my mother.

"Hold my mother's hand and kiss her face for me. Tell her I will come soon. Kiss Lazarus and Martha and all my cousins. Tell them I love them. Tell mother I love her, too. And Yosef."

Micah put his arms around my shoulders in a man-to-man embrace. He assured me that we did the right thing in sending them away. We had spent the last few weeks teaching them to call YHWH Adonai instead of Osiris. We had done our best to teach them about the living God who created us all and created Israel to be a nation of light to the world. We did not know how much was accepted out of gratitude and how much was truly believed. But, as Micah said, we know that God looks only in the heart and counts effort as righteousness, seeking as finding, and accepting as believing.

We walked slowly back to the village, and I pulled my thoughts away from the events of the past few weeks and applied them to my orientation. It was not easy, but it was necessary.

I spent several months studying the maps located in the Great Library of Alexandria, to which I was sent as part of my orientation. The maps were detailed and showed great land masses at the north and south poles as well as to the west of the ocean just beyond our own Great Sea. My special interest, however, was concentrated on the bodies of water around Egypt and India that I would soon cross. I committed to memory the names of villages, rivers, and mountains that I might visit or have to locate as guides to other places. When I finally knew them all by heart, I presented myself to Amen for examination. After a few hours he seemed satisfied that I knew the geography of the lands I was to travel. He drew out a small but carefully detailed map and handed it to me.

"This will take you to Kahanji in India. He is the magi who first made me promise to send you to him. There is a weaver in Bhavnagar who will show you the way."

I took the map and studied it closely. "I treasure it already," I said.

"You will study the Vedas and the Upanishads, the timely thoughts of ancient masters who have preceded you," he instructed. "Kahanji will be your guide, and you are to give yourself to him completely. It may seem strange to you at first, but eventually you will see the merit of our plan. You will learn their meaning of life and how they view God."

Early the next morning I bade Amen goodbye. I proceeded on to Micah's for the same purpose.

"Go with God," whispered Micah as he held me close, handing me a basket of good things and clean clothes. I could smell the freshly baked bread, still warm to the touch.

"May God keep you until I come again," I said as I kissed both cheeks in fond farewell.

With long strides and singing heart, I headed down the path on my way to that faraway land of mystery, India.

Chapter 10

India

At fourteen everything is exciting, and my sea voyage was no exception. Although we hugged the coastline most of the time while sailing from Egypt to India, there were times when all I could see was open water. It was there on a vast ocean whose depth I did not know and whose breadth I could not measure that I realized what truly insignificant specks we mortals are in the scheme of things.

In the desert I had peered through a wonderful glass atop the Great Pyramid that permitted me to see a billion stars beyond the average eye of man (perhaps a slight exaggeration, but who really knows?). We are tiny specks on tiny bits of matter floating through space, whirling around a giant star that is just one among many that also whirl through space. How could anyone own a plot of ground and believe they had anything at all, or own a lot of it and believe they had very much? Whether in the desert under the limitless stretch of stars or upon the ocean, the feeling must be the same: insignificance.

As our ship, a fragile piece of bark at best, bobbed endlessly from mountainous wave to perilous valley, or slid easily on waters smooth as glass, or pitched violently in a storm, I realized how small man really is.

Yet, when I first stepped on the ship, I thought it was very large and only I was very small. All things being equal, it was certainly so. The ship was a freighter, much like an Alexandrian grain ship, carrying a great deal of cargo and about thirty passengers. The captain was master of all he beheld on ship and at sea. The men who rowed the ship when the winds failed the sails were mostly slaves, some mere boys, like me. "Criminals" they were called, who stole or killed—or worse, those who claimed the emperor of Rome was not a god.

To those who believed in multiple gods there was no problem. What was one more? Because Palestine had a sort of peace with Rome, my own religion was protected and we were not forced to acknowledge Caesar as a god. But the rest of the hapless world had a problem. So I was happy to be escaping the influence of Rome for a while with its overpowering presence that demanded everything and claimed it all as a right.

My favorite place was a stack of ropes piled forward in the ship. I spent many hours sitting there thinking of all the things I had been taught since that time in the Temple in Jerusalem at the feet of Rabbi Hillel. As a huge moon slowly came up across the horizon and hung low in the sky, I would drift off into sleep, only to awaken to sea air washing my face with salty spray. I would discover a platter of food left by the young man who saw to the needs of passengers. He was about my age and seemed to love my stories—I practiced my Greek on him for he was from Corinth—he would sit squatting on his heels for hours nodding his head in seeming agreement.

Apollo was his name after one of their gods. When I mentioned the one God of the Jews he exclaimed, "Ah, yes, that is Zeus."

"How can you claim Zeus is one god when you say Apollo is also a god?" I asked.

The thought must never have occurred to him, for he shook his head, threw up his hands, and said, balefully, "Who knows?"

Practicing one's calling of rabbi must be much like a doctor or lawyer's practice, one never really gets the hang of it. One is always just practicing. How one's head does turn when such willing students such as Mina and Apollo present themselves. Yet I could do no more than share the things I already knew, knowing full well that there were volumes of information I did not have.

"Where is your God?" Apollo would ask.

"Everywhere," I would answer.

"Just like Zeus," he would agree.

"Can you see your God?" he asked.

"No," I answered.

"Just like Zeus," he would again declare.

And so it would go. He must have noted the frustrated looks on my face, for often he would just sit beside me in silence. Truly those were the best times. Our souls somehow filled in where our words could not, and I could see we really were one. How to explain all of that was what escaped me. I realized he, too, was aware of it and just could not put it all into words.

When the ship put into port, Apollo was free to go ashore with me. Although he assured me the captain would not be so foolhardy as to leave without his holy man, I was not sure, so we never strayed far away nor tarried long. Once we were in port for over a month, but I slept on the ship every night and amused Apollo by refusing to venture even to the other side of the great city. For some reason I saw our little freighter as my home away from home, and losing it was the last thing I desired.

Hugging the coast, we went up the Persian Gulf heading north for several months then down the coast of Persia before we finally reached India. The entire trip took nearly nine months. Sea legs were all I had when I finally set foot on Indian soil.

I turned fifteen on this sea voyage. Truly puberty was fast upon me. Nevertheless, Apollo and I celebrated. Only when demanded by the high priest of Osiris shall I ever say how.

We landed late one afternoon in that mysterious land that rivaled Egypt in antiquity. Bhavnagar was hot and humid and sticky. Adult men stood around clad only in loincloths and some had nothing on at all except turbans wrapped around their heads. Children, of course, wore no clothes. It seemed like a naked country, and I felt grossly overdressed with just my shift and sandals. The women, however, had on long flowing saris and wore veils, so I was forced to retreat from the naked country description. It was a naked male country.

I wondered if I would be mistaken for a girl with my shift. It left me feeling like I was standing in a shower of water as sweat poured from every opening on my body. I packed up my belongings, and departed the ship like a drunken sailor. The rolling, weaving sensation had not plagued me at other ports like this one and I had mistakenly supposed I was immune. Alas, it was not so. Staggering over to the nearest grassy plot of ground, I sank gratefully into a soggy heap.

A weird wailing sound gradually seeped into my consciousness, and I looked across the way to see a naked fakir playing a reedy flute while the flat head of a coiled snake slowly rose before him. The viper swayed to the music undulating like a throbbing wound. I froze. Surely the snake would strike him, but again I was mistaken. As the music slowly stopped, the snake sank back into its coil. The Indian then picked up a rope, threw it up into the air, and slowly climbed it. By this time, a crowd had gathered and I saw nothing but naked backsides.

Surely the sights and sounds and smells of India were vastly different from all I had ever seen, even imagined. The heat was more intense. Muggy. I only hoped the sun would soon disappear and send cool air. I picked myself off the grass and began my search for the weaver described by Amen.

As I was winding along a stony path, I suddenly heard the clacking of a weaver's bone needles. The shop was nearby. I listened intently. Then I spied an opening in a wall where interlocking pyramids had been carefully drawn about a foot from the top. The Star of David in India? Surely that was the place. As I drew closer, I saw a finely woven piece of material hanging from a protruding post and knew it was indeed the weaver's shop. I poked my head into the opening and called the greeting of an initiate, "Peace to this house."

At once the shop was alive with bodies. I was pulled inside with eager hands, seated at a low table, and a bowl of cold, sweet liquid was pushed into my hands. I drank long and thirstily, but to this day I do not know what that frosty drink was. Yet as I gulped it down it was as if the nectar of God flowed through my being. Eager voices babbled unknown tongues in my ears.

As I sat enjoying it all, a vision of loveliness appeared and announced in Aramaic, "I am Ishfani. We have been expecting you. Did you see your sign on our door? I drew it myself."

She was dressed in a gauzelike sari and moved like flowing water. Her voice was like a brook softly cascading over ageless stones. Like a hummingbird, she seemed suspended in air, yet constantly moving. She led me back beyond the shop into a courtyard that was filled with spray from a splashing fountain that bubbled up from stones arranged like the Great Pyramid. Everywhere flowers and shrubs gave off fragrances that were matched only by tiny tinkling sounds from chimes located somewhere within the branches of a giant banyan tree. The filtered sunlight bathed everything in prisms of light that flashed off mirrors located about the ancient tree. Reality and fantasy curiously mixed in the courtyard of my hosts. Now, when I need peace and beauty and serenity, I return to that carefully constructed garden with my mind's eye and drink in its sounds and fragrances and beauty.

Past the garden was another room filled with cool shadows and softly flowing air. There, sitting in the cool quietness, was an elderly man who looked vaguely like the Elder, only younger. His hair was snow white laced with silver, overhanging a strong face filled with wisdom gleaned from the ages. His skin was dark, which heightened the light of his hair and eyes, which were a deep blue. He was clothed in a blue robe that looked like pure silk but draped him like feathery gauze.

"I am Azata," he said simply.

"I am," I hesitated briefly before I finally added, "Jeshua."

"We have been expecting you," he replied, "and made ready for your comfort."

"It is my pleasure to have finally arrived," I responded.

Although I knew that Aramaic, or forms of it, was spoken throughout lands I knew of, I was surprised to hear it in India. As though he were reading my mind, Azata explained that Aramaic was the language of trade in that land since the many dialects of India were too difficult for anyone not native to learn.

"We do a lot of trading with men from distant lands. We learn their languages lest we lose out in barter," he smiled.

I had difficulty thinking of Azata as a trader, or any other kind of businessman. He looked so spiritual to me that I thought surely he dwelled far above the barter of the marketplace. Little I knew of India, where religion was everything and the marketplace was tolerated to support its pursuit. Having done with the formality of greeting, I asked about religion in India.

"I am a follower of Zoroaster," he noted, "which is not the religion of India. The bulk of worshippers here are Hindus, or Buddhists."

"Tell me about your god, Zoroaster," I politely requested.

"Ah, my young friend, you are truly an Initiate. Hardly in my house and already you pursue your goal. Lest you become confused, let me assure you that Zoroaster was no more a god than you are. In fact he was a student like you, an Initiate, whom we believe was in school in Egypt at the time of your Moses."

Somehow, I had never thought of Moses as being an Initiate like me. He was our lawgiver and surely he was educated in Egypt, but the comparison had never crossed my mind. The idea fascinated, charmed, and intrigued me all at the same time. Azata looked more like a gold mine of information than a man, so I eagerly awaited his words.

"Really? Tell me more."

He threw back his head and roared with laughter. It startled me to hear such a hefty laugh, like approaching thunder from faraway hills rumbling in the distance ever louder until it is upon you.

"So, you would make me your rabbi instead of a simple weaver?"

"Not so, kind host," I responded thinking perhaps I had offended him. "I am just so hungry to hear everyone's ideas about that One whom we call YHWH."

Azata sobered and spoke thoughtfully, "Yes, of course, my son. I am teasing you. I can only tell you about our view of the infinite in general terms. To get to the very core of our beliefs, you need to go to Persia and study with those who make it their business to teach seekers of the divine through the eyes of Zoroaster.

"Here and there you will hear of that great man, Zoroaster, as many call him. But do not become confused. He was a man gifted with light. He was so gifted that some now claim he was the light. But in truth he was a wayshower, reflecting the light."

Azata sat silently for a while and I could see I had all the information I was going to get about this Zoroaster, whomever he was. So I turned my head slightly and glanced at Ishfani, who was sitting silently to one side awaiting the call for something we might need.

"My daughter," spoke the host, quietly, again divining my unspoken question.

She was dark, even darker than Mina at her most unwashed moment. Yet, I knew Ishfani was spotlessly clean. Her eyes seemed black as the black pearls gleaned from the oyster beds of Egypt. Her hair was blue black and wrapped tightly around her head away from her face, which seemed sculpted from agate. She was a dream fully materialized. Azata finally acknowledged my admiration of his daughter with an astonishing sentence.

"Ishfani will be your guide to Ahmadabad and your next school."

"Wh-what?" I stammered, as I became aware of what it means to have one's thoughts perceived.

"It will be a favor to me, Yeshua, for she wants to visit her sister, and I cannot get away at this time. My business interests press me. It is reasonably safe to travel in this part of India, but no young girl makes such a trip alone."

"No, of course not," I breathed as my heart jumped with joy at such an assignment.

What had I ever done in this or any past life to merit such a blessing? She liked me. I could tell by the way she looked away quickly when I glanced in her direction. I could feel her eyes on me when I was talking to Azata, and I stared at his face even harder as I tried to concentrate on what he was saying. His lovely daughter kept flowering in a darkened corner of my mind and filling it with her presence. I felt her flush as I showed my joy at having her company to Ahmadabad.

Self-importance grew at the thought of being trusted with so valuable a treasure. I could not know that every man would trust an initiate of God with his daughter, for what kind of man would lose everything of value he possessed, including his life, for a moment of passion that would be gone in the twinkling of an eye? Our reputation for honor was part of our protection; trust was our savior. Still, that I, Yeshua, a humble Jewish boy, was to escort a glorious princess of India to her sister's house was all I could think about at the time.

The long sea voyage over, the excitement of reaching India, and the revelation of Ishfani finally overwhelmed me and I could no longer suppress a yawn. I clapped my hand over my gaping mouth, but fatigue plainly showed on my face. Instantly the ever alert Azata yawned loudly, while Ishfani followed with a small one of her own. My benevolent hosts closed down the day with a light supper, then servants led me to bed. I promptly sank into oblivion.

Chapter 11

Bhavnagar

Until one greets the new dawn in a country like India, daybreak has never fully been experienced. I awakened to the low moaning sound of some creature that created a crescendo at the end of each trill. As I lay on my bed of feathers, I tried to figure out what made the sound. At first I thought it was some person calling worshippers with the strange sound. But as I grew clearer-headed and the cobwebs of sleep disappeared, I realized it was a bird. From a distance I heard an answering call like the cooing of doves. A sound at my door brought me quickly to my feet and I threw on my shift. A silent form flowed into my room and handed me a cup of hot, strong, sweet brew. It was delicious and sleep was gone for the day.

Following the servant out into the main part of the house, I met Azata, who clasped my hand in the familiar grasp of the brotherhood and directed me to follow him. As we hurried along, we were joined by many natives emerging from the houses along the path. We walked until we came to the bay where, not stopping, we walked right into the water. Azata took some flowers from the arms of the bearer who had followed us, handed me some, and began strewing them about on the water.

As he cast the blossoms on the waters, he softly chanted a strange yet familiar chant much like the "om" chant of the Essenes. I followed him and felt a sense of joy with this form of worship. My sense of worship mingled with that of the Indians. Surrounded by sunlight and water and my own youth-filled heart, I was experiencing a renewing of spirit, the goal of worship. Soon the bay was awash with blooms and chants and happy faces. As the sun slowly lifted into the sky from the edge of darkness, I knew I was fully in India and YHWH was here also.

Azata seemed to be a leader among the faithful, and every eye appeared to watch his most casual move. As we carefully wound our way out of the bay heading toward his home, I remarked upon it.

"Ah, Jeshua, you miss nothing," he smiled.

"How so?"

"I am a simple weaver, a seller of cloth. But you are not following the outward appearances. You are able to look inside. You will learn much in this country where worship is everything if it is anything."

He did not answer my question and asking again about his leadership was out of the question. Nevertheless, it seemed strange that this ancient weaver of cloth, who claimed to be a follower of Zoroaster, was the obvious leader of the natives, who were mostly Hindu.

There were many shrines that lined the bay, the paths, the roads. Some were ornate and some were simple, but there was no mistaking them. It seemed as though every tree had its own temple beneath its branches. Was this country a nation of shrines? Was religion even more dear in India than in Palestine? The land was filled with symbols of man's reach for the infinite. There seemed to be a peace in the land of the Hindu where an entire village arose at dawn and gathered at the edge of the sea in daily worship.

Was my mind still a bit closed? I had thought it was open.

Their reverence for life was incredible. Such a gentle people. Without a complaint they walked around animals that stood in their path, bowing even to the flowers. What prompted this spirit, this overwhelming gentleness? It was all so different from Palestine, where violence was constantly erupting or at least brooding just beneath the surface, looking for the chance such that the Essenes had to withdraw into the mountains to create an island of peacefulness. It was so strange, so exciting, to see this contrast. Understanding it was yet to come.

After a breakfast of fresh fruit, yogurt, and bread, Azata suggested a tour of his village. We wandered endlessly through twisting paths flanked with flowering shrubs, trees, and gardens. A daily supply of fresh flowers for worship was a requirement in this village and the supply seemed endless. It must have been the major part of the village economy.

"Not so," declared Azata. "The flowers are free for worshippers. No one is permitted to profit materially from worship of the Holy One. The leaders of this village count it a blessing to have a community of devout worshippers, and the profit is a spiritual one, beneficial to us all."

"Amazing," I said as my mind flew back to Jerusalem, where our Temple was full of priests haggling over sales of objects with which to worship.

"Our shrines are places of prayer. Business is conducted elsewhere."

"Incredible," I voiced surprise.

"A man could sooner peddle his children than the flowers provided by God for the worship of the divine."

My burning question was who designed this concept, Azata or the Hindus? I thought surely I would explode before I found the answer.

"Is it like this all over India?"

"It varies, depending on the leadership of the village. The people are basically spiritual. But, as you know, they are also mostly like sheep."

"Is this village guided by the teachings of Zoroaster or the Hindu teachings?" I ventured.

"This is a Hindu village, is it not?"

Again he refused to satisfy my question.

The small shrines were adorned with wind chimes that softly sang in the early morning breeze. The heady perfumes, the soft gentle breezes, the music tinkling lightly in the wind from a thousand chimes–all these sensations wrapped around me. This experience alone was worth the long voyage from Palestine to India, even if nothing else was accomplished. These gentle people had created a reality that was only a fantasy in most parts of the world. Suddenly, Yochanan's face arose in my mind. It was stern, forbidding, disapproving of my romance with another people's worship.

How can Yochanan be offended? I mused. But in my heart I knew he would be. He would think me bereft of my senses to worship with the Hindu. "You are a traitor to YHWH," I could hear him scream. Surely there would be a way for me to show my conservative cousin the way YHWH smiles on all efforts to worship in spirit. Was not Abraham a worshipper of Brahm, the god of the Hindus?

How could anyone fault a gentle people who used flowers and wind chimes for worship instead of bloody sacrifice? A people who waded into the waters of life and mingled with the elements in joyous worship every morning of their life? Who respected every living thing above self? How could he possibly fault them? But I knew he would. I loved them and every moment of their worship and joined in, even trying their chants that began with "Brahmmmmmmm, Brahmmmmmmm, Brahmmmmmmm."

Even their marketplace was different. Unlike Egypt and Palestine, where bartering was loud and often hostile, the merchants here smiled a lot and displayed their wares artfully. A soft voice called, "Silk for the Sahib."

Row upon row of neat stalls were piled high with goods from the countryside. Everything–baskets to vegetables, sandals to fruit, small animals to birds–was available.

The vendors were mostly men, although there were women who willingly sewed a garment for you while you waited. Their hands flew as they draped and stitched and arranged the delicate fabrics around a person, their voices suggesting a "please turn" or "stand so, please" to speed the process along. Just as their worship was a study in devotion, so was their merchandising a study in crafting. Everything was orderly, even the children who played quietly just a few steps out of the traffic of commerce. Surely I was dreaming. Surely there was no such place on earth.

"Who is that?" I asked Azata as I noted a young man who wore a long orange robe. He had a shaved head with a single braid flowing down his back, and he carried a musical instrument that he beat occasionally.

"He is a follower of Krishna."

"Who is Krishna?"

"A part of Hindu beliefs that you will study later on. Suffice it to know that the followers of Krishna abound in India. You will see disciples everywhere."

It was now obvious that Azata would not usurp the place of my teachers in my studies. He had given me a taste of his philosophy, his worship, his hospitality. More than that was ahead of me, and he had no intention of altering the plan laid out for me. Yet, I knew without any doubt I could have remained in Bhavnagar for years and learned everything I needed to know from him. He simply would not permit it.

"When do we leave for Ahmadabad?" I queried.

"Tomorrow."

The School of the Open Mind was about to get one of its most devoted, enthusiastic students it had ever had. The paradox of wanting to go and wanting to stay struck me. The choices one must often make are often of equal merit. The making of the choice is the measure of one's soul development. Only occasionally is one truly right or truly wrong. Those are the easy choices. It is the subtle ones that try the soul. Until now, my choices had more or less been made for me. But I sensed that from now on I was on my own. It excited me a little.

I felt like a freshet in the morning of my day, loving everything I saw and heard and felt. It was all so new, yet it seemed ancient. Discovering Azata, not in the Hall of the Initiates nor the School of Prophets, but in a weaver's shop in a small village in India imprinted on my mind a truth that was to influence me the rest of my life.

When everyone can accept the truth from whomever it may come, the whole world will change. How to recognize the truth might be a problem, however, as I would later learn.

"You will enjoy traveling this land and those beyond, meeting its people, sampling its essences," observed Azata. "You are so accepting. It will be a pleasure for all whom you meet to tell you their stories. Listen carefully, for it is the people who will teach you the things you need most to know."

"So, why must I go to schools of learning?" I asked. Azata just kept smiling, as usual, saying nothing else.

Ishfani and I were not alone on the trip to Ahmadabad. The group that traveled was almost a caravan. My camel was enough for me. But two extra ones were needed to carry Ishfani's requirements. Her tent, cooking equipment, clothes, extra tent for private things, food, all the things that gently bred young girls must have were loaded onto camels no one would be riding. My mother and Judith loved sleeping under the stars, but Indian girls of means did not, or perhaps were not allowed such pleasures.

The camel driver walked, as did the cook, and two extra boys who did everything from making a fire to setting up the tents. Also traveling with us was a young woman who did nothing but attend the needs of Ishfani. She had her own camel. It was a mystery to me why I was needed, but I supposed a male of authority was required when all else were servants or females. Those lines of demarcation again–they seemed everywhere. I did not realize that I was viewed as holy, thus we were all protected.

As we moved along the trail headed for Ahmadabad, after taking all morning just to load and say goodbye, I pondered why this was such a favor to Azata. What might have taken me two days at the most traveling alone would surely take a week with this small caravan. My good luck, I thought. With such a charge, I could easily take forever and think it brief. My first disciple, Mina, was long gone from my thoughts, and it was clear to me that I was smitten with the daughter of Azata. What to do about it escaped me at the time.

As the sun began to set on the first day and our camels cast long shadows on the earth, Ishfani exclaimed, "Jeshua, your hair!"

Quickly I started brushing my head, thinking something had landed there that was poisonous or at least dangerous, but I felt nothing. Ishfani's laughter filled the twilight air.

"It's the color," she explained. "It is reddish gold with a shimmering halo as the sun glints upon it. I never saw such a sight. And the fuzz on your face–it's golden, too."

That hurt. What man in charge of a caravan wants to be reminded that a full beard or even a semibeard is beyond his reach? Especially by a slip of a girl. Gritting my teeth and forcing a grin, I turned to her.

"Older women notice everything."

She winced. "I am not old. I am only fourteen."

"Our women are married and mothers by that age," I persisted, a bit unnerved that she should be so young and look so mature, hoping she would not realize my mother (and Judith and Mina's mother) was all I really knew about women.

"Hmmmmm, our women marry at sixteen, a more proper age for managing servants and households."

Realizing that what probably started out to be a compliment was turning into a fuss because of my vanity of wanting to be a man in her eyes, I threw up my arms and exclaimed loudly.

"Oh, Ishfani, what a wretched soul I am to take your beautiful observation and twist it into an argument. I apologize to you for my vanity. I want to be a man in your eyes without earning it. Please forgive me. It was kind of you to notice me at all."

That wonderfully innocent soul melted at once and acknowledged she had as much to learn about men as I did about women, a kind way to put the fact that I knew nothing at all. From her I must learn, I thought, for which school would have a course in women, or even a female teacher? It was with no effort at all that I knew Judith had been my one and only female teacher, a most rare exception to a firm rule.

"I suspect they do not teach the mysteries of women in the School of Mysteries," I declared. "Would you be willing to take the task?"

She smiled appreciatively at my efforts to compliment her, but refused to be my teacher, even as Azata had. "I am not a teacher, but only a simple Indian girl who is half Persian."

"Really?" I questioned. "How is that so?"

"My father is Persian and my mother Indian. Did you not know?"

"No, of course not. I never even considered it. How did Azata come to India?"

"Zoroastrians are God's businessmen on earth. My father came long ago to sell his cloth. He met my mother and was persuaded by my grandfather to stay in India, if he wanted to marry my mother. So, he did. And, they have lived happily ever after," she smiled.

"What a wonderful story," I said, "YHWH has truly blessed you."

"Who is Y-H-W-H?" she stumbled over the letters.

"Those are the sounds of the letters that stand for Adonai, my Lord and my God, the Creator of us all, the All of the world. The Hebrews never speak those letters aloud, but I do," I cast my eyes around to see if she were impressed.

"Oh", she said thoughtfully, "you must be talking about Ahura Mazda."

"Who?" I asked, startled by the unfamiliar name.

"Ahura Mazda. That is the name Zoroaster gave to the great God of the Sun many centuries ago in the Zend-Avesta."

"Probably not before Moses gave the name YHWH to the Creator," slipped out of my mouth before I could stop it. Aghhhhhhh.

I was quickly learning that the tongue that praises God can also curse man, all in the same breath.

Again I undid myself in her eyes. She looked away, and I perceived she was withdrawing. Just as she had been about to give me the information Azata had refused, my wagging, vain tongue had cost me dearly. My sparring with her had cost me the pearls of her wisdom, a terrible price to pay for vanity. Surely if one could only control the tongue, he could control his entire body. Yet, I persisted.

"Will you give me an idea, now, about your God, your teacher, your ancient writings as we ride along together?"

"My father says you are going to Ahmadabad to the School of the Open Mind. Your teachers there will teach you all the things you should know, I am sure. I would not want to give you a false view with my simple thought."

At least I was right about one thing: I had shut her off forever. This wonderful girl who was about to tell me about her deepest convictions closed that part of herself to me, and I had only myself to blame. How could I ever know the mysteries of women if I would not listen to them? At that moment I promised myself never ever again, no matter how tempting it might be, to fail to listen and even to encourage women to talk to me.

Still, there is nothing so persistent as a teenage male who wants something, so I tried a final time.

"The School is one thing, but you are quite another. I really want to know about your god and your master from your lips."

She turned and smiled sweetly at me, "Rather, I should learn from you, Yeshua. Tell me about your god and your master, Moses."

I was completely undone. She had no intention of casting her pearls before swine. She retreated into that self-effacing position I saw women all over the world assume. She had been ready and willing to be my equal, my companion, riding through life beside me, and I had thrown it all away in order to master her. I saw clearly that the position of women on Earth was subservient because of me and my male attitude toward them. I had to change myself to change the world.

What a powerful lesson I learned riding a camel between Bhavnagar and Ahmadabad with a fourteen-year-old girl. I breathed a sigh of thanks to YHWH for the lesson delivered in so simple a setting. It would never be far from me whatever path I chose.

Azata had warned me to listen to everyone's story and the first day on the road, I failed. He had put me in the position of master and taught me the lesson of servant, for a good servant listens and hears. At that moment I could have left India forever and been fully educated. But I did not know that then.

Preparations for the night were a noisy affair. Every camel was unloaded, watered, and hobbled. Then disaster struck. The stakes for Ishfani's tent hit bedrock an inch below the surface and would not hold. Try as we might, there was no place suitable. The fire would not stay lit and green wood seemed to be the problem. The cook wailed in mournful tones while the rest of the group cast baleful eyes at me to do something. Even Ishfani looked at me as if magical properties were my domain. I realized that I could prove my manhood, or disgrace myself forever.

It was a definite choice between two evils. Taking the challenge was all I saw to do, so I made an announcement: "The Essenes often do not cook their food. I shall prepare an Essene supper for us all."

A look of horror froze on the face of the cook, who instantly saw himself as being declared useless. The camel driver declared water must be boiled for tea. It was clear that the solution for one was a problem for the other. To my delight, Ishfani came to my rescue.

Clapping her hands, she trilled, "This is a treasure. To be treated to the delight of an Essene meal is like delving into the secrets of life. We are so fortunate to have a master Initiate, a holy man from god, to feed us body and soul. It will mean a longer life for us all."

The group brightened considerably. After all, how could they continue to mourn when the daughter of their master was so happy? At once they began to babble and laugh and congratulate themselves for being so fortunate. Taking advantage of the positive mood, I directed the runners to scout the area for grasses and berries. I looked through the pouches of food to see what could be eaten uncooked. A wild goat appeared on the scene, and I milked her. The runners returned with berries, wild greens, and edible grasses. Taking the cashews and almonds and honey stored in the pouches, I put together a fine salad of nuts and berries and greens. Although the servants blanched at drinking the milk of an animal, the daughter of their master ate with the gusto of a day laborer.

I knew this delicate flower who usually ate like a bird was saving me, as women have done since time began, in the eyes of the other men. Another powerful lesson was aborning in my soul. How could I fail to love her? She made a man of me in the eyes of all other men. Like a mooncalf, I gazed upon her glowing face as she tasted each bit as if it were a gift from God. Her ooh's and ahh's were music from the angels. Even the cook was so charmed by her enthusiasm that he unwrapped a mound of cakes he had been saving for himself and served it all around. She whispered that the Hindus never eat meat or meat products, and I saw she was truly my teacher.

"Tell me about the Hindu?" I whispered.

But she only smiled and replied, "The majority of India is Hindu."

My stay in India could easily have lasted the rest of my life. No longer was my journey just about travel; it was a path toward enlightenment known only to those who seek the truth wherever it may be found. I resisted pressing her and relaxed into learning the lessons presented, content that YHWH had a better plan than I. My teenage feelings could easily overcome my mission, I decided, as I forced myself to become more disciplined and steadied my obedience to the will of God.

The problem of the unraised tents finally presented itself as the stars came out of hiding and flooded our campsite with light. Soon a golden moon would appear and chase away the stars. As I studied the problem, I saw some bushes rising out of what must have been crevices in the rockbed. I directed the runner to drape the tents over the bushes. It made a perfect frame and had the added gift of being night-blooming flowers full of sweet fragrances. The solution was so simple I grew embarrassed at the fuss made over it. I decided that potential campsites would get my undivided attention for the rest of the trip, thus adding another reason for my being there at all, which I sorely needed.

As dawn broke, I arose to greet the new day. Ishfani, glowing with youthful health, emerged from her tent and loudly proclaimed she felt like a new person. It puzzled me until I realized that the servants whose sleep had been punctuated with trips into the night were also smiling and nodding in agreement. Again she directed the response to my evening meal, the servants following her lead. As we loaded up, she confided in me that she meant every bit of what she said and from that day forward she would take her meals raw.

"It is a teaching of Zoroaster that we do not often follow," she explained.

I longed to ask again about this master she revered, but I knew it was useless. I contented myself with her hint that Zoroaster must have been an ancient forebear of the Essenes and Ahura Mazda was his name for YHWH.

My love for her was growing by the day. I struggled with the strange feelings that rose within me. I concentrated on the purity of her soul, the trust of Azata, and the chosen path of an initiate. She seemed to sense my struggle. Our souls joined in springlike bliss.

"Am I your disciple, or are you mine?" I asked one morning.

"It is all the same thing," she replied, and I knew it was so.

As our little caravan reached the outskirts of Ahmadabad, I experienced a loss I could not explain. Seeing it mirrored in Ishfani's face, I asked the question.

"What is it?"

"We are about to part," she said in her wisdom born of centuries, "to go our separate ways, never again to see each other in this lifetime."

"But I will return," I cried in protest.

"You will not. You cannot."

"Why not?" I almost shouted in my growing anguish.

"You are a son of Israel and your life is there. I am a daughter of India and my life is here. You are passing through, following a path laid out for you long ago. You will never come this way again."

How can this be, I wondered? How does she know? Surely she cannot truly know. But I reckoned without knowledge of that super sensitivity pure young women have as a birthright. Years later, after much study and purification, I achieved it. But Ishfani, my blessed star of India, was born with it.

We wept shamelessly at our parting before the gates of my school. I can see her still sheathed in wispy veils, waving goodbye forever. She was right. The week we had together, the love we knew, was all I have had or will ever desire. She set my feet firmly on my path and clothed me with a spiritual love that will never leave me. My soul is entirely satisfied.

Chapter 12

Ahmadabad— The School of the Open Mind

The School of the Open Mind was not a very large place, as schools go. The gates opened onto a small garden much like the garden of Azata. There were stone benches placed around the pool, where a bubbling fountain flowed continuously. A shower tree rained blossoms onto the paths and the ever present bells of wind chimes gave sound to the wind that moved among them. Set off to one side was an open-air structure of intricate design, delicate, fragile like a white vapor hanging in midair. Beyond that was a house of white stone that served as an administration building housing records, charts, and other papyri. A small room beyond housed Kahanji, the director of the school.

He was ageless. Unlike the elderly Essenes, mystical Egyptians, and even the venerable Azata, he had no hair at all on his head or face. Even his eyebrows were missing. His stark brown eyes were set in a brown, sunbaked head that set atop a mostly naked sunbaked body. His gleaming white teeth matched his cotton dhoti, and the contrast between the dark and the light accentuated both. His neck, a common indicator of age, was weathered rather than withered and wrinkles were nonexistent. Kindness poured forth from his ever smiling eyes that proclaimed centuries of life and light while his light airy step proclaimed eternal youth.

Although Kahanji was the most stark of the guides, he was by no means the only ageless monk. There were twelve of them who looked exactly alike at first glance. Closer observation showed a mole, a chipped tooth, a birthmark, or some other slight difference that distinguished one ascetic from another. Kahanji, like Amen, had heavily hooded eyes.

"Welcome," he smiled as he warmly took my hands in his. "Your arrival has been awaited for fourteen years Earth time and hundreds star time."

Surely I heard him wrong, I thought, and leaned closer to hear better his soft voice. He spoke Aramaic, but it was heavily accented and broken. Asking him to repeat his welcome was out of the question since I did not wish to be reminded that babbling kids full of pestering questions should listen to their master's every word. Looking about for other students, failing to see any, and not wishing to appear stupid, I waited.

"A boy of few words," continued Kahanji, "is even more welcome. Filling your mind after it is opened will be a pleasure we have not had since Gautama was here."

Having made a good first impression by saying nothing at all, I nodded my head and bowed a little to show my appreciation. Smiling, I listened to Kahanji outline my course of study and introduce me to the other priests, called "guides" at this school.

"You will be our only student for a while and our first task will be to completely cleanse you, body and mind."

The Essenes had taught me much in that area, and I wondered how there could be much more. How clean can one get? Little did I know. "Clean" and "open" reached new dimensions in the land of the Hindus.

"A closed mind is a dirty mind too full of musty thoughts and dusty ideas," said the monk Raj as he carefully shaved off the hair on my head, face, arms, legs, and everywhere. "Hair especially holds dust. It stands as a shield between you and truth, between you and Brahm. It must all go and remain gone while you are here."

Naked also reached new dimensions as the old monk even pulled a few hairs from my ears. "The better for you to hear," he said.

Rather than the final act, the removal of hair was just the beginning. Dried sponges were used to scrub what felt like the very skin from my body. Spreading a white powder over my body, Raj scrubbed until I thought surely I would bleed.

"Mites, dead cells, scabs, and a multitude of organisms live in the folds and crevices of your skin," he explained. "We must make sure there is nothing between you and truth."

Still they were not finished with my body. Lowering me into a pool of limewater, the sting increased until I passed out. Had they torn my skin from me section by section, the pain could have been no worse.

When I came to, I was lying on cool, dark green leaves freshly pulled from a rubber tree. It was all my stinging body could tolerate for nearly a week. The guides poured cold water over me regularly and suggested that I cleanse my mind in exactly the same way my body had been cleansed. Fearing they might discover a way to do it for me, I concentrated on the task.

Slowly, my mind began to empty of all the thoughts, ideas, remembrances, and beliefs I held closely and dear. Away went Palestine, Nazareth, Carmel, Judith, Egypt, Yochanan, Mina, the ancient writings–everything. The last to slip from my mind was Ishfani; only then did I know it was empty. A deep, deep sleep filled with shades of emerald green and cobalt blue enveloped me, signaling the guides that a pure clean new mind was ready.

Healing came quickly and my body was dressed in a filmy, gauzy loin cloth and sandals. Kahanji appeared and motioned for me to follow him.

"You are in the land of the Hindu," Kahanji began what proved to be a new look at life, "and you must learn this way of life with a clear, clean, fresh mind. Do not attempt comparisons, for to compare is to judge and you are not competent to judge. Accept what you see and hear for exactly what it is, no more and no less. Drink it in as though you have just been born. Go with it. Do not resist. Drink deeply.

We walked out of the school and into the village of Ahmadabad. Smells that once might have been a stench were now just smells, neither good nor bad. Sights that might have once revolted were now just sights. People no longer seemed strange or unusual but were just people, no different from me.

Stopping beside a holy man who was sitting in front of a wooden statue, Kahanji said, "He has been gazing at Krishna for seventeen years in this trancelike state. Who can know what a man thinks in his heart from only his outward appearance or acts?"

Another man stared at the sun and had gone blind; it was his way to know God. I could have judged the facts as I saw them or measured without knowledge, had I compared; it is the way all men judge, I learned. And why YHWH commands "Judge not."

"Krishna is the eighth incarnation of Vishnu, a part of the Hindu holy trinity of the Godhead. Staring at the symbols of Krishna brings one into attunement with him, so we believe."

Over the next few months I studied the Dharma, as their laws or doctrines are called. I studied the Vedas, their ancient writings, and learned yoga, the mental discipline of directing one's attention totally and exclusively to a single object. Their supreme being was named Brahm or Brahma and their priests were called Brahmin.

"Tat twam asi," I chanted the ancient Sanskrit phrase that means "Thou art that, God and I are one, He who is yonder, yonder person, I am He." It produced attunement, the power to become one with my surroundings. It is all the same, as each phrase means the same as the other. Grasping the full meaning is grasping an eternal truth: we are all one.

The atman, or soul, is the only truth, the only true self. All else is illusion. All else will pass away. The eye with which one sees God is the same eye with which God sees that one.

The immutable law of Karma begins and ends in India. Whatsoever a man sows, that is what he shall reap, in this life or the next one.

"Karma," declared Kahanji "is the basic universal law for man. It applies to everyone and everything equally."

"Even thoughts?" I asked.

"Even thoughts," he replied. "As a man thinks in his heart, so he is. That is the real man, not his outward acts and appearances. Those acts may not be his true thoughts at all, for he may give you a piece of bread while he poisons your field of wheat."

In India, the companion teaching of reincarnation is not just a theory to be argued. It is accepted as truth, and it is as immutable as karma. You must be born again and again until the soul accomplishes perfection, for only a perfect soul can attain oneness with God or be fit for companionship with the deity. "Willing" seemed to be their definition of "perfect," and I have found it so.

The Upanishads sum up the teachings and consequences with a few simple words:

He who sees himself in all beings,
And all beings in himself,
He enters the supreme Brahma
By this means and no other.

The Rig-Veda contained over a thousand hymns matching word for word the beauty of the Psalms that I loved so much. "Veda" means spiritual wisdom and is thought to have been composed some eight- to fifteen-hundred years before my time. It must have been during the Vedic period that YHWH filled all the Earth with music heard clearly by the psalmist, the poet, the singers of songs all over the world.

A year passed and one morning Kahanji announced it was time to visit the land of the lamas high in the distant mountains.

"Those mountains are so high they disappear into the stars," declared Kahanji, his eyes sparkling with a mirth that always loomed just beneath his surface.

"Am I ready so soon to leave?" I inquired of my master.

"You were ready when you first arrived; it is all the same."

I smiled.

"You will go first to Sarnath and Kashi. Sarnath is the village of Gautama the Buddha. Kashi is the sacred village of the Hindus. From there you will travel to Katmandu, where Rabat awaits you."

It seemed only yesterday that I had said goodbye to Ishfani and arrived at this school. Had a whole year really gone by? I supposed it had for Kahanji said so. What did it really matter?

"Only when your body, mind, and soul are in perfect harmony can you hope to find harmony with the Infinite," said Kahanji. "Time has no meaning in soul development."

Truly it must be so, or so I believed at the time.

Now, I have come to believe that "willing" is enough. Perhaps "willing" puts body, mind, and soul into harmony? The sole purpose of the school was to open the mind. Refusing to judge others was evidence of an open mind. I had a way to go. It was a good thing to learn, as I was to spend time filling it at the schools without names from teachers I only see in retrospect about men who became gods against their will.

Chapter 13

Sarnath and Kashi

We made the long journey to Sarnath by elephant. The rocking of the elephant was smoother than that of the camel; the animal also seemed more intelligent than the "ships of the desert," as camels are called. Once when I fell asleep with the gentle rocking, I tumbled off. A headlong fall from the top of an elephant can be a devastating experience, often costing a broken neck, or at least a leg. Awaking to discover that my fear of falling was now capped by actually falling, I let out a blood-curdling scream that shook our end of the caravan.

Had my elephant not been worthy, I would have been crushed by the one behind us. But mine reached down and picked up my body without breaking a step and plopped me back on her back. The caravan runners chortled and giggled uproariously; even I thought it funny. As I laughed along with them, the boy from far away became one of the natives. They seemed impressed that my elephant was my friend, for the Hindus think the animal sacred and a friend of God. My white shift and silver medallion had not gained me any reverence at all, but my relationship with my animal carried me to great heights. These people knew nothing about Initiates, but they knew a lot about elephants.

As I rode along, I thought about all the things I had learned at the school, such as a Sumerian air bath. Lying in a small, shallow, pool-like place with nothing on, soaking up sun and air, was my idea of how to bathe. It was for cleansing the soul. The body is a manifestation of the soul, I was taught, and it must be aired regularly. Mind is the builder. The mind must keep itself constantly cleansed to achieve purity of thought. Thoughts will show up in the body. A pure soul is what all must try to achieve. Of all my lessons, working on my soul while taking an air bath was my favorite.

Soon I learned to sink into a reverie that nourished my soul, or was it my mind? At sixteen, one is not aware of the meanings of all one is learning, nor at seventeen, eighteen, not even when an adult, in reality, instead of only by law. Awareness must grow like everything else. Only the fool believes he knows it all.

The Ganges River is like no other river in the world. It is said that everything in India and lands beyond is dumped into its waters and instantly purified. Many crowd into the river to purify themselves. It was exciting to see such a body of water flanked by its magnificent flood plain. Water is a very spiritual body, so the river is a natural place for worshippers to gather.

Seeing the river for the first time was a kind of milestone for me in India. Imagining that it divided the world, I rode across it into Sarnath with a sense of adventure.

At the time I thought a week's stay in Sarnath was in order to catch a horse caravan heading for the mountains. The change from elephants to horses was required because of the steep, winding trail into the upper regions. The elephant caravan was going to the south of India. Changing caravans seemed reasonable, but a week's layover impressed me as a long time and surely an unproductive one. However, making the best of the situation was part of my makeup, so I unloaded my things and searched for an inn. Walking along the Ganges, which was still awash with multicolored flowers from the morning's worship, I noted the hundreds of shrines along its banks.

"No Hindu may eat or go about his daily life until he has first bathed in the sacred stream and worshipped at the shrine of his favorite deity," Kahanji had said. "Study it carefully. See everything. Feel it. Open up to it. It is India."

Life along any river is interesting. In India it reached an unimaginable extent. Sarnath and Kashi are near the banks of the holy river, and are constantly full of pilgrims. Worship was the main business. Everything was geared for religion. To die and be burned in Sarnath or Kashi guaranteed a quick return to a full and happy life on Earth, they believed. The idea was that one might return to the same place from which one left. Many saved coins for a lifetime just to be able to pay to be cremated near the sacred river. It was a big business in Kashi, reminding me of the Temple in Jerusalem.

Burning pyres were everywhere. The lifeless body was laid on a bed of woven twigs, leaves, and bits of material, all placed in the special pit and set afire. Happily, the smell of burning bodies was just a smell to me with my newfound way of receiving odors neutrally. Otherwise, I might have rushed for the river and thrown up my latest meal.

The Inn of Light caught my eye, and I walked over to the small place. Many pilgrims slept under the stars, for few could afford an inn. Along the river a tree was as good as one could desire. Knowing most of my travels would require that I stay at the "Inn of the Stars," that is to say, sleeping outdoors under the stars, I took advantage of being in a village.

"We put our special guests in this special place," the innkeeper explained, showing me a wonderful room.

"How am I special?" I asked in surprise, forgetting I was dressed to look special and that hanging from my neck was a sign for all to see.

"You are an Initiate from Egypt," he proudly exclaimed.

"We are blessed when such a one comes from so far away to visit our city. There is always a place for such as you."

"Are you a Hindu?"

"Buddhist," he replied.

"Tell me about Buddha," I urged.

The innkeeper plopped himself down on the floor and began a wonderful story.

"You are in the village of Gautama Buddha, the Enlightened One. He gained life in that incarnation five hundred years ago as a prince living in the Tarai on the northern edge of India. His father, the King, determined because of a prophecy that the prince should never see anything unpleasant. To protect the young boy, the King had him carried everywhere in a covered chair borne by four young men. The carriers were charged on pain of death never to allow the boy to see poverty, illness, pain, suffering, or ugliness in any form. His days were filled with music, poetry, gentle conversation, and happy scenes of every kind. He believed he lived in a perfect world of happiness and light.

"One day as Gautama was being carried to another place, a maimed beggar failed to remove himself from the path. The four carriers shuddered and shouted at the lame beggar to clear the way. But the piteous man, try as he might, could not drag himself away. His hands were broken and bleeding and useless. The helpless cripple wailed and struggled as the carriers set the carriage down and rushed to remove him.

"The prince, hearing the commotion and noting the activity, threw aside the curtain to see what was happening. There for the first time in his life he saw reality. Life was full of pain and suffering. Astounded, he jumped from his chair and rushed to help the poor lame man.

"'Touch me not, oh Prince,' begged the helpless unfortunate, 'for I am unclean, broken, and ill.'

"'Then healing help is what you need, my brother,' spoke the gentle Prince 'and I will give it to you.'

"He quickly lifted the man into his princely chair and ordered a return to his father's castle. Prince Gautama walked, soothing the tortured man who feared his wretched life was now over. It was such a walk to the kingly domain that Gautama wondered why he had never in his life sought to walk down that road and see for himself what was there. He was amazed that he had never thought of it.

"By the time the small entourage reached the palace grounds, a crowd was following. The prince, glancing back at them, noted that they were clad in rags, unkempt, and thin from illness or hunger. His heart broke. He quickly invited them all into the king's palace and commanded a sumptuous feast for the entire lot. They fell on the food like starving dogs.

"After carefully placing the lame beggar on a brilliantly brocaded couch made solely for the prince, he requested an audience with his father. Of course the king was furious, but he could deny his only son nothing at all. No one knows exactly what went on behind those closed doors, but it is said a broken-hearted father left the room several hours later, and the young prince left the palace forever. It is rumored that the carriers and captain were retired with good pensions, and the beggar lived in the palace the rest of his life. It is whispered that Gautama told his father that whatever he did to the beggar would also happen to the son.

"Gautama came here to Sarnath and made his home under a bodhi tree. At first the people wandered about, thinking he might be insane. His bearing was princely and his dress obviously costly, but he would not satisfy the curious with one word about himself. Except for his regular trips to the river in worship, he refused to leave the tree. He welcomed all who would share his humble surroundings, and soon he was surrounded by disciples who loved to listen to his teachings.

"He reinterpreted the Vedas, giving new life to the ancient words and new vigor to the worship of the Hindus. He claimed Brahma was unknowable, and some thought he did not believe in the creator of the universe; but it was not so. He taught that nothing is ever lost in the universe, everything is constantly changing, and whatever happens produces an equal and appropriate response. He made clear that those who are powerful and oppressive today will be the weak and oppressed tomorrow. He taught that no man can change that immutable law of the universe. He called it karma.

"Slowly, the story of a young prince from a faraway kingdom who had turned his back on princely wealth and power to live among the poor and helpless trickled into Sarnath. Many asked Gautama if he were that prince, but he would never say. When asked why he chose the life of poverty when he could be so rich, he would only smile mysteriously and say, 'Lucky is the man who has charge of his own life and can choose how it shall be lived.'

"It is rumored that the king came in secret and tried to persuade his son to return to the kingdom, offering to use all his wealth for the poor as a bribe, but Gautama refused and invited the king to stay under the tree with him. Both were sad at their parting. The king believed his son quite mad, and Gautama believed his father had lost the rare opportunity to take control of his life."

As the innkeeper concluded the story, I was exceptionally moved. I think perhaps I would have become a follower of the Buddha myself except that I recalled Moses having given up a kingdom for a stray band of slaves a thousand years before the time of Gautama. Renouncing material riches for spiritual riches seems to be the path to God. I was beginning to see a clear path and decided to concentrate on the why of it all.

"Thank you for such a wonderful enlightenment," I enthused as I settled into my room. I wondered if the Gautama mentioned by Kahanji was the same one in the story I had just heard.

The next morning at dawn I waded into the Ganges with all the Hindus and Buddhists, casting my flowers on the waters in worship of YHWH. Glancing up I saw a Brahmin standing high on a stone, motionless, balancing on one leg. He was clasping his hands and turning his face full into the slowly rising sun. As he muttered prayers toward the brightly glowing eastern sky, I could see how some would believe he prayed to the sun, rather than God. The image of a Pharisee standing on a street corner praying loudly for all to see flashed through my mind. Were they very much alike, or very different? One difference was that the Pharisee would go to the temple and commit a bloody sacrifice while the Brahmin would consider his flowers and prayers enough.

Oh, oh, I thought to myself, my mind cleansing seems to be wearing thin. There I go with a comparison, a kind of judgment. Who am I to judge anyone? I want to save the world, not judge it.

The children frolicked in the water. What mother might have a former prince in her care, or a child who was an incarnation of her favorite deity? There was much to be said for the gentle view of life called reincarnation, where one chooses the path of rebirth with one's own thoughts and acts.

Angels of mercy, as women carrying jars of water on their heads were called, carried water to the aged and infirm who were unable to get to the river, much less into it. Thirst was not all the waters of India quenched. Parched souls were constantly born anew in the river.

The fires at the burning pyres were smoldering as I passed, and bodies were laying there ready for cremation. The last wish of a devout Hindu is to be burned after death on the bank of the Ganges at Kashi, which is miles from Sarnath, and have his ashes scattered over the waters of the river. I could not help but wonder if the ashes of such devout worshipers scattered in the waters along with the multitude of flowers was what purified the waters.

There were many wells in the city: wells of wisdom, wells of fate, wells of purification. They reminded me of the Essenes' pools of purification at Carmel. It occurred to me that from someplace this single idea must have sprung all over the world, like perfume wafting in the wind. Water for purification is an outward manifestation of what is happening within.

Stopping for a drink from one of the wells, I was given a cup made of a single leaf. A leaf was for the poor and for strangers, for natives carried their own bowls. The caste system of India did not permit the upper classes to drink from a bowl that had ever touched the lips of one deemed "unclean," as the lower classes were perceived. The kind of work one did determined cleanliness and no amount of constant purification seemed ever to cleanse the lowly laborer who did the dirtiest work. So Brahmans were the highest class and garbage collectors and refuse cleaners were the lowest. Birth seemed to be how one got into a particular caste and death seemed to be the only way out. Karma was the explanation. As Kahanji explained, what one does with knowledge is the true measure of one's wisdom.

"Be very careful what you choose to do about the unfortunates of this world, Jeshua," he taught. "Just because they have incarnated at the lowest ebb of status or chosen the life of a cripple gives no man the right to kick him also, lest he find himself having exchanged places with the unfortunate in a later life."

It made a great deal of sense to me why Gautama was called a Buddha after hearing the innkeeper's story, for "Buddha" means "the enlightened one." I supposed enlightenment grew like a billowing cloud towering in the sky. Mine certainly was growing. I could see it, feel it, even revel in it a little. I enjoyed water from the leaf cup of the stranger more than from the wooden one I carried with me.

The trinity of the Indian belief system were named Brahma, Vishnu, and Shiva. The shrines had images, wooden carvings mostly, of at least one of these gods, and some had all three. Other shrines had an empty place, indicating it was for the unknown god. I fancied that was for YHWH and worshipped there.

My desire to tell those standing about that the empty shrine was for YHWH was overwhelming. Although Amen had cautioned me against starting my teaching too soon, I finally succumbed to temptation and struck up a conversation with one from the lowliest caste.

"The empty place is for my Holy Father," I whispered.

The ragged man stared at me in surprise. Looking closely into my face, he seemed to grow brighter and more excited by the moment. So I continued.

"My Holy Father loves everyone everywhere and has no favorites. In the Kingdom of God everyone is equal and the same."

"Where is that kingdom?" gasped the man.

"Why, it is right here where we are, within us," I proudly explained, happy that I had his attention.

The man began to call others to come hear the son of God who was incarnated in this young boy. My knowledge of his dialect was limited, and I did not quite understand what he was saying in his excitement to hurry each word out of his mouth. But a crowd began to gather. I sensed I had probably overstepped myself and wanted desperately to run away. It was no use. Soon I was surrounded by a large number of obviously poor, ragged, and often crippled people. Even children gathered.

As they waited expectantly, I began. "The Kingdom of Heaven is at hand. The God of all creation welcomes you into that Kingdom. The poor, the laden, the weary are invited to come in and rest. There is room for everyone, for in my Father's house are many rooms."

I tried to keep the message as simple as possible and talk in terms the poor and uneducated could understand. A house with many rooms would be heaven to people who slept many in just one room, and I knew that is how the poverty-stricken all over the world lived, especially in India.

The crowd grew excited and urged me to stay, but I insisted I must go. It saddened me to see the hungry hearts so ready to hear words of encouragement. As I walked quickly away, I could hear them whispering among themselves.

"It is the Buddha returned." "No, no, it is Krishna," they argued among themselves, allowing me to slip away unnoticed.

The words of Amen rang in my ears: "Many a false teacher rises who is only partially prepared. Do not become one of those. Wait upon God." It tore my heart to walk away, but I was comforted somewhat by the feeling that I was an obedient son of a divine father.

Hurrying back to the inn, the words of Amen repeated themselves over and over in my mind. What had I done? The image of the innkeeper flashed into my mind, and I sought him out to tell him what had happened. His face grew solemn as I explained. He studied me carefully.

"When the great God of the universe moves you to speak, you must do so. There is no guile in you. The Buddha urged India to do away with the caste system. What words did you speak that were false?"

"I do not know."

"I will tell you. None at all. Everything you said was so."

"But now they think I am the son of God, the Buddha, or Krishna," I cried.

"Men will always want to put you in a pocket," mused the innkeeper. "Let it not worry you. Pray and meditate. Keep your mind on the infinite. Follow your path. That is your concern."

What would I have done without the wise words of the innkeeper? Again it occurred to me that all my teachers were not at the schools, but were often in the great school called life.

I voiced my appreciation for his care and concern and mentioned my thoughts of him as a teacher. Although he seemed pleased he raised his hands in protest. "When someone asks a question, I must answer as best I can, that is all," he modestly replied.

"As I walked up the river to Kashi everyone everywhere seemed to be in constant prayer. This is a very religious country, much like my own, only much more gentle," I continued.

"Some were in meditation," he pointed out.

"Meditation?" I repeated with a slight rise in my voice that even I could hear.

"Yes, meditation is not prayer."

It seemed I knew exactly what he was talking about, and I cast about in my mind for a word or words that I had known before. Nevertheless, I stood before him in awkward silence waiting until he explained.

"Prayer is when you do the talking. Meditation is when God does the talking. A simple way to explain it."

"Is that the same as entering into the silence, putting the atman at one with Brahm?" (Kahanji had explained it so.)

"Yes, that is it."

It sounded like what my mother called "being in the spirit," and what the Essenes called "communion with Adonai," covering a two-way communication.

Amen had briefly discussed it and seemed satisfied that I had a system of sorts. I decided that, by whatever name, it was all the same thing, that state of listening to the call of the spirit, an attuning of the mental and physical bodies to their spiritual source.

The innkeeper continued: "Meditation is the key to our spiritual growth. It is how we expand our consciousness and become greater than we ever dreamed possible. Some, through meditation, even travel through space and time to the stars and beyond."

"Ah, yes," I nodded my head, "I practice that, and I have learned it takes practice, and quite a lot of it."

"You have another key to mastery, my young friend," said the innkeeper.

Changing the subject to something lighter, he said, "The monsoons will be upon us soon."

"And I shall soon be in the cool climate of your mountains and beyond."

"You are going to the roof of the world?"

"The Himalayas."

"Yes, that is the name of our grand mountains that wallow in the clouds, yet kiss the stars."

"You describe them like a poet," I exclaimed.

The innkeeper dropped his heavily lidded eyes and sank into a reverie. As he summoned images of his youth, I discovered I could see them clearly, too. He was young again, crossing the plains of the Hindustan toward the Brahmaputra River that divided the wilds of Tibet from the plains of India.

"The Himalayas are where Earth pierces heaven and the spirits soar with the wind. The Hindus call them the dwelling place of the gods. It is a wilderness staggering in solitude, a region of everlasting snows. At their incredible height, the silence roars. When the winds come howling down the mountains, a thousand rocks tremble with fear and sound achieves a new dimension. It lifts one completely out of one's skin.

"The 'cuds' (the tops and bottoms of valleys) are fringed with tall, straight poplars, pines, and firs, while the bottom of the valleys admit gushing streamlets rushing to join their sisters as they heave up boulders. The river, gathering up its brood, tumbles rocks the size of cities as it cascades onto the plains of our tropical land. The voices of sighing winds and many waters clear the path of all other sounds. No mortal soul can experience those mountains and ever again be the same."

"It sounds grand and exhilarating," I said. "What an adventure!"

"Not all adventures are pleasant," sighed the innkeeper as he excused himself to attend to his tasks.

For the next few days I wandered through the marketplace shopping for provisions needed by those going into the mountains. Food, water, a bedroll and a few other items were suggested in the event that I got lost. Woven blankets, displayed everywhere, functioned as a source of warmth for travelers as well as a bedroll. A coat or warm cloak was on my list and it seemed like a good idea for time spent in snowy mountains. Even so, it seemed odd shopping for cold weather as sweat poured off my body.

Keeping in mind that travelers are not pack mules, shopping got to be a game. The barter, bantering, smells, sounds of the marketplace–they all fascinated me. The sale of flowers, forbidden in Bhavnagar, was a booming business here. Little girls, mere flowers themselves, constantly bobbed up and pulled on one's robe. Turning brown eyes fringed with long lashes full upon me and lifting up a fistful of blooms for sale got to me every time.

Every afternoon I arrived at the inn loaded with my purchases and flowers. As I handed them out to the other guests and laid a bunch on the innkeeper's table, he smiled broadly at my foolish grin.

"Jeshua, you have bought out the marketplace again. At this rate you can become a flower boy."

"Lo and behold, innkeeper, these flowers fill the inn with sweet odors and bright colors that produce an inn of happiness."

He laughed at my reference to the fishy smells and foul drafts that floated through his inn when the winds blew from the river. His guests nodded in agreement. They sensed a closeness between us that was beyond friendship.

"Like attracts like" was a universal law taught at the School of the Open Mind, and Kahanji had declared that proving the universal laws to oneself should be an ongoing activity until one mastered them.

"Do you want to know exactly what you are like?" he asked. "Look at your friends and acquaintances. They will be mirror images of yourself. The thing you like least about them will probably be your own worst fault."

That was stunning. Nevertheless, looking around at the happy guests at the Inn of Light, it occurred to me that the innkeeper attracted a warm group, people like himself. Even his children were warm little berries bouncing around everywhere, helping with the chores, assisting the guests, respectful of everyone and one another, never intruding on one's thoughts–little copies of the innkeeper, who seemed young and elderly at the same time. Was that a characteristic of the wise? Did I have the characteristics that I most admired in others? Truly these universal laws were knotty things requiring constant thought and study, and a lot of simplifying for my people.

The night before my departure I went to the innkeeper to pay my bill. To my amazement, he refused to take even a single rupee. He threw up his hands and rolled his eyes in pretend shock.

"What is this that you should insult me with your coins? Have I offended you? Was your room unsatisfactory? Did my children disturb your rest?"

"No, no, nothing so terrible. Everything was wonderful. This is an inn where people pay for their keep, is it not? I seek to pay my fare as all others do. That is all."

"But, my fine young master, you are an Initiate, and even more. You are a prince from a faraway land, like Buddha. You are the scion of the kings, David and Solomon, heir to a kingdom without end. I cannot take pay for sheltering you. My family was blessed by your having chosen us."

"How do you know all this about me?" I cried out. "Who are you?"

"I was a shepherd in the hills of Judea near Bethlehem when you were born. I saw your star and talked to the magi. They said the king feared your birth and sought to kill you. They told me of the prophecies concerning you, and that you might be the one who was to fulfill their law."

"Why were you in Judea, and how did you get there?" I asked, breathlessly.

"My parents were merchants who traveled the silk route, and we all went together. When we left the caravan one evening and headed for the hills of Judea, we were attacked and robbed. Without our goods and coins, we were penniless. So we got jobs to collect some money in order to return to India. I, being the youngest, found work as a shepherd. We were ready to return about the time you were born, so we accompanied the magi back to the East, which is when we learned all about you."

"But, how do you know I am that one?" I embarrassed myself with my prodding for answers.

"How many Jeshuas from Palestine who are also Initiates of God can there be? It was simple for one who seeks truth," he smiled. "I can see your aura; everything about you fits."

He continued, "There are not many Hebrew boys wandering around India, you must admit."

I laughed at that. It was pretty easy to figure out if you know how to put two and two together. Getting five puts one on notice something could be amiss, but getting four pretty well puts the cork in the bottle, or the patch on the wineskin as Yochanan liked to point out.

"I am amazed that I chose your inn," I commented. "Of all the inns in Sarnath and Kashi, why yours?"

"There are no accidents, coincidences, or happenstances. Everything that occurs is part of the divine plan of the Divine All. Like the sea, the soul tides ebb and flow. We were all one once, and we will all be one again, even as God is one. It is written on the sands of time and embossed in patterns on our souls."

"I love listening to you. I could sit at your feet and feast forever."

"We are always together, my Prince," he gently repeated. "You must learn from everyone, for everyone is a teacher."

"And I am a devoted student."

"Everyone is a student. He who stops studying, ceases to learn. It is called death."

King or teacher, student or prince? Who was I, really? Surely the time would come when I would have to decide. But not at sixteen years of age, and not in India. One would think from all I have written in this journal so far that my whole journey was from one philosopher to the next, one spiritual precept to another, and that it was always uplifting.

Not all my experiences were uplifting.

My experiences took a decided turn in the twin cities of Kashi and Sarnath. It was there that I began to really interact with people.

I joined the storytellers in the evenings as they sat by their campfires and spun tales of ancient times. They sang stories, more than told them, of the places they had been and the things they had seen. Some of them were bawdy, and there was much laughing and guffawing and punching of one another as the turbaned men listened. Although I was unused to such revelry, I could see the closeness it produced among those hardworking men. Their old faces, withered and weathered from long hours in the blistering sun, spread in broad grins, exposing snaggled or even toothless gums. Some had had their teeth knocked out as penance for wrongdoing, others to show deep sorrow at the passing of a loved one. These gaps were displayed as badges of honor as the men squatted together for a few hours free from earthly cares.

The women formed their alliances at the river as they did the wash, bathed children, and sought each other's companionship. Wives were bought and sold like cattle and treated with much less respect. Daughters were viewed as a sign of disfavor by the gods, to be sold as quickly and when as young as possible. Five years was not too young to sell off a girl. Occasionally, a daughter might be believed to be the incarnation of one of the divine goddesses, such as a wife of Shiva named Doorgha. It might be a blessing of sorts, but its occurrence was considered highly unlikely in the homes of the lower castes.

In the center of the square was the grim-faced statue of Doorgha. It was there that baby goats, bleating piteously, were sacrificed. Their heads were placed in a forked stick and whacked off with a knife while worshippers plunged their hands in the gushing blood and smeared it on their foreheads then stood before the idol.

It startled me to see this blood sacrifice in India. But I discovered that some sects continued ancient practices and only lately had substituted animals for children. That humbled me a bit. Whereas I wanted to believe that India was a land of perfection, where everyone was enlightened, I learned it was much like Palestine. Some, like the Essenes, had achieved a higher level of consciousness, while others like the scribes and Pharisees, preferred tradition over spiritual enlightenment. Slowly I grew to understand that it is all the same everywhere, a mix of many belief systems, good and bad.

In my wanderings, the monkeys, sacred to the Hindus, kept catching my eye. They had the run of the temples and kept a lively chattering going while peering at one from every niche of a building. Making the mistake of throwing some grain on the ground, I was suddenly surrounded by the strange creatures. Not only did they pounce down from the building, but from trees, fences, court enclosures, even from faraway Calcutta, I fancied. They gobbled up the grain and began to pull at my robe, begging for more. The older monkeys boxed the ears of the younger ones, who then turned somersaults in an effort to get away. Laughing at the sight, I scattered more grain and drew a crowd of people, also. Feeling like a minstrel traveling with his monkey chorus, I quickly withdrew from the scene. It was important for me to be "correct" in my travels in foreign countries. I did not want to do anything to embarrass my teachers or to make a public spectacle of myself. I had come to realize I was no longer a carefree boy with no responsibilities, but rather an initiate representing my schools.

"He's a god," one man called out to the others as I sped away. "He is the incarnation of Vishnu."

In my heart of hearts I was happy my stay in Sarnath was drawing to a close. Being called a god was not my chosen path, and I wanted to distance myself from such a claim. It seemed to be my responsibility to refuse claims not really true, especially when made about me. At sixteen, I ran away from all that. But now, I make a stand.

Chapter 14

The Himalayan Caravan

It was early in the morning when I bade farewell to my friend the innkeeper and his family and found my way to the caravan staging area. Already in the half-light of early morning, men and horses were in preparation for travel. Locating the horse assigned to me, I loaded my packs and got used to the animal. She was a sturdy mare that nuzzled my hand for food. Fortunately, the innkeeper had told me how to win the friendship of a horse forever, and I held out a pear. She deftly took the fruit from my hand without so much as touching her teeth to it. Her huge lips just lifted it and sucked it in. Dainty is not the word one usually uses in describing horses, but that is the way my horse ate that pear.

Pure white horses trained to be part of a fast-moving pack caravan ordinarily are not affectionate. They are trained to obey, and I soon discovered mine was alert to my slightest lean or touch. A slight nudge and she was instantly at a gallop. A slight tug on the reins, and she almost threw me as she came to an abrupt halt. My mind and hers were in tune. Who could help but love such a horse? And I fancied she returned the love.

All of the animals were beautiful and in obvious good health. They had been well groomed and trained. The caravan master was apparently an outstanding man, and I was anxious to meet him.

My first encounter with him was one never to be forgotten. I saw him striding along the path checking various details of the preparations. He was a brawny man with full beard and flashing eyes. His hair flowed in a mane that whipped about in the early morning breezes. Clad in boots and softly hammered yak skin breeches, he shifted his cloak with a flick of his burly hand.

He came to a full stop beside a group of travelers. He looked them over and spoke in a direct manner.

"The boy cannot go."

A frail youth about my age looked to one of the men and began to whine. The men began to protest loudly and bordered on threats.

"The boy was not mentioned when the booking was made," the caravan master said, annoyed at the affair.

An older man stepped forward. He was the leader of the group and apparently by consent had been appointed to speak for them.

"We paid a lot of money for this trip. The boy either goes or none of us will go."

"Fine," said the caravan master. He turned and ordered the animals of the protesting group to be removed from the caravan. Instantly the guides began to remove the horses and detached several pack animals that carried provisions for them. The master turned his back and strode away, continuing his checking. The small group was shocked.

It shocked me also, for there were five in the group, not counting the young boy. That was a large sum of money the caravan master had just cut out of his income. However, to watch him and his offhand manner one would think it mattered not at all to him. As he headed toward me, I shuddered. My already thin frame seemed to lose ten pounds, and I felt eight years old.

Because it was a fast-moving caravan, no one under sixteen years was permitted to travel with it. Trembling, I stuck out my chest and tried to stand an inch taller than my modest height. I feared I might be seen to be too young to make this trip. I could feel my heart pounding and my whole life passed in review right before my eyes. (At that moment I almost made an irrevocable decision to remain in Sarnath the rest of my life.)

"Ahhhh," he exclaimed as he approached me, "so you are the young Initiate traveling with us? Welcome!"

Those flinty gray eyes melted into a velvety blue, and the stern caravan master changed into a warm, jovial fellow.

"I always feel better with a holy man in the caravan," he continued, "or should I say holy boy?"

He laughed loudly and clapped me on the shoulder with his huge hand, nearly knocking me over. I laughed along with him, so relieved was I.

"Call me anything you like, sir, er, sahib, er, master," I stumbled for the right title.

My eagerness cost me, for he called me "holy boy" throughout the long trip. Not that I cared, for I was so happy to be allowed in the caravan that he could have called me "it" and I would have been delirious with joy. It was only with effort that I allowed myself to wonder why the other youth who was my size and age had been denied, while I was accepted. He was so astute that I feared he might be a mind reader, so I pushed the question away.

As he moved on, the forsaken group's elder rushed up to him. A much more contrite and wiser man, he pled with the master to allow them in the caravan as they had urgent business in Lhasa. He whined and groveled as disgust filled the master's face. Nevertheless, after determining that the frail youth had been sent home to his mother and after extracting extra money for his wasted time and trouble, the caravan master allowed himself to be persuaded to take the group. He reluctantly ordered the animals returned to the caravan and walked away smothering a grin as he counted the extra coins. It was a masterly display of having one's cake and eating it, too, for he had made extra money on the deal while eliminating anticipated trouble. The added benefit was that the caravan had no doubts who was in charge.

As the commotion ceased and everyone settled down, a lone business traveler whispered to me, "I'll feel sorry for any bandits who attack this caravan."

"Me, too," I muttered.

We laughed, and the businessman grew friendly and began asking me questions about my dress, my medallion, and my title, "holy boy." It took a while for us to find a common language, but soon we were speaking comfortably in a form of Aramaic. Explaining as best I could about myself, I returned the favor with my own questions.

He was Persian, a merchant traveling between Calcutta, Lhasa, and Isfahan. His name was Omar, and he dealt in salt between Calcutta and Katmandu, herbs between Lhasa and Katmandu, and picked up silk from China in Lhasa for trade in Isfahan, near central Persia. We became companions on the journey.

Omar was a strong man, and his oval face and deep-set eyes gave him the appearance of men I had seen many times in the marketplaces of Capernaum. However, he claimed he never traveled to Palestine, as his long circuit from Isfahan to Calcutta took him two years for just one trip. Still, he looked familiar.

"Didn't you know all Parsis look alike?" he smiled, his twinkling eyes signaling he was joking.

"I knew all businessmen see alike. Does that count?" I returned.

He laughed at my joke. I loved his jokes and funny asides, and he seemed to enjoy hearing about my studies as an initiate. We became friends.

"I don't have much time for religion," Omar explained, "but it interests me greatly. You are the first holy man I've seen, much less one I can talk to about holy things. Is it a business?"

I cast my eyes at Omar to see if I were being tweaked, but he seemed serious. The question flitted through my mind, how could he travel through India and Tibet and never see a religious man? So I answered his question with my own.

"It isn't that I never saw one," he explained, "it is that I just looked through them, hardly noticing they were there."

"Ahh, yes," I nodded. "We all have eyes that do not see. Would you mind repeating your question?"

I needed clarification since I did not want to get into a discussion that might prove over the head of one of us.

"What I mean is," Omar began, "are you training to go into the God business and make your living off the people? Or will you teach people about God and make your living some other way? Zoroaster was a farmer, I hear. They say he gave away his teachings free for all. What will you do?"

The question was a good one. I had learned the public trade of carpentry from Yosef, not to mention helping the shepherds and farmers around Nazareth at Yosef's direction. There were a lot of things I could do for money, but it just never happened to be a need of mine. Yosef was well-to-do and provided for my needs. Most Initiates were princelings; it certainly was a privileged group to which I belonged and making a living was not one of the things we thought about. Nevertheless, I could not be dependent on a generous father all my life.

"You have asked a good question, Omar. May I have a little time to give some thought to my answer?"

"Of course," he laughed, "you can understand that my business must show a profit or my family of six children and a wife would starve. So I am interested in how you will provide for your family in your God business."

Within his question was another question. I had no wife or family to support. However, suppose I did at thirty years, when Initiates are free to marry? My love for Ishfani was so great that had I been older and free, I would have asked her to marry me and I would have remained forever in India. I knew in my heart that my chosen profession of rabbi would have vanished with such a marriage, for I would have devoted every waking moment to the passion of my soul. I could not have served God and a wife without dividing my time at least a little.

Many Essenes do not marry, choosing to serve God with a wholeheartedness that is difficult with a wife and children who make demands on a daily basis. Yosef had determined that he could best serve God as a devoted husband to Miryam, my mother, and to me as a loving father. He had no problem putting his business second. His business grew and prospered. As devout Essenes, they had chosen a path that fitted the will of the Infinite as they understood it.

But I planned to travel the length and breadth of Palestine. Sleeping under a tree might always be my home, even as Gautama Buddha had done. No wife could accept that, and certainly no children should be treated so. Silently, I closed off the idea of ever having a wife or children. My path must be traveled alone, with those who chose to come with me, free to come or go at any time.

The Brotherhood of Initiates had a tradition that whosoever could not pay his bill simply left a note for the next member who chanced that way with funds. It was acceptable. The bills were always paid and soon.

The law of Moses commanded a portion of one's income to be set aside for the living of those doing God's work. Although I was not of the House of Levi, a priest of Aaron, I knew my Heavenly Father would provide for me, even as the lilies of the field and the birds of the air had provisions made for them. Was I any less important to YHWH than those? Did I need to live more luxuriously?

As evening fell and we began to make camp for the night, I wondered why it had taken me hours to form an answer to Omar's question. Sitting around the campfire, I declared I was ready to answer his question concerning my livelihood. He smiled, waiting expectantly.

"I am not only an initiate, but am also an Essene and a Nazarene, dedicated to God even before my birth in Bethlehem of Judea. Thus, I plan never to marry nor have children to support, for my whole life is dedicated to the will of God. I expect to be free to follow that will without divided loyalties. Those who accept me accept the God who sent me. Likewise, those who reject me also reject the God who sent me. I cannot concern myself with what I shall eat or what I shall drink, for God knows what I have need of and will provide it even before I ask.

"Nevertheless, I am prepared to spend my life on a hillside, fasting and wearing only the skin God has provided for my clothing. If God chooses to clothe me in the finest of silks or the poorest of rags, it will be all the same to me. If God chooses to feed me from banquet tables or from leaves of grass, house me in palaces or under the stars, fill me with the wines of kings or water from the river, I shall breathe happily the air of creation and be thankful I am permitted to do the work of God.

"Therefore, I cannot be concerned with how I shall live nor how well. My only concern is that I do live and as long as I do, my every thought will be about the will of God for my life. What would it profit me if I gained the whole world and lost my way? All that I am or ever hope to be I owe to God, and I shall give it freely to my fellow beings even as it has been given freely to me. I can do no less."

We sat in silence for a long time as Omar considered my answer Then he gave a deep, long sigh, turned his eyes on me and said, "You are truly a holy man. For the first time in my life I want to know all about God."

I breathed a sigh of relief, for already I knew that businessmen think spiritual teachers are parasites who go about teaching men not to work, or to rob the rich and give to the poor. They often believe (correctly so) that many teach poverty while living in wealth and splendor. Holding to this idea, businessmen have had a distorted view of God and often used the concept for shortchanging their customers, failing to realize they shortchanged God and themselves.

I wanted no one to fault YHWH because of me. Yet it required an act of faith to think of a lifetime depending on the generosity of gift-givers for my needs. But it was so in my heart, my work demanded it, and I learned from Omar that my actions were more important than my words.

The Persian merchant was a man accustomed to inspecting goods, evaluating merchandise, and securing the most profitable bargains. He understood clearly that what men say about what they are selling is often colored by the profit motive and the selling process. He also understood that there is a relationship between a man and his merchandise. That is where one looks for the truth.

"How can I have faith in a God in whom the salesman has no faith?" he questioned. "Such have been my few contacts with so-called holy men."

Then that shrewd and brilliant man asked me another probing question. "Should I quit my business, abandon my family, and follow your lifestyle in order to worship your God?"

Again I begged for time to consider my answer. I was happy Omar did not demand an instant answer, but wanted a serious, thoughtful reply. Such would not always be the case, and I saw why I was not yet ready for my mission. Hard questions require careful answers; to give less can easily destroy a man's life.

Through the night I prayed, seeking a careful answer to Omar's question. Marriage is a holy union between a man and a woman, especially when it is blessed with children. Surely what God joined together no man had a right to divide. And, most certainly what no man had a right to do, neither would God do. Even so, there are men who leave a wife and children, claiming to follow God. It seemed not so to me. It was clear to me that I needed finer tuning. Who was I to determine right or wrong for others?

Then I slept. As I slept, I dreamed. Omar was surrounded by his wife and children. White clouds settled upon them. They seemed to glow with a bright light. From the light came a voice: "My servant Omar will take the message throughout Persia of the One to come. Send Omar first to the Zoroastrians; they will prepare him."

As the dream faded, it was clear to me what I must do. As I thought about the dream, I recalled that the Zoroastrians were God's businessmen on Earth. They put God first and business second, even as Yosef did. If Omar became like Azata, I would be truly successful as a wayshower. My heart pumped with joy as I awaited the first light of dawn to give Omar the dream's message.

As we loaded up, I told Omar the dream. Simple as it was to me, he failed to see the meaning, so I explained it for him.

"God is a spirit and seeks those who will worship in spirit. It matters not what profession you follow, nor whether you have a family. It is your spirit that is important. You would certainly destroy your spirit if you abandoned the family you love so much. God does not require that of you, or of anyone.

"To learn about God and the ways of God, go to the Zoroastrians who abound in Persia. They will gladly take you in hand and teach you how to be one of God's businessmen on Earth."

"Who is this One in your dream?" he asked.

"There is One coming who will make all things clear. He is prophesied in the ancient writings of the Hebrew. When that One comes, you will know it if you are in tune with the spirit of God. Preparing the way is what the dream seems to say–getting people along your way ready for the One who is to come. I have heard he is already on the Earth."

"Does that mean I am to remain a merchant, traveling about?"

"Ah, Omar," I cried. "Let no man tell you how to serve God. Listen only to God. If you listen to men, they may tell you wrong and you will blame them for having missed your calling. But, if you listen only to God, who will never lead you down a wrong path, you will have no one to blame but yourself, and only for a failure to listen."

"How can I ask God, whom I have never known, what I should do with the rest of my life?"

"Because you have not known God does not mean God has not known you. You have but to ask and you will have your answer," I replied, suddenly, without thought. It startled me, for the answer came from my lips and in my words. I heard it, but it did not seem to be from me at all.

"Can anyone do this?" asked Omar.

"Anyone."

"Why then does not everyone?" he wanted to know.

"They have lost their way. They know not God, even as you have not known. They know not how to listen."

He seemed satisfied. As we rode along in silence the rest of the day, I could hear him make many starts in questioning God for himself. I wondered if I should teach him how to pray or meditate, or how to listen for the voice of God.

It was clear the seed had been planted and must have time to germinate. To fill Omar with too much too soon could smother the seedling. Nourishment for one who has been spiritually starving all his life must come slowly.

Chapter 15

Katmandu

Katmandu is a great distance from Sarnath across a plain, through a jungle, and into great mountains. As we ended our second day, we could already see the beginnings of the great mountains in the distance like thin blue lines marking the horizon.

Horse caravans travel much faster than either camel or elephant, so I expect we were making a good distance every day. There were about fifty of us and everyone was mounted. The pack animals that carried only provisions traveled as swiftly as the rest. Nothing slowed us. The caravan master had informed us the travel would go more slowly as we climbed into the mountains and that was the reason for the extra speed across the plains.

As the late-afternoon sun hung low in the sky, the distant hills turned purple and the caravan master finally called a halt for the night. I was so weary I was ready to fall off my horse and roll into my yak skin bedroll, skipping mealtime. Had the frail young boy been with us, I suspected, someone would now be taking him back to Sarnath. The ache in my bones was exceeded only by the fatigue in my body. Yet I knew I must eat something. Losing weight might send me back to Sarnath.

My years of walking across Galilee, through Samaria, and around Judea had made me strong despite my thinness. With my recent toughening at the School of the Open Mind, I was strong for a boy of my years. I wondered if the caravan master could see that when he looked at me. I supposed he could or else I would have joined the frail boy back at Sarnath.

We made camp and I unrolled my bedroll, carefully picking off the bugs that had caught in my blanket during the ride. Nothing worse than an unknown crawler on one's body in the middle of the night. The drivers were busy building fires and setting up cooking places. We always had one hot dish, usually a kind of meat stew. It was not only hot from cooking, but also was hot flavored. As a matter of fact, the food was still hot when it passed from my body the following morning. I liked the spicy foods. They were so different from the fresh, uncooked foods of the Essenes, who believed dead foods produced dead men; even their fruits and vegetables were left on the tree or vine as long as possible before eating.

The Indians regarded food as secondary to everything. The devout fasted to show they did not need food and ate heartily to show they were in command of their bodies. Most were vegetarians. But the robust men who traveled the world declared that men needed meat; they ate everything.

Even if the schools I had attended did not exist, I would have learned much by observing people with their different lifestyles. It was the similarities that I loved and sought. The similarities seemed to make us all brothers under the parenthood of the divine, the creator of us all.

Omar and I talked long into the night, for after an hour's rest and a bowl of that hot, stimulating food I was ready to go again, no longer tired or sleepy.

"The energy of the young overwhelms me," smiled Omar, as he noted the way I came alive.

"No need to grow old before my time," I replied.

We talked mostly about the Adonai. I told him about the slavery of the Jews in Egypt, the exodus, the promised land, the mission of the Jews to become a kingdom of priests. I even told him about their failure and captivity by the Persians and Babylonians. It was my first experience of being a rabbi, and I was happy my audience of one was not learned in religion.

As I kept trying to portray YHWH for this man of the road, I kept coming back to comparisons with Yosef, my father.

It was here that Omar and I met on familiar ground, for Omar's father had been a wonderful man. When I compared YHWH to my mother as a loving, nurturing personality who was always forgiving and accepting and ready to be helpful, Omar seemed to gain a clear picture of the God I worshipped. It was around the evening campfires as our caravan gradually ascended into the magnificent Himalayas that I developed my teaching concept of the Creator. A perfect parent with the best attributes of one's mother and one's father seemed the best way to describe that universal spirit all peoples called God, by one name or another. Omar asked another question.

"How do you portray God to those whose parents are cruel and unloving? Or who abandon them when they are still young?"

My mind flashed back to Mina, whose father was a stranger she never knew and whose mother was a prostitute. That presented a problem.

"Like the Indians who name three facets of God and describe them with many characteristics, I must find many ways to suit the many seekers. I love taking the wonderful characteristics of my tender parents to describe my God, which is far better than picturing the Infinite as a jealous, vengeful, murderous God who demands bloody sacrifice as appeasement, horrible punishments for reconciliation, and a life of denial in exchange for salvation. Abundant life is what my parents want for me, and I am sure that is God's will, also. You are right, however. That may not suit the needs of those whose parents may have been less than loving." It was years before I learned how to relate examples that those whom I would teach could understand. Omar was wonderful at making me think.

"Should I be circumcised, as the Jews are?" he inquired.

"In your heart." Another unforeseen answer popped from my mouth. "Circumcision is a sign between man and God, a ritual of cleanliness opening the lines of communication."

"Will I be a Zoroastrian or a Jew?"

"Does it matter what followers of the One God are called?" I answered with a question.

"No, of course not," he answered thoughtfully, "not any more than it matters what man calls God."

My heart jumped. My pupil was standing on his feet already. He was putting simple truths together and getting answers. What a joy to teach an earnest seeker, a mind open and ready to receive. How God must love such a one.

"Find your ideal and follow that," I advised.

"I think you are my ideal," he whispered softly.

"Not me," I protested, "I am just a boy, a messenger from my Heavenly Parent. You are just beginning your journey. The One to come will be someone you can follow all the days of your life and never be fearful he will fail you."

"The Mashiyah?"

"Yes, that is the One. He is coming and will soon be made known. In Him you can put your trust; He will be the perfect pattern, the ideal ideal.

Omar stared at me, and I saw he believed I was that One. I shook my head to clear it. Still it was there like a monument looming before me. Omar crossed his arms across his chest, planted his feet firmly on the soil, and set his mouth in a determined line.

"I shall wait," he declared.

The first glimpse of the Himalayas was at sunrise. They had been a purple haze in the distance as we made camp the night before. But in the clear, early-morning air, they loomed like massive temples lost in masses of clouds. Nothing prepared me for such majesty.

"You have not seen anything yet," exclaimed Omar. "Wait until we are in them."

"They look three times larger than anything in Palestine," I gasped.

"They are the roof of the world," laughed my Persian friend.

We took half a day crossing the tiny strip of tangled jungle lying at the foot of the Himalayas. The lushness of the forest was the result of monsoons clashing with the mountains and washing fertile soil down to the edge of the plains. The tarai, they called it.

As we began the ascent toward the fabled valley of Katmandu, "slow" took on a new meaning. We passed along narrow and dangerous gorges full of turbulent waters cascading over acres of stone, and dropping steeply to icy rivers, which we had to cross.

Frequently we got off our horses and waded through icy streams. We crossed bridges of a single giant tree or several smaller ones held by twigs on which heavy flat stones were laid. The ends were held by piles of stones that seemed ready to topple any minute, plunging us, horses and all, thousands of feet to the rocks below. Falling rocks constantly tumbled down the mountainsides. The wildness of the place enveloped the soul.

Hardly daring to look up and not daring at all to look down, I noticed shrines where the Brahmin paused to tinkle bells and present prayers to Brahm. The urge to leave the perilous travel and to worship forever at such a shrine was strong. But I resisted and slowly grew less terrified at what seemed like a perpetual invitation to disaster, and continued on my way.

At sunset the peaks lit up in a fantastic glow, changing from crimson and gold to a range of hues that defied description. Deer leapt up and down the mountainsides followed by dappled fawns moving like mists in the afternoon glow. I might have been a poet, my soul was so full of beauty and its delights.

Coming upon a clearing of level ground, we stopped for the night. Nightfall in such mountains could easily spell catastrophe if one were caught still traveling. Several wooden huts were at the edge of the clearing, and even in the near-freezing air, barefooted children came rushing out begging for sweets. I gave what I had to the children, who seemed happy for anything at all. They did not seem to notice the cold, but I shivered just watching them.

Omar, knowing I had spent a lifetime in subtropical climates, became my adviser on coping with the mountain cold. I was grateful I wore boots and sturdy breeches. Pulling my cloak around me, I dismounted and stood among the children for a while. I drew warmth from them and hoped they gained something from mine. They crowded around, giggling and chattering in a language I did not know. I decided that talk would have to be by sign language. So, I sang to them and waved my arms in descriptive ways telling the story of the song. They laughed and clapped and jumped up and down, begging for more. However, Omar waved them away and said they would be there the whole night if we allowed it.

Reluctantly, I turned away and we gorged ourselves on the spicy foods, resuming our conversation. It was much colder as night closed in and I snuggled closer to the campfire. Only the night before it had seemed too warm. Omar laughed and chided me.

"You will be a snowflake yet. That is what happens to teenage boys who do not adjust quickly."

"Please leave off the snow, Omar," I begged. The very word "snow" raised visions that sent my teeth chattering. Yochanan's lessons on warmth and chill seemed insufficient in these mountains.

Omar would have none of it. "Think warm," he would urge. "Go with the cold instead of resisting it. Soon it will be as stimulating as the hot food."

But, stubborn youth that I was, I shivered, believing it protected me from freezing. How wrong could I be? I urged we cut short our talk and crawl into the warm bedroll fully clad, boots and all. He smiled and agreed, knowing that I would learn the lesson sooner or later.

As we descended from a mountain pass down into the enchanted valley of Katmandu, I knew why it was legendary. Getting there at all was a feat beyond the grasp of most men, and once there one never wanted to leave.

The Valley of Katmandu had once been a giant lake, an inland sea trapped by the surrounding mountains. Legend had it that the ancient god Manjusri opened a passageway to drain the water with just one swipe of his mighty sword. The waters flowed south out of the valley, leaving land fertile beyond a farmer's wildest expectation. The soaring mountains protect the blessed valley from the bitter cold of the north, while the encircling Mahabharat Lekh range protects it from the effects of the monsoon rains. Those monsoons create jungles and floods with equal ease. The valley, high above sea level, boasts a year-round growing season and is usually free from snow or even freezing temperatures. This fact enthralled me.

The Baghmati-Nadi River drains the valley and is revered as a sacred stream. A Buddhist temple straddles the river in the center of the valley, and a Hindu temple tops a hill above the river's curve. A tiny settlement formed around the temples and that section of the stream and was called Katmandu, also.

Over the centuries, the village of Katmandu became a crossroads for traders traveling from India to China, Tibet, and other far-eastern destinations. The lushness of the valley was a welcomed rest from the rocky crags, wastelands, and howling winds that one encountered in the cloud-shrouded mountains.

As we entered the settlement, I remarked to Omar that I hoped to find Rabat before dark since I longed for a good bed.

"There is only one resthouse, or dharmsala, in Katmandu, and it belongs to a fellow named Rabat," he laughed loudly. "How lucky can a holy man get?"

"Truly?" I asked in amazement.

"Why is old Rabat important to you?"

"He is to be my teacher, my guide, for a while. He was present at my birth and for some reason requested I be sent to him."

I drew out the map Amen had given to me in Egypt. It ended at Katmandu as though finding Rabat would be simple once I arrived in the village. How lucky that the man I sought had the only dharmsala there!

Omar guided me to a large wood-and-stone house also on the river. The caravan master waved us on and called he would join us as soon as he finished stabling the caravan.

"Take your horse, holy boy," he called. "I will get it later."

Some of the travelers would be going on to Lhasa with the caravan and preferred to sleep beside their merchandise. Not so Omar. He claimed that stealing salt in Katmandu would be like stealing air.

"There are always those who believe imported things are better than homemade," he winked as he explained business to me. "And the belief gets me a fancy price. I sell a dream more than a product for salt is salt whether from India or the mountains around Katmandu."

As we walked up to the open wooden door, an elderly man strode vigorously through it and enveloped us in a warm hug, much like that of the Essenes. He seemed to know Omar very well, but how did he know me? Or perhaps he greeted all potential lodgers this well.

"Welcome," he boomed. "I've been waiting for you both."

Chapter 16

Rabat

Omar seemed as surprised as I, but neither of us did more than return the hug and bask in Rabat's warmth. Unlike us, with our heavy boots and woolen cloaks, Rabat had on a simple cotton shift and sandals. His hair was snow white, yet his face seemed years younger; he was ruddy with good health. His blue eyes contrasted with the warm, brown almond-shaped eyes common to the people we had seen in the mountains along the trail. His lean body was strong and firm. He glowed with the goodness that comes from good thoughts, a quality I was beginning to notice had no boundaries of nationality.

Dusk was almost upon us when torches and lamps were lit. The torches were soaked in oil, but the small lamps seemed fueled by butter. A table was laden with ripe fruit and green vegetables so crisp they seemed to still be growing. Flat bread stuffed with honey, nuts, and cheese caught my eye and I fell to the banquet with eagerness. I was eating my way around the world and learning as much about people by the food they served as by the words of the language they spoke.

Rabat enjoyed our appreciation of his table and waited until we were finished before urging conversation. As we sated our appetites and sat sipping the warm tea, he asked about our trip.

"It would have been a mere repetition for me had it not been for my companion here. Let him give you his story," remarked Omar.

With great enthusiasm I recounted the high mountains, the winding trails, the mere paths along ledges that scarcely had room for one foot, much less a horse, the deep ravines, the loud, crashing waters. I described worrying that lions and tigers were lying in wait ready to pounce any moment; I recounted the sudden storms that lashed us with rain, then winds determined to tear us from our thin hold on craggy rocks. I went on and on now that I was safe in Katmandu.

"You have seen nothing as yet, young master," Rabat said. Both men laughed as much at my innocence as at my enthusiasm. "Oh, to see the world again through the eyes of the very young," sighed Rabat.

A shiver ran up my spine as I envisioned higher, craggier, colder mountains and steeper, narrower, slipperier paths. How could it be?

"There are mountains north of here twice as high as those we have just crossed," chortled Omar.

"Impossible!" I scowled.

They laughed and banged on the table with their fists. Omar winked at Rabat and nodded as if they had a common secret. It was the way older men taunted younger ones good-naturedly, so I was not offended. Rather I was pleased they included me in their discussion and cared enough to tease me.

"You shall see all in good time, Yeshua," said Rabat, using my birth name.

It was pleasing to hear that after all these months of hearing "Jeshua." Omar immediately picked it up and turned it over in his mouth, decided it was too difficult, and spat it out.

"Jesu," he said in Greek. "I like the Greek better. I have trouble with Jeshua."

"Just call me 'boy,'" I smiled, joining in the good humor.

Rabat's continual good humor was deceiving. I surmised he had never had a day of tragedy in his entire life. Little did I know what kind of life lay just beyond his smiles and warm-hearted jests. His laughing eyes and happy face showed a genuinely joyous man who spent his days running his dharmsala, taking in strangers day after day. He made us feel like we were family to him.

"Listen with your heart," Amen had urged, "and every man will tell you his story."

Other travelers appeared, ate, then wandered off to bed. But we sat just outside the door long into the evening, talking away the hours. Omar sensed my teacher might have words for his own enlightenment so he stayed to listen.

"How did you know to expect us?" I could not refrain from asking.

"I have a magic ball," teased Rabat. "Don't you know Orientals are magicians?"

"Hmmmm," I took up the challenge. "I know your land is mysterious and mystics are supposed to be magicians. Is it all the same thing?"

He laughed at the way I repeated the Indian beliefs. "You are such a one. Guess again."

"A runner told you we were coming?"

He started a bit at that and almost exclaimed aloud that I knew. But, he held himself in check and murmured that I was surely fresh for one so old.

We all laughed and the evening flashed on with bits of story swapping, observations, and entertaining notes of wisdom. Soon, Rabat began to tell us about the mountains and people.

"The shaman is an interesting fellow. He believes, and therefore the people believe, he has the ability to know the wishes and intentions of supernatural beings. Here in Katmandu they are known as the jhankri. They are in every settlement no matter how small and claim to be holders of messages from God. They are mostly Hindus now, although there is a shaman in Buddhism.

"Shamanism is the oldest of spiritual beliefs. It is a daily, practical belief that covers everything from why it does not rain to why a man's wife does not show him proper respect. A good shaman is also a good healer.

"The initiation of a good shaman is frightening and some do not survive it. Those who do are never again the same, and some rumors have it that a new spirit has taken over the old body. There are quite a few shamans who are uninitiated. They must resort to sleight-of-hand tricks and often give poor advice. But in the past they all were good men who loved their people and considered it a service to God to live among them."

I wanted to ask Rabat whether he was Buddhist or Hindu. It was difficult to tell, but I leaned more toward him being a Buddhist. However, when he talked about Vishnu and the supposed many incarnations of the god, I changed my mind and thought him a Hindu. He told us of the lamas who devoted every waking moment to the worship of the universal consciousness they called God. They lived and studied and worshipped in lamaseries.

Rabat talked about Krishna and Buddha as the eighth and ninth avatars, or incarnations, of Vishnu. He gained my undivided attention as he told us that the tenth avatar of Vishnu would be the Perfect One and was yet to come.

"He is the One who will truly be the Light of the World, the salvation of man, and the reconciliation between the lost souls and God," explained Rabat.

"The tenth avatar will be much like the Buddha. He, too, will be a prince from a faraway kingdom who will leave a kingly domain to live among the poor and oppressed of mankind in order to teach them the ways of God. He will be free of the sin of desire that the Buddha declared was man's undoing. He will already have achieved nirvana, the state of oneness with deity, and will choose to give it up to show man how to achieve it too. He will even overcome death so that all men who believe in him and follow his path will never taste of the death that keeps man tied to the endless cycle of births."

Omar's eyes were as big as bowls, and so were mine. When Rabat stopped talking, we realized he had been in a trance, and we had heard the message from on high.

"Are you a shaman?" whispered Omar with the question I dared not ask.

"No, no," he protested. "I am a simple man who came to this valley long ago when my fellow monks refused to allow me to return to my home in their lamasery."

"Why was that?" Omar pressed Rabat to tell us his story, as eager as I to know all about this mysterious man of Katmandu.

Chapter 17

The Magi

Rabat breathed a deep sigh and began a fascinating story.

"It was long ago," he began, "when I was a very young, very rich, very spoiled man in another land. My father showered me with riches and splendor and power. I had everything my heart could desire or my mind conceive. I even had a beautiful young wife who was as good and kind as she was lovely. Along with all my many blessings, I had a fine young son. I not only adored my son, I worshipped him. His every cry brought me running, and I berated both his mother and the nurse for allowing him even to whimper. They seemed not to mind too much, for I rewarded them handsomely for their loving and devoted care. They knew I was just an anxious father fretting over matters about which I knew nothing.

"'There, there, my lord,' my beautiful wife would say, 'Your son must exercise his voice or perhaps he will never learn to call out for you.'

"It sounded reasonable to me, but so anxious was I that I could hardly leave the house for the marketplace for fear my son might call and I would not be there. By the time my son could stand alone and take a few steps, my father sent me away on a trip for his business that he vowed no other could make. I pled with him to send someone else, but he refused. So with much weeping and wailing and hugging of my little son and his mother, I finally tore myself away and departed the city.

"My trip took only a week, but when I returned my horror of horrors had happened. My son had been stolen in the night.

"In my rage I immediately had his nurse put to death, followed soon after by the guards of my household. For days I sat in deep gloom and brooded. I hired servants to seek my child and offered a king's ransom for his return, but all to no avail. My father tried to comfort me, but I turned him away with much hatred, blaming him for sending me on the trip. My wife, whose heart also must have been breaking, sought to comfort me, but I lashed out at her with my wicked tongue and finally cast her out into the street in a bill of divorcement. That was certain death for her because in that land on pain of death, or worse, no man dared help the cast-off wife of another man. Soon, word came she had died. She had taken no nourishment since the moment she discovered our son was missing.

"Still I was not solaced. So selfish, so focused on my own sorrow, I saw nothing else but my own sad plight. I put on sackcloth and covered myself with ashes and departed the city of my fathers not knowing or caring that I was breaking the heart of my own father and mother. It was my loss, my grief, my tragedy that consumed me. For months I searched far and wide. At last, not knowing what else I could do, I climbed a high mountain and threw myself off it for I no longer wished to live my now-shattered life.

"When I came back to consciousness, I was in a lamasery. Hovering over me was a lama, clean shaven, dressed in a long cotton shirt, wiping my face with a wet cloth. His words soothed me although to this day I do not know what they were. I could not speak. My legs were broken and I was in a wooden cast from head to toe. For days I floated in and out of consciousness. Slowly, I recovered.

"I learned that as I was falling, I hit some trees jutting out into the path of my fall, bounced over into a nest of leaves intertwined along the limbs of another tree growing out of a crevice in the rocks. It was just enough to break my fall. My cloak caught on a branch and held me until some traders who saw me could lower a basket and lift my broken body from its perch. Not knowing what to do with a bruised, bleeding mass of nearly lifeless flesh, they left me at the gates of the lamasery, more dead than alive.

"As I mended, a lama told me I had failed the test of grief. 'It will take many years and an act of great courage to recover your soul's former place in the progression of souls,' he said.

"Strangely, I no longer wanted to die. My physical pain was finally equal to the anguish in my soul, and I wanted to suffer daily, intensely. I was twenty-two years old. So, I did. Nevertheless, my body was young and strong and finally healed. The intense pain ceased. Eventually I could walk again. But I did not recover my power of speech. Even so, the lamas knew who I was and what had happened to me. Not wishing to leave, I beseeched them with my eyes to let me stay. They did, although they made it clear it was only to prevent me from harming myself again.

"No one is idle in a lamasery. It is a refuge of sorts, but everyone must always be busy. I took up the study of astronomy as well as astrology. From that mountaintop retreat, I could see stars that most men have no idea even exist. The lamas had a most marvelous device that magnified the skies and brought the stars as close as my hand before my face. The stars became my family, and I learned them like one learns a beloved friend. I learned to read them like the pages of a book. They spoke to me of things past and things to come. It was a most solemn and holy relationship.

"During those years, my soul seemed to grow. That peaceful, silent sanctuary spread a balm over me that defied description. Daily I came to the observatory and sought out the stars. I was privileged to see the herald of the Great One who was coming. It was the Kalki Avatar, some said. Others said it was the Hebrew Mashiyah. Others claimed Krishna was on his way as the tenth incarnation.

"I saw the star rising slowly in the east. My guide told me it had been prophesied two thousand years before, long before the Buddha's star rose and set again. They said astrologers all over the world could see it and marveled at its brightness and promise. They claimed that when it was fully risen a new king would be born who would unite the whole world with God.

"I watched the star for years. Daily I plotted its path and charted its course. Soon it became apparent to me that the birth of the Promised One was soon. I would jump for joy, show the charts, and point with enthusiasm to my calculations. The lamas enjoyed my activities, nodding their shaven, shiny heads, and giving faint smiles.

"The years passed, and suddenly one morning as I was watching the star, something within me whispered, 'It is time.' Quickly, I plotted the location of the star on an ancient map and discovered the star was over the land of Palestine, a small country far from Tibet.

My heart sank, for I could not pinpoint the exact time of the event predicted, nor even the exact place; all I knew was that I wanted to be there for the blessed event.

"I went to the Grand Lama for an audience. For the first time, I was permitted to see and talk with the Grand Lama of Tibet. He sat on the cold marble floor of the inner room, which was flooded with light. Flickering candles were set behind him. From his eyes poured the wisdom of the ages. He was simple, but in that simplicity, he was magnificent. I fell before him on the floor.

"'Oh, Great Master, wisdom of the universe, God's holy servant on Earth, please grant me my desire to attend the birth of the coming One whose star I have observed for all these years,' I cried out.

"'Arise, my son,' said that voice of antiquity. 'You are not a prisoner here. You are and always have been free to go anytime.'

"I rose and sat before him and waited. I had heard his words, but they were meaningless to me. I did not know if I had permission to go or not. He seemed to be staring at me quite a long time. Then he spoke again.

"'We, too, would like to be present at that long-awaited birth for we have been waiting for the star to rise to maturity for centuries. We are very anxious, for there is much turmoil in the land of Judea. Already the life of the new king is in danger.'

"'No,' I gasped.

"'It is so,' he replied.

"In my eagerness I failed to note the subtleties of his words. He waited. I waited. After a while he spoke again.

"'You seem to have recovered your voice. You must want to go to Judea very badly. We welcome your willingness to go. It is the earnest wish of many of us.'

"Still I did not hear what he was actually saying. In my selfishness I believed I heard him put his blessing on my request, and, of course, recovering my speech put the whole thing in a place I thought was made just for me.

"He remained still and silent for a long time. Finally, he said that they would provide me with the fastest horse, the best maps, and the shortest route. It seemed the answer to my prayer.

"'We will send a gift to the new king; you will guard it carefully, for it is priceless.'

"I was ecstatic. Not only did I get to go, but they trusted me with a precious gift to the newborn prince. It humbled me beyond all my dreams. I even thanked the Lord of the Universe that my lost son was to be replaced by God's own son to fill my hungry heart.

"I spent many hours in prayer and preparation for the long trip. Fortunately, it was spring, and melting snow is better than falling snow at a great height. All the lamas, including the Grand Lama, turned out for my departure and bade me farewell with tears and more affection than ever I had seen in that monastery. It puzzled me, but I dismissed it all as part of my anxiety at leaving. Nevertheless, they seemed to be acting like they would never see me again. Surely they would tell me if misfortune were ahead. No one said a thing. I failed to use any of the many gifts I had learned at the monastery, like mind reading. I was so eager to be on my way. I concentrated on the Grand Lama's instructions.

"'Send the new king down to Egypt with one whom you will meet in Jerusalem,' he said, 'for the prince's life is in the greatest of dangers. We are not the only ones who have watched his star and heard the promises of his divine rule.'

"He handed me a tiny bag of precious herbs mixed with myrrh and cautioned me again about the gift's value. (It is only now that I realize how truly precious it was.) I loaded up the pack animal that was waiting and together we plunged down that steep mountain path to the plains of India, where the fastest camel awaited my trip toward that faraway land. As I studied the map provided, it did look like I was going the long way around, but I believed firmly in the wisdom of the lamas so did not deviate one mile nor stray one day from my quest.

"Months later I saw the city of Jerusalem sitting on a hill in the distance. Beyond was the star hanging low in the sky. I urged my camel on and, as I was nearing the Damascus Gate, a young priest from Egypt joined me. He was Amen, a newly mantled initiate. We rode into the city and found an inn for the night. As we talked over our quest, I learned that he, too, knew there was danger about. Neither of us knew from whence it was coming, however, and so we went together to the palace of the king the next morning. We both believed that a new king being born must be the son of the present king.

"Imagine our shock when we beheld a sickly, insane man unable even to conceal his alarm that a new prince had arrived and was close by. Old King Herod made a great pretense of eagerness to see the child and called his seers into the throne room to discover the whereabouts of the babe. The seers professed ignorance, or should I say they quoted contradictory writings? It alerted us that they knew the danger of telling the king the whereabouts of the princeling.

"'I shall call my son out of Egypt,' quoted one seer 'The Holy Scriptures say the boy is in Egypt.'

"'No, no,' exclaimed another, 'he shall be called wonderful and counselor. Obviously the child was born in Rome.'

"'Not so,' claimed another seer, 'the babe is to be a Nazarene like Samson of old; he must be in Zorah.'

"As the seers dissembled, both Amen and I realized their argument among themselves was to give us time to steal away. We quickly begged leave of the insane king. He was so intent on the arguing seers that he failed to notice we were rushing away. Then he called out to us, 'Return and tell me where the young prince is so that I may worship him, too.'

"The squabbling of the astrologers grew louder and we stole away without promising anything. As we descended the steps out of the palace, an old man hobbled up to us and whispered the exact location of the blessed event.

"'The babe is in Bethlehem, a few miles south of here, in a cave behind an old inn. Take him out of Judea, for our king is sick with many fears and will murder him if he can.'

"The old man limped away into the shadows of the palace and we saw him no more. Coming up the steps, some magi from far countries recognized us and asked about the king.

"'He is not here,' whispered Amen. 'Only a sick old dying man named Herod who is not a real king at all, but a lackey of Rome. The babe is hidden away in a manger in Bethlehem. Come with us. We will show you.'

"'Someone must wait here and warn others who may arrive,' whispered Baungha from Persia.

"'I am weary from travel and need to rest here for a while. I will stay,' volunteered the seer from Gobi. Magi are the ones who deal with things of the spirit. There are many magi.

"Three of us set out immediately for Bethlehem. It did not take long to get there, but we searched far into the night for the cave, for there were many. Finally, just as the morning sun rose to meet the brilliant daystar of the new prince, we found the child in a stable behind an ancient inn. The entrance was covered with trees, and cattle lowed softly at us as we entered. Some shepherds from a nearby field were all that were there. The young mother was radiant.

"The proud father had wrapped the child in swaddling, and stood hovering over the mother and babe. We all had gifts and presented them, describing their value. The youthful mother accepted them gratefully. But when we warned her they were in grave danger and must flee out of the country, she refused.

"'I cannot go until my days of purification are over,' she cried, 'and my son dedicated to the Lord God!'

"We trembled with fear for her and the child, but the father backed her up, and we could not persuade them to change their minds. Achlar, the magi who had just arrived, heard her cry, and gave them some frankincense; he bade them burn it and stand in its fumes before going into Jerusalem.

"'It will protect you from evil eyes,' he claimed, 'but only for a few weeks. As soon as your purification and dedication are over, you must surely leave Palestine and flee into Egypt; otherwise you and your precious child will surely die.'

"The blessed couple gave us their promises that they would follow our instructions. Amen gave them a map, assuring them it would lead to Alexandria and safety. He urged them to follow it closely. Through all of this the cattle lowed continuously, a dog howled mournfully in the distance, and the hairs on the back of my neck stood on end. As a cock crowed loudly three times, we realized we were surrounded by unseen beings charged with the safety of the babe. So, we bade them farewell and left.

"My heart sang as I retraced my path back to the high mountain retreat that was home to me. Oh, what wondrous stories I planned to tell the lamas now that I could speak and had seen such events. Little did I suspect what awaited me as I finally trudged up the winding trail months later to the lamasery. All too soon I discovered what I had done to myself.

"The gates of the retreat loomed above me, and I ran the remaining steps to those portals. The sun setting beyond the clouds cast a golden glow upon the copper lacings of the wooden gates. I jangled the brass bell that hung on the copper stand. It clanged loudly and echoed through the mountaintops. As I stood waiting for the gates to swing open, unaware of my fate, I hummed a hymn of thanksgiving to the great Lord of the Universe for bringing me safely home.

"Alas, the great doors failed to open. Only silence greeted me. I rang the bell again, thinking (foolishly) they must not have heard it ring; or perhaps they did not realize it was I, their companion and student of the past thirty years, recently returned from the journey they had sent me on. I leaned against the stone wall that surrounds the base of the monastery and turned my face westward to watch the last crimson rays of the disappearing sun as it turned the sky a glorious reddish gold, slowly fading into ever deepening hues of purple. I watched the stars come out followed by the new moon. Still the gates refused to open.

"As the night wore on, I began to call out and pound on the great gates with my fists. I shouted until I grew hoarse. When fatigue overtook me, I slept across the gates, lest they open in the night and fail to waken me.

"When the first fingers of light streaked across the heavens, I awoke and began anew to clamor for admittance. All that day and most of the following night, I begged and pleaded for just one word from any of the lamas, for I had finally realized they knew I was there and were refusing to open the gates to me. I could feel the stony silence that proved deaf to my pleas. Still, I begged them to open the gates.

"A light snow began to fall and soon covered me. I fainted from fatigue and hunger. Only my deep anguish kept me from freezing to death. For over a week I begged, and for another week I lay across those great doors blocking the entrance lest they open while I was unconscious.

"Late one evening, I saw a lone figure coming slowly up the winding trail. At first I thought I was dreaming, but no, oh no, oh great God of the Universe, it was my own dear guide, Lopsam, who had nursed me back to health years before. In my joy at seeing him I believed that he who had set my broken legs and opened my shattered mind was once more my salvation. I threw myself in his path and fell upon him with tears. I felt his body go rigid as though cast in stone. I pulled back and looked into his face. It was set in a stern look and his eyes refused to look into mine. He folded his arms beneath his cloak, a sign of rejection.

"I went on my knees before him and begged to know what crime I had committed that closed my home of many years to me. He stared at me in surprise and asked, 'Did you not know that once you leave our lamasery you are never again permitted to return? Did you not know that only those sent on missions for the Grand Lama may leave and return again? It is an ancient rule. No one is forced to stay, but once one leaves voluntarily, it is forever. We do not have in-and-out privileges.'

"'No, no, there must be some mistake,' I cried. 'I did not know the rule. And, I was on a mission for the Grand Lama. I carried his gift.'

"'It is not the same, my son,' soothed the old lama. 'Another had been chosen to go when you asked to go yourself. We all wanted to go. But you rushed in and put yourself first, ahead of us all. Did you think you were the only one who wanted to greet the divine prince? We had labored for years to earn the privilege, and one had earned the right to go. He gave up his prize because you asked. Cyani is a gentle soul and never pushes himself ahead of others, even when it is his right.'

"'I did not know,' I wept.

"'You did not ask,' he reproved me, gently.

"'I put myself first, again?' I asked.

"'Yes,' he replied

"It was at that moment that I finally learned the terrible price we pay for selfishness. Sadly, sadly, I turned and walked away, knowing that nothing I could say or do would change their minds. I stumbled through the mountains for days, hoping I would die, but not daring to bring it on myself. After many months I came upon this valley and collapsed, a sadder but much wiser man. I built this dharmsala beside the sacred river as a refuge for lost souls, strangers, wanderers, even perhaps for my own lost son.

"It is my hope that I can repay all that was done for me by doing for others. Whether it is a bowl of soup, a warm bed, some magic herbs, or months of silence, I am here for them all."

Rabat's eyes glittered brightly with tears as he continued with his story.

"When Amen sent me a message from Egypt that you, Yeshua, were coming, and that with you would be the answer to my prayers, my heart leapt. I hoped against hope that my own beloved son might be with you. But, alas, only my old friend, Omar, who is much too young to be my son is all I see."

Omar and I professed our sorrow to disappoint him. To laugh and smile after such a long, tragic life of loss must take a great soul. To come to this valley and spend the remainder of his life serving mankind–his example reminded me of the Buddha. As the Hindus say, "It is much the same thing."

"Are you not bitter from all the blows life has dealt you?" questioned Omar.

"How can I be bitter when I did it all to myself?" he responded with a question indicating enlightenment.

"But," cried Omar, "you did not steal away your only son!"

"Perhaps I did. I worshipped him instead of God. That led to all kinds of evil. Perhaps my fears that something would happen to my son brought it on. Whereas, if I had worshipped God and trusted God, perhaps my son would still be with me.

"I blamed others for what I failed to do myself. My innocent wife, my son's nurse, the guards were all killed by me when I could have spent that time and energy searching for the robbers. I dwelled on punishment instead of salvation, and, in so doing, I killed myself. I punished myself. I committed the most selfish act of all: I tried to kill myself, free myself of pain while filling others who loved me full of that pain.

"Even after the good lamas took me in, shared their secrets with me, healed my sickened soul, I snatched away from them the treasure they had all worked for. Was that not the same thing as bandits stealing away my only son?"

"But, you could not know." started Omar.

"Ah, yes, I could know. That is what all men say, how they rationalize their selfish deeds."

"How?" exclaimed Omar. "How could you know the results of your acts in advance?"

"Every act has an effect, a result that can be determined with careful thought, prayer, and meditation. If we are in doubt, we have but to ask, for it is in the seeking of truth that it is found. Alas, more often than not, we turn our heads and say it is not meant for us to know so we can go merrily on our evil ways."

"If you want to know, you will know."

Omar's eyes widened, and he began to moan. "Oh, oh, oh, I am undone. Woe is me. My retribution comes!"

Rabat put a gentle hand on his arm and soothed him. "Omar, knowledge is the beginning of wisdom. You can begin now to undo those things that worry you. Seeking to undo wrongs often saves you from having to suffer terrible consequences."

"Did you do that?"

"All my family and servants died long before I stopped thinking about myself long enough to care about them or the effects of my life's acts. Now, all I can do is care for each one who comes my way as though he were my own son, my long-dead wife, the nurse, my hapless guards, or my father and mother, who died from broken hearts."

Omar sat silently in deep thought. As we all sat thinking about the story of Rabat, I thought surely he must be a Hindu. But still I could not be sure. So much of Hindu and Buddhist thought seemed the same to me. One produced the other, and I could not tell where one ended and the other began. I hit upon the idea of making a fool out of myself by saying I could not tell the difference between the two.

Rabat looked at me with amusement as the merry twinkle jumped back into his eyes, "Why, Yeshua, what a pleasure it will be to teach you, when already you dwell upon the similarities of two great religions rather than the differences. You truly are a worthy Initiate."

I know I blushed. I could feel it. It started at my toes and swept up to my face in a flash. Burning hotly, I sought to refrain from putting my hands to my face. It was a mighty effort.

"I am embarrassing Yeshua," the gentle Rabat said. "It is difficult, I know, to handle compliments, but drink them in now and store them away against the day when men speak evil of you and spit upon you. For it will surely come!"

"Jesu is a holy man," said Omar, "for he has taught me all about the Lord God. I am now a believer."

At that point the caravan master arrived. Sticking his head through the door, he called, "Have you a place for me in this warm little gathering?"

"But, of course, Bat. I always have a place for you," answered Omar.

"Bat," so that is the caravan master's name, I thought. No one dared call him anything but master during our travel, and his servants called him sahib, which probably meant the same thing. I was struck by the warmth and familiarity between the two men. They seemed to be friends of many years.

Bat picked up his bags and heaved the heavy pile onto the floor of the dharmsala. He paused only a few moments, grinned, patted me on the head, and said, "Goodnight, Holy Boy. Sleep in the arms of the gods." He laughed as he made his way to his room.

"Tell us about him," I urged Rabat.

But the old man merely laughed and said, "Yeshua, you are young. You could sit up all night listening to my stories, but we old men must rest, eh, Omar?"

So that first evening in Katmandu closed. It was a fabled land, and justified its legend. There was no way a man could describe it accurately. It occupied a place in the heart, like the sense of home. I could scarcely sleep that night, even in the comfortable bed that took the place of the ground and a bedroll.

Chapter 18

The Valley of Life

Early morning anywhere in the Himalayas is spectacular. In the valley of Katmandu it exceeds one's wildest fantasies. The dusty Indian air had already faded into a dim memory, while the clear, crisp, cool air flowing into the valley off the snowcapped mountains filled my soul as well as my lungs.

I breathed deeply and chanted a mantra I learned from the Ahmadabad monks. I wandered down to the river and eyed the clear, sparkling water. Recalling the hundreds of Indians who would be pouring into the Ganges on the plains below, I wondered why no one was in this river, as it was called the most sacred stream in the mountains. I looked about and noted not one soul near the river.

The ring of mountains shimmered in the early rays of light like great bars of silver and gold; everywhere there were treasures of reflected light like diamonds, rubies, emeralds. Picking a handful of flowers, I proceeded into the Baghmati-Nadi. Too late, I realized not only that the water was freezing cold, but was deeper than I thought.

I sank like a sack of stones. The cold took away my breath and the sudden depth overwhelmed and disoriented me. The gentle slope of the plains was absent and the shock of the sudden drop shattered my senses. I knew I was drowning. My arms refused to move.

As I plunged under the water for the second time, I opened my mouth to cry out and immediately paid for the mistake.

When I came to, I was face down on the grass. Someone very heavy was on my back forcing the water from my body with strong pushing strokes. I gagged and threw up. Even in my desperate gasp for air, I looked over my shoulder to see who was astride my back and who else was observing my humiliation. The lone savior was all there was, now gently massaging my back, expelling the last bits of water from my lungs. Then the massive hands sat me up like a rag doll and wiped my face.

She was a Sherpa, a yak herder who ordinarily made her home higher up the mountains. She grinned at me with a toothless smile, clapped me on the back, and roared with laughter.

"You lucky you no die, dumb boy, jump in sacred river like rock," she correctly described me.

"Yeah," I muttered in agreement.

She threw her heavy cloak around my now-shivering body, asking, "You at dharmsala?"

I nodded, still too weak to speak.

She picked me up like a sack of potatoes, threw me over her shoulder, and headed for the inn. Bouncing on her shoulder, I protested loudly, "No, I can walk," but she paid no more attention to me than she would to a lump of clay.

I struggled to get my feet on the ground while she made shushing sounds at me. Finally, she gave up as I managed to slide from her grip and allowed me to stand. "You better, dumb boy?"

I tried to thank her for saving my life, but she would have none of it. She hustled me into the main room of the resthouse and plopped me down on the yak rug, stoked a roaring fire in the fireplace, and began boiling water for soup. She was much at home in the dharmsala.

As she pulled fresh vegetables from a storage bin and began chopping and dumping them into the boiling water, Rabat appeared. He surveyed the scene and immediately went over to the busy woman and hugged her warmly. They spoke briefly in a tongue I did not know. She continued with her cooking while Rabat came over and put his arm around me.

"You are such a dear boy," he sighed. "I should have known you would worship with the dawn. You Essenes are all alike, greeting each new day before it wakes. Lucky for you Pema was about. In these mountains water is just melted snow and does not lend itself to anything more than being watched from the banks. We never get into it voluntarily and certainly not to worship, at least not without some training, which you have not had."

At my questioning look, Rabat continued, "In the land of eternal snows, the people never bathe. Getting into the water is an initiation you will have later on."

"Never bathe?" I gasped. "Icy initiation?" I asked.

A loud giggle erupted from Pema. "He try drown heself," she snorted, "to wash he body. He insides get washed more so." She howled.

Rabat laughed, and I had to laugh, too. How could one fail to find happiness when everything that happened brought peals of laughter from the natives? No sour looks on those faces. I wondered if Katmandu meant "happy."

My teeth had only recently stopped chattering, so I kept my mouth closed in hopes no more heat would escape my body, as well as no more stupid remarks. I recalled the wise words of my Egyptian mentor that made so much more sense to me now. "The most stupid man in the world will seem wise if he is at least smart enough to keep his mouth closed and not disclose his ignorance to the world."

It was clear that what made good sense in warm countries made no sense in cold ones. I glanced at the Sherpa woman and sniffed slightly, wondering if she smelled. At that moment, however, she would have smelled like jasmine to me, for I owed her my life.

As I studied her, I wondered how Pema had gotten into that frigid river to pull me out. How had she gotten out clad as she was in heavy boots and many layers of clothing? Although much rounder, she was not as tall as I, so the bottom of the river was even "deeper" for her. Yet, she did not seem to be as wet as I was, even after I had sat by the fire for an hour.

Later, I learned that Pema had roped me as I was going down the second time and pulled me ashore like one of her yaks without getting any more water on herself than fell off me. The Sherpa were never without their ropes. Falling off cliffs was a way of life in these mountains and the rope was a lifeline. Whether hauling a fallen animal from the depths of some ravine or hauling oneself, it was all part of the life on the steep trails.

I had purchased a rope in Kashi in the hope that someone would teach me the Indian rope trick. As I learned the marvel of the rope in Katmandu, my hopes of learning to use it expertly grew. Nevertheless, I asked no one to teach me. Amen had warned that no one should ever get ahead of their teachers, and that was particularly true for Initiates.

"Everything comes in its own time," he had said. "The foolish rush ahead and eat apples out of season. It causes a man to fail." Amen smiled as he added the bit based on our holy writings. He always impressed upon me that the writings of the Hebrews began in Egypt.

After a few days' rest, the horse caravan was prepared for the trip to Lhasa. Omar would pick up a load of silk from China for the trip home to Persia. I embraced my beloved friend who had taught me the yearning of all men for God.

"Goodbye, dear Omar," I whispered, clinging to him. "I learned so much from you."

"From me?"

"Yes, from you."

"How so, young friend?"

"You asked the questions that demanded deep thought and required perfected answers. They forced me to consider my mission and the path it must take. Before you, I merely flowed with the river."

"Ahhh, Jesu, you make all men stand a little taller. You tell me how to make life even more abundant, then claim it is I who have helped you. Be careful, lest men fall down and worship you."

"See, there you go again, teaching me," I quickly responded. "We all need to be reminded that God shall be the true teacher, while we are merely channels through which the great messages come. Because of you, I have learned that God's messages are for everyone, not just a few ragged souls in Palestine."

We bade each other a fond farewell. His route to Persia would bring him back through Katmandu, but who knows what can befall a man of the road? I promised I would come to him in Isfahan even before I sought my Persian guide, Baungha. Omar promised to seek out the Zoroastrians and tell Baungha my whereabouts.

Bat appeared to collect Omar and called out, "Goodbye, Holy Boy."

"Goodbye, King of the Road," I gathered my nerve to jest with him.

He came to a dead halt, turned, and walked slowly back toward me. "Is this my holy boy I hear dropping my accustomed title of 'master' now that I have delivered him safely to his destination?"

I trembled a little for Bat towered over me, and his mountainous frame seemed to grow. "Is the change from 'master' to 'king' a step down?" I replied, softly.

He stared at me a few moments then threw back his head and roared with laughter, "You'd better watch this one, Rabat. He will be teaching you a thing or two."

He gave me a hug that surprised me, for I never expected a display of affection or any emotion from the tough caravan master. As a last surprise, Bat left the white horse with me, saying he would pick it up on his return from Lhasa. Rabat warmly hugged Bat and tenderly kissed both sides of his face in a display of affection that alerted me to a feeling I could not quite define. I shrugged it off, however, as I realized Rabat was warm and affectionate with everyone. As he himself had said, everyone who came to him represented a possible reappearance of his beloved son.

Rabat walked to the staging area with an armload of baskets filled with food for his guests and Bat. The long trip to the fabled holy city of Lhasa was not only dangerous, it was sparsely settled. Food was welcomed on any caravan, but especially that one.

As the caravan slowly moved out across the valley, heading for the mountains, Rabat told me some facts about the distant city. "Lhasa is closed to strangers. Omar is one of the few traders allowed inside. We hear it is because he gives precious gifts to the Grand Lama, who dotes on surprises from Calcutta. The rewards are great, but the penalty for betrayal is quickly exacted."

I could not help but wonder if Lhasa were the city from which Rabat had come, but I did not ask. A man is measured by the questions he asks, and some questions are too personal to be intelligent, or even safe.

Pema had been gathering herbs at a farm she owned with another woman. She returned, and I learned her story, as both she and Rabat related it. Pema's husband had fallen from a cliff trying to save one of their baby yaks. The chasm he had fallen into was inaccessible and after two weeks of waiting and listening for some sign that he was alive, Pema had given up. She lived alone high on the mountain where she tended her herd, coming down into the valley occasionally for supplies.

Pema always stayed at the dharmsala since she was the one who helped Rabat build the resthouse, kept it furnished with blankets she wove herself, and decorated with intricate wall hangings. She also made glorious rugs, which provided much of the warmth of the resthouse. She busied herself with the dharmsala cleaning, cooking, and fussing over Rabat, and now me.

There was something about Pema that was different from all other women in the valley. I noticed it in some Egyptians and a few Indians. When I mentioned it to Rabat, he explained she was an original descendant of the root race.

"What is the root race?" I inquired.

"The root race is what survived worldwide catastrophe."

"Like Noah's flood in our ancient writings?"

"Yes, like that one. There have been others."

I looked at him with a mixture of surprise and questioning. He seemed reluctant to go on.

"The Earth is not young. It is millions of years old. Civilizations have arisen and fallen like the ebb and flow of the tides. You will study that later."

He would say no more on that subject, so I busied myself about the resthouse helping Pema. Occasionally I found myself sniffing as I passed her. At first I did not realize I was doing it, but she noticed (according to Rabat). I began to pay attention to my nose.

As I worked on my attitude, Pema seemed to acquire a warm, earthy odor. While some Essenes might call my acceptance of the odor a miracle, I acquired new respect for the mind and its powers. It was one thing to accept a casual passing thing of repugnance; it was quite another to live with it daily. The discipline I learned from the guides in Ahmadabad began to take effect. YHWH's great gift of free will took on new meaning. It was a monumental way to celebrate one's birthday, practicing prior lessons at a deeper level.

A week later Rabat asked if I would like to travel up the mountain with him to Pema's home. I was overjoyed.

"I help her carry her supplies up the mountain as a token of my appreciation for all she does for me," he explained.

"A good exchange," I commented, happily.

"The scale tips in her favor, but it is the best I can do."

It took a while to load the pack animals with bags of fresh fruits, vegetables, grains, and herbs. Soon we were ready and headed out across the valley floor. As we began the steep climb up the mountain,

I feasted my eyes on the majestic mountains ahead. Like a snow-capped sea of peaks and valleys they towered above us, climbing ever higher and higher.

Toward the end of the day we heard a faint cry coming from deep within a bottomless cud. It was weak, but sound travels far when echoing through mountains, and we heard the hollow yell reverberating feebly from the walls of the chasm. I could not tell from whence the cry came, so unused to echoes were my ears. Pema, however, seemed to know exactly where it was. She expertly unwound her rope and tied it to a tree that seemed no more than a sprig clinging tenaciously to a rocky ledge. She attached the other end of the rope to her waist and was over the side, quickly lowering herself down the stony cliff. In what seemed no time at all, she hauled herself back up the cliff with a man draped over her shoulder. Rabat and I pulled them up onto the path. As we gently rolled the man over on his back, we saw it was Omar. He was nearly dead from thirst, hunger, and broken bones.

"Must hurry," Pema commanded, as she crushed some herbs and placed them inside Omar's parched mouth. "He no last long," she declared pouring a single sip of water down his throat. Omar roused slightly, but then lapsed back into blessed unconsciousness.

We were not far from Pema's house, so we carefully loaded the broken man and cautiously proceeded up the trail. An hour later we arrived and soon had Omar bundled into warm blankets and soft furs. Pema set his broken bones and wiped the blood from his head. She soothed him with soft words as he groaned, and she filled his mouth with little sips of water and crushed herbs. Soon his moaning ceased and he fell back into a deep sleep.

"Is he dead?" I cried.

"No," she fairly shouted. "He no die. He no dare die on Pema."

She was right. Omar did not dare die. She pulled him back from the edge of eternity and breathed the breath of life back into him. We sat anxiously by his pallet for hours. But not Pema. She was much too busy. She put her all-purpose soup on the fire and unpacked her many precious herbs and fruits. Rabat and I were left to do all the worrying and fretting.

When Omar awakened, he seemed relatively free of pain. He thanked God we had found him and declared his newfound faith was what had brought us to him.

"What happened?" asked Rabat, as we leaned near him to hear what he had to say.

"A boulder came crashing down the side of the mountain. We heard it coming, but on such a ledge, we were all helpless to move. It hit my horse on its head, knocking us both over the edge, killing the horse and throwing me onto a protruding tree far down the canyon. The fall must have knocked me unconscious, for I could faintly hear someone calling my name, but I could not rouse myself to answer.

"As I drifted in and out of consciousness, I thought perhaps it was spirits calling to me from the Other Side, or perhaps a dream. By the time I was conscious enough to collect my wits, I could no longer hear anything except the calls of the wilderness."

"Bat would have saved you, had you made the weakest of sounds," murmured Rabat.

"Yes, I know," wheezed Omar, "but I could not seem to utter a sound, no matter how hard I tried."

"Karma!" sniffed Pema.

I stared at her. There was that strange word again that so many in India applied to every unfathomable unfortunate event. Here it was in the Himalayas, too. Was everything karma?

Pema busied herself turning her home into a dharmsala of luxury. There were long, low benches running along the front wall of the main room under a row of windows. Low tables in front of the benches were soon laden with food. She sat Rabat at the head of the table as the honored guest, at the place nearest the fire, as was the custom of the Sherpas. Pema placed me next to Rabat, while she squatted on a rug where she remained when not serving us or ladling soup into Omar's mouth.

While I was surprised Pema took the role of a servant in her own home, Rabat seemed not to notice, and poor Omar was too weak to care. Custom dies hard in the soul of a simple people, I surmised. The moment men entered her house, she had reverted to her "place," which seemed to be somewhere between servant and dog. She who had sat at table with us in Katmandu now refused even to consider it. She who had hauled both Omar and me from the jaws of death itself was now our servant. The mysteries of women deepened. The word servant took on new meaning.

It was amazing how quickly Omar healed. Pema's herbs were miraculous. They grew in soil rich from the minerals washed down the mountains into the fertile valley of Katmandu.

"I tell you secret, boy," Pema explained. "Herbs no help if mind sick."

Rabat patted me on the shoulder and declared I was some special person to merit receiving Pema's secrets. "She guards those precious herbs with her life, for she and her partner sell them for kings' ransoms, and usually only kings can afford them."

How novel, I thought. Pema gladly risks her life to save a stranger, but charges a fortune for herbs plucked from the field that anyone could grow. I mentioned this to her.

"Shhh, no tell my secrets," she laughed. "Special grind, special mix, special bag of life. What price a bag of life?"

Merchants came from faraway China, Palestine, Greece, Egypt, and all over the world for her special mixes. Watching Omar heal before my eyes proved Pema had something powerful going. I was not surprised to learn she was a very rich woman, along with her partner, another widow. It made her subservience to her guests even more mysterious and precious. Again I realized all my teachers did not sit in the halls of fine schools. Was there anyone from whom I could not learn?

"Open your mind," the Ahmadabad monks had exhorted me every day, They whispered it in my sleep, wrote it on my wall.

"The open mind sees all, hears all, feels all, and knows all."

How could I miss? They had prepared me for anything and everything. Even the tea Pema prepared was from a magical herb. Ginseng, she called it. It was terrible. Omar slurped it up, but I filled my cup with honey to mask its taste.

"Some tastes must be acquired, Yeshua," Rabat assured me. "The Mongolians have centuries on you in liking ginseng. Their civilization was ancient when Abraham left Ur of the Chaldees."

My surprise prompted Rabat to tell me the stars were not all he studied at the lamasery. Again the idea came to me that I could stay with Rabat and Pema forever in Katmandu and learn all there was of value. But, when I said so, Rabat denied it was so. "You have no idea," he assured me.

Idyllic as it was at Pema's, we could not stay forever. So, early one morning a few days later, Rabat announced, "Omar must stay here until he can travel comfortably. Then Pema will bring him to Katmandu, where he can catch another caravan for Lhasa."

"Not so," spoke up Omar, "I cannot go to Lhasa now. I have missed my shipment of silk. It will be sold to someone else, for it is precious. I shall go on to Persia when I can travel."

"So sorry," murmured Rabat.

"It is the will of God," Omar said, easily. "I am more interested in getting back to Isfahan and the Zoroastrians than in making a profit from silk. God has spared my life for some purpose, and I must seek the divine will more than ever now."

Surviving the fall was enough to convince any man his life must have some purpose other than the one he was following. Being rescued by the happenstance of coming up that trail at the very moment he gave his final energies to one last call would be enough to astound even the hardest of unbelievers. Not to mention Pema's role, a woman who could pluck a tooth from a tiger's mouth. If ever God had touched a life, He had touched Omar's.

My great lesson in that year was that not all schools are labeled so. I much preferred this kind.

Chapter 19

The Soul

Bidding Pema and Omar farewell, Rabat and I wound our way down the mountain back into the valley. I felt as if I were coming home. It was strange, that feeling that I had been there once before, long, long ago. I could not shake it.

We spent the spring and summer traveling around that wondrous valley. I came to know Hindus and Buddhists. Some, like me, saw not much difference between the two. Rabat explained that in the isolation of the mountains the people tended to cling to what they knew rather than accept the strangely new. They believed there was only one God, Brahm. Gautama Buddha had taught them that, along with the teaching that God could not be limited, described, defined, or even explained. Buddha's effort had been to wean the people away from thinking about Shiva, the destroyer, being a god or even a facet of God. He wanted people to acknowledge the Spirit.

Many years after the passing of Gautama, there were little statues of him everywhere. The story that he was the ninth incarnation of Vishnu, another facet of God, was not what the Buddha intended. Many claimed they had the statues to remind themselves of what the Buddha taught, how he thought, what he saw. Certainly, it was a worthy goal. But the Law of Moses that forbade such images had merit, considering what tended to happen as the centuries went by. There were probably many simple folk who believed the statue of Buddha and the statue of Vishnu were the image of God. The Law of Moses was designed to create a consciousness of God. How can one have a statue of consciousness?

"Hurt not others with that which pains yourself," declared

Gautama, the Buddha. "Go now, O monks, and wander for the benefit of many, for the welfare of mankind, out of compassion for the world. Preach the doctrine. If it is not preached to them, how can they know the path to salvation? Proclaim to them the life of wholeness."

Such worthy teachings–who could fault them? Every one could be found in the teachings of Moses, the prophets, the Hebrew law. And Buddha taught love, the practice of love in compassion, truthfulness, and purity in all walks of life. He laid out an eight-fold path, teaching that when one followed that path, he or she would find nirvana, or heaven, or oneness with God, which are all the same thing.

The eight-fold path was really very simple: right views, right intentions, right speech, right action, right livelihood, right effort, right mindfulness, and right concentration. Who could argue with that?

Nevertheless, people did argue with it. They argued over what was "right." What is right speech? One would say no speech at all, complete silence. Another would say it is speech that is free of curse words, while still others said only speech about God was right speech. That could go on forever. The Essenes seem to agree with the idea of right speech. They are very careful about their speech. If you say "yes," why then mean "yes," they teach. If you say "no," mean "no." Speaking the truth is their idea of right concentration.

What is truth? That is a question that can lead to eternal arguments. Seeking the truth about oneself is about the best one can do. That leads quicker to the truth about God than anything else; it was my belief then and still is.

Meanwhile, my guru–another interesting word that means spiritual teacher or guide–instructed me in herbs, their names and what they aid in the healing process.

"This one," said Rabat, "is good for the blood."

There was one we burned like incense; it had a calming effect, slowed things down, relieved tension, increased appetite. It was especially good for one who was losing his sight. There were herbs for every malady, including the dreaded leprosy and the shaking disease.

At the end of summer Rabat announced, "Now you will learn to heal without the use of herbs."

Novel, I thought, just novel. You wasted six months on me.

"A number of people are sick in their minds," Rabat began. "Once their minds are healed, their bodies will heal. The body does whatever the mind commands. Many do not realize that when they say, 'I cannot stand that thing,' their legs will start to lose their energy. Very often the legs will cease standing. Negative thinking produces negative results."

We went around the valley seeking out examples of what negative thinking had produced. "Be careful what you think, for as a man thinks in his heart, so is he." Surely this was the "right mindfulness" taught by the Buddha. Right and positive must have the same meaning. I decided to put all the teachings of Moses in a more positive way when I became a rabbi.

"What about the atman?" I asked one evening.

"Ah, yes, the soul," mused Rabat. "Some men get very sick in their soul. That was my illness. I am not clear about healing a man's soul. The lamas spent thirty years working on mine, then I failed the test of selflessness, which had been my problem all along."

"You certainly are whole now," I observed.

"Perhaps," he mused. "The lamas claim the body and the mind are manifestations of the soul. Most people are aware of their bodies and their minds. Few are really aware of their souls."

"If I work on a person's soul first, perhaps no one will need ever be sick in the mind or body," I mused.

Rabat stared at me, studying my face and looking deeply into my mind. He hesitated for a moment, then went somewhere, beyond. After what seemed a long time, he spoke again.

"I can see you have the keys to eternal life . . . Heal the soul of man and his whole world will change from death to life."

I clapped my hands in boyish delight, "Rabat, you are so serious. Surely healing a poor sick soul should be much easier than mending a mangled leg or a crazed mind."

"Not so easy, not so easy," he muttered.

That worried me. Surely forgiveness for the sins of the soul would heal it, make it whole. What was difficult about that? The spirit is always willing. What seemed clear to me seemed unclear to Rabat.

He seemed to dwell on his past sins, his murderous soul. I could see it was a gentle soul now, full of love and selfless. What else did a soul need to be?

It occurred to me that my Heavenly Father had given a precious gift to man: the forgetting that comes with being born again and again. Certainly remembering the deeds of a past life could sicken one to the point that it would be all the mind would dwell upon. A fresh start in a new life with a clean mind is a gift that helps more than anything for man's soul to heal, so that he may be made whole as God is whole, for that is the perfect pattern.

"Yochanan will love it," I cried out.

"Wh-what? Who?" stammered Rabat.

"My cousin, Yochanan, in Palestine. We talked about reincarnation and had fun playing around with who we might have been in a past life. I thought he might have been Elijah, one of our prophets. Or that I might have been Joshua, one of our generals who was a son of God. It was all in fun, of course."

"We accept being born again as truth," declared Rabat.

"Yes, many do. The Sadducees do not, however, and are constantly preaching against it. The Jews are divided."

"You will see your past lives at the next place you study," he remarked.

"Really and truly?" I exclaimed. "I can hardly wait."

"Wait," he replied. "It is a sobering event. Only the truly strong in God can bear it."

"God forgives what man forgives, but that is very difficult to believe. You will see," I cried, even as I wondered where it came from. These odd remarks that flowed out of my mouth from somewhere deep within were coming to me more often. I learned from them myself, which was strange, too.

"Before the snows come we should travel to Lhasa," he said. "We shall see tomorrow whether we can make it. Already it may be too late, for the trip is over rugged mountains and terrain for three hundred and fifty miles. It may already be impossible."

The next morning I learned we were too late. It was snowing in the passes. Spending the winter with Rabat was not the worst thing that could happen, I decided. Drinking at his fountain of wisdom was more than any man could hope for.

Men, women, and children were already in the fields harvesting their summer crops and preparing the soil for winter planting. Children were winnowing the grain in flat, hand-woven baskets while older ones were grinding the grain into flour and meal with wooden pestles pounding into wooden bowls. Laughing and chattering rang across the valley as everyone worked.

Women with huge straw baskets strapped to their backs carried everything from loaves of bread to babies. The women loved jewelry and had rings in their noses and all over their ears. The people were almost black from constantly being in the sun. As they worked, they waved and smiled at Rabat. It was plain they loved him dearly and he returned their love. Who could believe he had once murdered members of his household? All of that was gone. He had been born again within one lifetime. Perhaps that was what it was all about, being born again and again until one could achieve that feat of purity within one life? The thought excited me, and I longed to tell Yochanan.

Suddenly, the earth began to tremble. Everyone stood still. In Judea everyone would run screaming when an earthquake struck. But these people stood very still as though waiting silently for something.

"They believe it is the god Shiva speaking to them," explained Rabat. "They believe the beauty of the mountaintops is for the gods alone. The gods live there and we are intruders for daring to live in their valley at the base of their mountains. The people send up prayers explaining that they live here to be close to their gods in worship. When the earth shakes, it is Shiva sending a reply."

I wondered if Rabat believed that.

"I believe in one God, Yeshua, and it is the same God in whom you believe."

"Adonai?" I blurted out.

Rabat laughed loudly.

"You call God Adonai. I call God Brahm, since it is the name the people here use the most. Universal consciousness might be a better name. Your Moses said God told people to use I AM, 'Call me I AM,' it is written."

"Right," I said, realizing I knew nothing more about Rabat's religion than before.

Fall and winter flew by. Pema came and went. Omar went through on his way back to Persia. Just as I settled into the comfort of being at home with the people and the valley, Rabat announced it was time to go. The snow was melting and the passes were clear once more. We loaded up and crossed the valley floor, finally heading for the holy and eternal city of Lhasa.

I imagined this city was golden, its streets shining with gold ingots and its palaces made of precious jewels. I supposed the fear of bandits was what made it a closed city. Surely the people wore pure white, shining robes and everything was filled with light and purity. That must be the reason for fearing people from faraway places; they equated it with evil, as many do when confronted with the strange, the unique, or the different.

Rabat called on Tengsing Mahat to take care of the resthouse while we were gone. Tengsing was an educated man from India who had come to the valley ten years before, sick with malaria. A devout Buddhist, he had sought Rabat, whose fame as a healer had spread throughout the East.

A few days taking a dark brew had healed Tengsing, and he had refused to leave Katmandu. "I want to stay close to the source of my healing," he had declared, and stay he did. He farmed and kept Rabat stocked with the choicest produce from his farm. Between Tengsing and Pema, Rabat had a fine family that gave him time to be away from the dharmsala.

As we began climbing the tallest mountains in the world, Rabat said we would head for the village of Rasua Garhi and the Girange Dzong Pass. I breathed deeply, taking in the freshest, purest air and enjoyed one spectacular sight after another. The lush vegetation of the valley soon became verdant forest up to eighteen thousand feet. Cattle mingled with goats grazing on almost vertical inclines. The mountains glistened. The valley mists mingled with the frosty clouds that kissed the snowy caps of mountains. Lazy clouds drifted down from the peaks like herds of sheep following a shepherd, only suddenly to fly off across the blue expanse.

I could hear the sighing of the winds high above our heads, as if caroling the ancient Vedas wrung from the heart of Brahm:

He who knows the pathway of the birds
That fly through heaven
Sovereign of the sea
He knows the ships that are thereon.

He knows the pathway of the wind,
The spreading high and mighty wind

He knows the gods who dwell above.

Varuna, true to holy law, sits down among his people
He, most wise, sits there to govern all.

From thence perceiving, he beholds all wondrous
Things, both what hath been
And what hereafter will be done.

How like my beloved psalms are these ancient writings known as the Rig-Veda–majestic like the Himalayas, beautifully soft and gentle like its people.

The Hindu philosophy seemed to me the same as that of the Hebrews, only expressed differently. The sum of it all could be found in the Upanishads.

He who sees himself in all beings,
And all beings in himself,
He enters the supreme Brahma
By this means and no other.

That was what Gautama Buddha must have understood when he saw himself in the lame beggar and willingly changed places with him. How important it is to know one's holy writings as if they were written upon the soul.

Climbing ever higher into the mountains, I continued my musings. The many gods were used to explain the one God. Images of gods in every household were simply a way of saying, "Thou, O God, art the cherished guest in every house . . . father, son, cherished friend, brother, benefactor, guardian, all in one."

Was it any different in my own household in Palestine, where the ancient writings are tacked on the wall, written on phylacteries tied to the wrist and forehead? Our synagogues are like shrines. Then there is our own Temple with its many courtyards and holy of holies–how are we different?

"The Himalayas are still growing," Rabat said, interrupting my musings. "Long ago India crashed into Nepal and Tibet, lifting them up into lofty mountains."

"Is that a legend or fact?" I asked, smiling.

"It is all the same," he laughed. "Remember, it is all the same."

Certainly when I looked up, the mountains did seem to grow

and move. My imagination soared with them and wove fanciful stories during the five days it took us to get to the pass and the village of Rasua Garhi.

In Rasua Garhi we stayed in a Sherpa's house. She was called Yatna. There are no dharmsalas in Tibet. One either has a friend or one sleeps wrapped in yak skins next to yaks in hopes that freezing will not be part of the night's experience. Rabat had friends everywhere, and I noticed that more often than not they were widows.

"What is your attraction for widows about?" I asked.

"You notice everything, Yeshua. Usually, it is the men who fall off cliffs, fall sick and die, or just wander away in the shadow of their minds. The women cling to their houses. In Tibet the house belongs to the woman. Yatna has the distinction of having one of the few tubs of heated water available for those who insist on bathing."

Good Rabat. He had made sure I had bathing opportunities in Katmandu. Providing me with a bath in the wilds was just short of a miracle.

Cheerfully, I undressed and sat down in the warm water. It was only about six inches deep, but heavenly nonetheless. As I sat soaking, I felt something behind me. Glancing around, I saw Yatma standing with brush in hand, preparing to scrub me down.

"No," I yelped as I tried vainly to disappear beneath the shallow waters.

Yatma chuckled. She was slightly deaf and shouted every word. She told Rabat that the skinny kid needed more meat on his bones. And what did he have he was ashamed to show? I had to give that some thought. What indeed?

As I approached my nineteenth year, I began to feel more like a man, a real man. Although I was still a teenager, I was now tall. Still thin, but more filled out, somehow I was feeling clearer about my path, my journey. My schooling in the Valley of Life gave me time to practice all I had learned. Every day. Yet, it was not called a school by anyone. What more can I learn? Yet, the best was still in my future. Resolutely, I looked forward to Lhasa and the School of the Lamas.

Chapter 20

Lhasa

Although the Indians of the plains claimed all the Himalayas as their own, I discovered the Sherpas claimed they were all theirs, as did the Tibetans, the rulers of China, and each independent kingdom near them. The teachings of Buddha had traveled throughout the mountains north to China and around India. A kind of peace reigned and territorial claims more or less were less important than religious practices. Buddha had taught that life must not be taken from another, so armies were few.

"Who wants a bucket of snow enough to fight about it?" asked Rabat as we trudged over the last mountain before we reached Lhasa. Outside of his valley the land was all wasteland anyhow in his mind. What can you do with a mountain?

As I huffed and puffed behind him, he remarked, "Not much air up here." Passing up and down trails that wound around mountains of dizzying height, where no trees could grow, I was inclined to agree with him.

As we came off those trackless wastes of eternal winter and headed down toward Lhasa, I could scarcely contain my eagerness to see the Forbidden City. In my mind's eye I could already see it shimmering in the crystalline air and feel the warmth of happy souls. I even transplanted the lushness of the surrounding forests of Katmandu to the city we were about to enter.

Then I saw Lhasa. It was only a village—a dirty, scrubby collection of ugly, squat huts nestling in a sterile valley of dust and rock. I caught my breath as I sought a reason to call it holy. At this awesome elevation we were on the edge of the snowline. There was nothing green anywhere.

No chimneys were visible above the low, flat roofs of the brick-and-stone houses. Oiled papyri covered the few windows, giving the place a lackluster sand-colored blankness.

As we drew closer, I saw men, women, and children, some in various stages of squatting in the streets to relieve themselves. It was just about a degree above freezing and rain mingled with snow that began to fall. Offal was piled everywhere, in towering heaps. Dirt and grime covered everything.

Swarms of beggars surrounded us, whining for coins. Children and monks alike begged. Begging is an honorable profession in the holy city, I soon learned.

There seemed to be no idea of cleanliness here. Dead animals littered the streets where they had died. Carrion birds ate the dead bodies. Dogs and pigs roamed the streets scavenging for food, competing with the birds. No self-respecting Essene could ever wish to die here. Only the most ignorant of Jews would dare enter such a place. I was undecided as to whom the title "forbidden" was benefiting. No wonder Lhasa was forbidden: who would believe this or call it holy?

We walked toward the center of the miserable stone huts and stopped at a large stone house called the "Place of God." It was the winter home of the Grand Lama of Tibet, the real ruler of the Himalayas. It was full of lamas busily scrubbing the great house, for the Grand Lama was insistent that everything about him be clean. Such a contradiction with life in the streets. Suddenly, I realized I was judging, comparing. I stopped, with great effort.

We stayed at the Place of God. Since there were no gates and it did not sit atop a great mountain, I surmised this was not where Rabat had spent so many years studying with lamas. There were stone fireplaces in the large rooms, but nothing to heat the cubicles in which we slept. The lamas were dressed in bright orange robes; their bald heads were shaven clean, and each face bore the perpetual suggestion of a smile.

Yak-butter lamps flickered along the walls. The main room, larger than all the others, was for cooking and eating. Huge pots held water kept at a boil—one for tea and one for gruel. It took only ten minutes to feed all thirty of us. We sat at low tables that were like the window seats at Pema's house.

We spent a day or two walking around Lhasa. As a trade center, it left much to be desired. The marketplace was sparse. Most of the trade was done at the staging center, where the caravans loaded and unloaded their wares. The traders swapped stories and goods.

The women of the village daubed black pigment on their faces to protect them from the glare of the sun and the harshness of the icy winds that whipped through the village. They gathered at the well to draw water and gossip, always laughing and nudging each other in spite of the harshness of the weather and the land. Occasionally I saw a small black patch the size of a pea stuck on someone's temple. It was to cure a headache.

"We can go now," Rabat said early on the third morning. "I have permission from the Grand Lama to take you to Sat-cit-ananda, my home for thirty years."

My joy knew no bounds as it pulled me up in a dance of excitement. "I am ready," I shouted. "Let us depart."

As we rode out of the Forbidden City, Rabat mentioned that the Grand Lama had refused to see me.

"Why?" I asked, daring not to think the worst, lest I bring it upon us. Yet it came anyway.

Rabat stopped, looked long and lovingly at me, sighed, and explained: "He said there would be great divisions on Earth for a long time because of you. That millions would be slaughtered in years to come because of you and even in your name. That many would claim you are really God. He said he could only see a dim light through a very long, very dark tunnel and could not be sure whether it was yours or that of another.

"He said that he, therefore, could not greet you as a friend, so he has chosen not to see you at all."

I fainted dead away and fell off my yak. Rabat was horrified.

"Yeshua, Yeshua, wake up. Surely, the Grand Lama has lost his mind. He does not really know. He is just trying to frighten you. It is a test, surely."

But I knew in my heart, as I slowly gained consciousness, that it was probably all true, every word of it.

At the time, however, I could not conceive of a mission of peace producing war. Did not the apple tree produce apples and the fig tree produce figs? Surely, peace produces peace.

I finally convinced myself that my way was the way of peace, the path to peace, and sooner or later, peace would come. However, gone was my joy and light-hearted spirit. Somehow, I must change the course of history as seen by the Grand Lama of Tibet, whose priesthood, he feared, I sought to abolish. Of course, I did not realize that outcome at the time I began my simple teachings.

I was to meet this specter over and over, I feared. What is best for many often is tragedy for others.

Chapter 21

Sat-cit-ananda

I quickly pulled myself together and we headed farther into the wilds of Tibet. That strange wilderness of snows grew on me. It was much like Yochanan's desert if you shifted your view just a little.

Two days later we arrived at the wooden gates I had envisioned many times since hearing Rabat's story. The place was exactly as he had described it, only more breathtaking. There was a wild beauty to the lamasery that seemed to grow out of the mountains and was surrounded by bottomless ravines. Mists hung like lacy veils along the lamasery's walls. What miracle had built such a place at twenty thousand feet?

Rabat pulled a cord to ring the brass bell held by a small copper bracket.

"I shall leave you here, my son, for I am not permitted inside."

"No," I cried. "Unforgiving hearts have nothing to teach me. I will not stay."

Abruptly the gates swung open. The entry filled with clean-shaven lamas gowned in white shifts and sandals. They were like flowers, nodding and bobbing and smiling in the sunshine that splashed over us all. They invited us both inside the gates. Rabat was wiping tears from his eyes as he hugged and kissed his old mentors, and they returned his warmth and affection.

The "why" of his great old heart–why had they let him in–did not need sound as it hung in the air.

"Because you brought him to us when you could have kept him for yourself," said a lama named Lopsam. "A selfless act, to be sure, to give up a second son."

"He must be shared with the world," I heard Rabat say. "No

man may take such a light and hide it under a basket."

Were they talking about me? Surely not. To blush now would be to show everyone I thought they were talking about me. I thought of the snow and ice and storms in an effort to keep the crimson shades from flowing to my face. It was a monumental effort, yet the words of the Grand Lama rose up and everything balanced. Why? I asked myself.

There was much rejoicing. I loved every minute of it and was so glad to be a part of the joyous reconciliation. We were ushered into a large hall where tables were abundant with exotic foods. Who would have thought to find such a feast table in the wilds, many miles from the nearest farm or settlement? Just to find the lamasery was a feat impossible without a guide. One could stand almost beside the gates and fail to see them. From a distance the clouds blocked the view. So much a part of the mountain from which it seemed to grow, the splendid structure looked like another mountain peak. It was a most strange and mysterious place, unlike anything I had ever seen before or probably will ever see again.

The marble floors were curiously warm. Within the lamasery there was a springlike atmosphere. The old lamas made clacking sounds as they padded across the marble floors. The opulent bath was magnificent, drawn from natural springs bubbling up from somewhere within the mountain; flowing over the rocks the springs cast mists that covered everything. The heat of the springs formed steam that condensed back into water and dripped from ferns and tropical flowers, creating a little rainforest.

"Did I not tell you there was more to learn that required your presence?" asked Rabat as he prepared to depart.

"True," I returned. I realized he was distracting me from his departure. "But, why are you leaving? You can stay now. You do not have to go back. You are forgiven."

"I must return to my dharmsala and relieve Tengsing. My life is deep into its mission, which I would never have found had I stayed here where it is so safe and secure and isolated. Always remember that we are not here to entertain ourselves with easy living, especially you."

"Forgive me," I urged. "I keep forgetting that we are not here to entertain ourselves with selfish desires, nor even to sink into comfortable places, repeating the easy life over and over." Surely, the Grand Lama's words made this clear.

"Keep that idea ever before you, my young friend. You discovered it quite young, and it belongs to you."

I debated telling him what I had finally come to realize. Should I tell him, or merely give a hint? Surely his life merited the information I had acquired while studying at his feet. So I took a deep breath and decided to hint at it.

"You never did tell me Bat's story," I said, as I gave him a questioning look.

"Well, I do not know much about him. One day years ago, soon after I built the dharmsala, he appeared wanting a room. He made such a good offer that I realized we would spend a lot of hours together over the years. I fixed up a room that would always be his. He started leaving his personal things in it and now it is his home. I never thought to question him about his life before that. It is part of my acceptance of whomever comes my way. They can tell me what they wish, or not. It is their choice.

"Ask him about his parents some day, will you?"

"After all these years?"

"Certainly. Why not?"

"I don't know. I guess it would be all right. Surely he would know it was friendly interest and not prying."

"Surely, he would."

As Rabat was saying goodbye to his old teacher, Lopsam, I studied his face–such a dear and wonderfully kind face. At the back of his mind, I knew there was the nagging question of why I wanted him to question Bat about his parents. It was so clear to me, yet even with my suggestion he still did not know. One can be surrounded with the answers one seeks and fail to see them.

"Let me know what Bat tells you," I called to Rabat as he reluctantly took leave of us and turned down the trail. Then, he was gone.

A tear trickled down my face as I turned back into the lamasery where I would spend the next three years. One kind word and I would have dissolved in tears. The lamas knew this and retreated to their own places leaving me to wander sadly back to my room, where I could overcome my sadness. It was probably as sad for them as it was for me, and we needed to get our emotions under control. Parting is tolerable only when you truly know you will see your loved one again.

The truth of reincarnation grew more precious to me every day. Rabat was not dying, but we both knew we would never see each other again in this life. Knowing we would spend eternity together, though, lightened my mood considerably.

A number of lamas remained year round in the high mountain retreat. They preferred the soaring heights, where snow poured off the peaks like waterfalls while winds howled and moaned. Tall, thin windows allowed one to peer out into the eerie ice world while preventing the cold from seeping through. The snow whirling around the stone mansion always melted when it touched the lamasery on any spot.

There was a strange garden within the lamasery walls that had many dwarf fruit trees that always had delicious fruit. Each tasted like honey. The apricots were special; their flesh was excellent and the seed produced oil. The lamas used the apricot oil for everything, rubbing it on their skin to keep it youthful, putting it on their greens.

The garden seemed exposed, yet snow never fell into it. I spent a lot of time there studying its mysteries. In fact that was the one place my guide, Cyani, knew he could find me when all else failed. One morning as I was sitting in the garden gazing at the falling snow, he came for me.

"Come, I have a lesson for you today," he declared.

Cyani was such a gentle soul that a command from him almost seemed out of place. But one must never be fooled by gentleness. Often a lion's heart beats beneath such an exterior. He turned and headed down a long hallway, his sandals flapping rapidly. The hallway became a tunnel lit by torches as the path gradually descended. We went down for what seemed like an hour, finally halting before a massive door. There, hanging on hooks protruding from the frame of the door, were several heavy cloaks with hoods lined with fur, and beneath the cloaks lay several pairs of fur-lined boots.

"Put those on," Cyani again directed in tones of command.

I put on the heavy clothing, glad to get a little warmer since the torches gave little warmth in the tunnel. I wondered if the lesson might be about how to freeze gracefully, or some such Oriental test. My imagination almost got the best of me as Cyani slowly opened the heavy door.

The room was brilliantly lit, yet the light source was hidden.

There were no torches and the room was freezing. We could see our breath as we exhaled. We walked across the frigid chamber. In the center was a large waist-high table of pure white marble. As we approached it, I could see two figures lying there, seemingly asleep. I whispered to Cyani lest I awaken them.

"Who are they?" Then I gasped as I noticed they each were about ten feet long.

They were giants, blond and young. They looked warm although surely not, for I was now shivering and chattering from the intense cold. Cyani shivered not one bit. He appeared as warm as the sleeping giants. A thousand questions filled my head and struggled for form, but it was hard to speak through my chattering teeth.

"Th-they s-sleep s-s-so soundly," I managed finally.

"They are dead," whispered Cyani respectfully.

"Dead!" I stopped shaking in my amazement.

"Yes. They have been so for at least fifty thousand years."

"What happened to them?"

"The nearest we can surmise is they existed before the breaking up of the Earth's land masses into continents, eons ago. They were probably sitting on a beach when they were instantly elevated into the freezing cold of more than twenty-five thousand feet and froze suddenly. Lamas before my time placed them on this table, where they have been ever since. We think the intent was to try to rouse them, but they could not agree on what to do if they still lived. It is my understanding the problem is still in discussion."

"You jest," I exclaimed.

"No, I do not. We have the knowledge to restore them to life, but we are not sure we have the right. Their souls may have incarnated many times since and be somewhere else. We never want to interrupt karma. Then, even if we did do that, we do not think they could live a normal life. She could not stay here with us. In the world outside they might be treated like oddities. There are many problems, not a few of which are our own."

I nodded in agreement as I stared at those young faces so full of youth and hope and beauty. In the twinkling of an eye they were gone forever into a world of sleep, ice, entombment. Was that karma? Or was something else at work? A lesson is as good as its application, no more and no less. As I began to shake again with cold, Cyani drew me out of the room. "You are not yet ready to stand such cold for very long," he said. "Your nose and fingers will freeze."

Wondering what Cyani meant by "not yet," I gladly followed him from the room into the tunnel and back up the winding path to the lamasery. He took me by the hand and shook his head.

"Ahhh, Issa, your fingers froze. You are so sensitive." He wrapped his warm hands around mine and slowly his hands grew warmer and warmer. I could feel mine tingling as his grew hot. He looked deep into my eyes and my body flushed with heat.

My fingers were no longer frozen. They worked perfectly. In this house of miracles, what was yet one more? How long would it take for me to learn them all, I wondered as I gratefully slid into the bubbling springs of the bath.

The next morning Cyani appeared in the garden. It was clear my days of roaming free were over; it was also clear that Cyani was my chief teacher. "Come," he commanded.

I followed him. Obedience is my nature, yet understanding obedience without questioning it was something I had yet to learn.

"You must learn to control your body, Issa, for it is the temple of your soul. It is where you meet the universal mind we call God."

"I am ready," I responded.

"You must teach yourself."

"That could take years and years," I blurted.

Cyani laughed, understanding that boys of nineteen years hardly ever have control of their bodies. I was no exception.

"I will show you a place where there are the answers to every question you will ever have," he said over his shoulder as he padded down another long hallway. I was sure he had no idea what questions I had.

Rolling my eyes a little, I followed after Cyani, hoping it was not freezing there. Overcoming frost while I searched for answers might put more strain on my quest to know than I would be willing to cope with.

Perhaps it would be a crystal ball, I thought, as we climbed a winding staircase, or a magic screen or some other sort of wizardry. Nothing seemed impossible to the Tibetan monks. Who could question their knowledge? Where did it come from? At the top of the stairs was an opening into a huge room with a domed ceiling. The dome was clear and through it I could see the distant mountains, and the sun sparkling clear in a dark blue sky.

It was a library and observatory combined. There was an elevated platform with a device used for scanning the sky. It contained a series of magnifying glasses that made viewing the stars as simple as watching the snow falling on the dome. It was larger than the one I'd seen in Egypt. The dome could be opened and the device moved for a better look.

"Can I look?" I asked even as I was running toward it.

"Of course," Cyani said. "That is why you are here, to look, study, and learn."

Getting all my many questions answered was a wonderful way to study. As Yochanan had once observed, I loved to study and cheerfully could have spent all my life at it.

"You seemed to know already what it is and how it works," explained Cyani.

"There is one like it in Egypt."

"Oh, yes," Cyani pled ignorance, "I quite forgot you came to us from that faraway country. You seem so much like one of us." He smiled at that. He knew I was a long way from being a learned Tibetan monk. But, perhaps in another life . . .

As I looked through the device, I saw worlds hanging in space, looking different from the stars. They were planets, but now I could see great mountains on them and wide valleys. I could not see if any people were there and turned to inquire. Anticipating me, Cyani held up his hand. "Stop," he cried. "Your answers are over there," he said as he pointed to the shelf-lined walls.

The library looked much like the one in Alexandria, with manuscripts everywhere. Some were scrolls of rolled papyrus in earthen jars; others were on copper and stacked on the shelves; still others were written on the hides of animals.

In the center of that part of the room stood the largest of the books. Resting on a stand, it was written on skins and great gold rings held its pages together. The inner leaves were of the thinnest parchment, while the outer cover was strong like tanned hide. It was a warm, rich brown and glowed with its own light.

"This is the sacred book of the ages," Cyani spoke in a hushed tone. "You cannot grasp its meanings at one time, so do not try, but drink it in over a period of months. That is how to drink from the fount that is the Light of the Ages."

Cyani took me around the room explaining the various sections. For example, everything about the body was in the same section. The library was organized in that way throughout. "I suggest you start your study with practical matters and progress to the mysteries. It will have a logic you can understand and apply. Too often students rush to the mysteries and fail to learn anything of value."

I could see the logic in that. Orderly study is important. Cyani explained that I would be examined by practical application, but usually I would not realize at the time that I was being tested. "Truth is not truth that has never been tested," he smiled. "Every test confirms itself."

Cyani said I should learn control of the body, so I began my reading in this topic. He left me alone in this room of knowledge, so I pounced upon those ancient manuscripts. I longed to devour every page of every manuscript.

Although I did not spend the next three years reading every day in the library, it seemed as though I did. For I was there more often than not. I studied the body until I knew every part, every function, all the interactions of all the parts. I finally learned that a strong liver keeps one free from all ailments. I learned that a strong mind will keep the body healthy. That was not all there was to it, but a goodly part. Clean thoughts produce a clean mind and cleanliness is next to godliness. Purity, that is the key.

Studying in Tibet, so close to China, I was directed to reading about the Tao, which translates as "the Way." I was surprised to learn that a good general will never have to go to war. The philosophy of these ancient writings suggests that harmony with the environment produces good behavior. I can see that. Everyone, from time to time does a good deed, some more than others. But to be in harmony with nature, that is something. I incorporated the Tao into my own philosophy and practiced it as my way.

My teachers had no limitations. They claimed man limits himself only, and I could feel myself growing out of such limitations.

One subject seemed to affirm another and require research into still another. Daily I walked in the garden and talked to Cyani or Lopsam or one of the other lamas. Always I enthused some about what I was reading. They seldom commented, but enjoyed listening to my prattle. I am sure now they knew all about my current topics, yet they received what I said as if hearing it for the first time.

Late one afternoon Lopsam came for me. A group of us went down to an icy stream just outside the lamasery walls. Lopsam broke the ice off a sheltered pool that was frozen only on the top. He carefully dipped a sheet into the freezing water and draped it around a lama who had disrobed and was sitting on the snow beside the pool. He looked like a statue of the Buddha. I shivered from the cold, and my teeth began to chatter. I realized I was not practicing what I had learned. Concentrating, I tried to raise my body temperature at least to keep from shivering. I warmed up a trifle, but lost my concentration when I noticed the formerly wet, freezing cold sheet around the lama was now steaming and beginning to dry. As it dried and fell off, the lama was now bright red instead of his usual golden hue.

Lopsam dipped the dry sheet into the frigid water again and threw the wet freezing mass across the lama. This time the sheet snapped and sizzled like water hitting glowing coals.

"What a mind!" I gasped as I stood shivering and shaking. "Such control!"

The lamas turned and stared at me in deep silence. I grinned helplessly as I tried to regain some control over my own body. It was apparent I could freeze standing there even in shift and sandals and cloak. No one returned my grin. Cyani took away my cloak.

"One does not need heat if one is already warm!"

As the frosty wind whipped through my thin shift and lashed my body, I felt the need to survive. It was obvious they would stand there and watch me freeze to death. Every other thought fled. My mind triggered the command, and I could feel the heat rising in my body. Soon I was standing in a veil of steamy mist.

The lamas cheered and clapped their hands.

"You have passed your second test," declared Cyani.

"My second?" I inquired.

"When you would have given up your status as an Initiate in loyalty to Rabat, you passed your first test, even before you entered our gates."

"But I thought coming here was voluntary," the argument poured forth.

"Not for you, Issa. Not for you. Your course is laid out for you. Avoiding difficult parts defeats your study, and the parts will grow more difficult as time passes. The mysteries are for the selfless. All others are not ready. Some would even die, as you could have done just now. You are always free to turn away from difficult study and hard testing, but sooner or later it must be faced."

The lamas smiled, nodding as though they, too, had passed. I took my cloak and filed back up the trail perfectly comfortable. With practice, I knew that distractions need never again interfere with my concentration.

A week later I found myself seated by that stream, nude, draped in an icy sheet. That was a bit different from just keeping one's body warm. Generating enough body heat to completely dry a freezing, wet sheet while sitting nude on snow is something that could easily distract one's concentration. My first efforts failed. Thoughts of freezing were too strong for me.

"It is all right to fail the first time, Issa," Cyani assured me. "You can take all night, if necessary."

It is amazing what motivation can do for the mind. The idea of sitting alone all night whipped me into extreme concentration. Off came the sheet, steaming!

To be sure I could repeat this at will, Cyani dipped the sheet into the stream and draped it across my hot, steaming body. As it crackled and fell off, he handed me my robe and remarked, "Spring is near. It is a good time for testing."

Cyani's almond-shaped eyes ranged over my face and settled on my full-grown beard. Without a word between us, I knew that shaving my face and head was the next order of business. As I became aware of that idea, I realized I was communicating more often with thoughts and less so with words. There was no need for words between the monks. Thoughts are things, and soon I perceived the thoughts of all the lamas. I no longer asked questions. The need had passed.

I spent the next few weeks watching the lamas levitate. They rose from the floor slowly up to the beamed ceiling and floated gently back. This was amazing to me. One minute they would be sitting silently, on the floor, and the next they would be bumping their heads on the ceiling. I worked at this with all my might, but I could not do it. Back to the library I went and searched for an answer to the mystery. There was not much written on the subject, so I surmised its mastery involved several things. Still I could not learn the secret.

I could feel amusement growing in the lamas as they watched

me search. They blocked the key element from me as I searched their minds for the answer.

"Quick to come, quick to go," whispered Lopsam.

"Mysteries must be like breathing and heartbeats," whispered Cyani.

Were those hints? What did they mean? Raising one's body should be like raising one's body heat, but it was different somehow.

Even though Cyani was my day-to-day counselor, it was apparent that Lopsam appeared when things went beyond the usual. He was the oldest and surely the wisest of them all. Even the Grand Lama deferred a little to Lopsam. There was a funny gait to his walk; he scurried around with his hands held tightly in front of him.

One spring morning Lopsam arrived at the library just as I settled down to read about the will. He beckoned me. He wore a strange robe with many folds; it was a rich blue trimmed with lighter blue piping. As we reached the gates, the other lamas joined us, and they were dressed in similar robes. We filed out of the gates and took a trail that led up the mountain. We seemed to climb for about half an hour, finally reaching a cliff overhanging a deep valley. Birds drifted lazily on the wind.

Dipping now and then, the birds would catch a draft and slowly rise higher and higher. Yet there seemed not to be any wind at all where we were standing. The air was thin and soon euphoria set in.

Suddenly, one of the lamas fell off the cliff. I screamed and ran to the edge in an effort to catch him. Lopsam caught me by the arm. Slowly, the falling lama spread his arms like the birds and the rising thermals caught the folds of his robe, lifting his frail body as easily as a feather. Incredible! The lama was flying! He dipped and turned exactly like the birds, his robe acting as wings.

He was truly an adept. As he maneuvered himself back toward the cliff, he hung for only an instant, then deftly let the air out of the folds of his robe and stepped lightly back to solid ground.

No sooner did I catch my breath from that sight than all the other lamas flew over the edge of the cliff and moved among the birds. A great distance below, yawning chasms waited to devour a hapless body that might suddenly forget how to fly. The lamas seemed oblivious to the danger.

Lopsam landed lightly beside me and looked intently at my

fear-filled face. "One can fly if one believes one can," he said.

The lamas dipped and swirled back to the rocky ledge. I breathed a deep sigh of relief. Cyani put his arm around my shoulder and cooed, "Even Rome was not built in a day."

I laughed. "It took me a hundred years to get the nerve to hurl myself off this ledge," Cyani confessed.

I looked carefully at him. His clear brown eyes, smooth, taut, golden skin, firm strong body, pearly white teeth with not one missing–How old is this monk?

"I am two hundred years old," he said, proud of his years.

Two hundred years old and he's the youngest lama? What about the others?

Soul journeys were my next subject of study in the great library. The why of my existence was of consuming interest to me. The thoughts of Lao-tzu were particularly interesting. "It is better to travel hopefully than to arrive," he said. This master who developed the Tao taught in terms of simplicity. "Water gives to everyone, but never competes." What a wonderful way to describe the perfect spirit, the God spirit, the goal of man on his way to perfection.

The thoughts of Confucius, Thales, and many others in the volumes I studied were alive, glowing. One theme from every age of man seemed to dominate: selfless giving, selflessness, wholeness, know thyself, always self, the great I AM.

I thought about many things. Socrates drinking the lethal hemlock because he spoke the truth in the marketplace. What an ignoble end–or was it? He "birthed" Plato, his student, for the world. Does it take death to produce life? I pondered the "three perfections" of Pythagoras: to realize truth in the intellect, virtue in the soul, and purity in the body.

Studying those great minds, I began to feel new powers flowing through me. I felt myself surrounded and protected by invisible, luminous beings. It was heady and humbling. Filling oneself with the highest and noblest thoughts achieved by man seemed the path to enlightenment.

A little over three years after I arrived at Sat-cit-ananda, Lopsam appeared by my side as I studied the stars. A cold chill settled over me. A vague feeling of impending disaster lay over me like a fog. I raised an eyebrow in question. "Move the device a little higher," he directed. "It is time you see your past incarnations."

"Through this?" I inquired in astonishment.

"No," Lopsam smiled for the first time. "Through the mists of time. The Akashic Records that are written there."

"God's Book of Remembrances?"

"That is the record."

I waited.

"Concentrate. Focus. Look deep into the past," he ordered. "Remember. Recall. Deep into the past."

A strange calm took over my mind. My body seemed to float. Waves of light passed by my eyes. I could see images. Although they did not look like me, I knew who they were. One by one, some of my past lives flowed before my eyes like a living tapestry of events and people, times and places. Just as quickly as they came, they disappeared. I was shaken, drained. I fell into Lopsam's waiting arms.

"Sleep, Issa. Fall into a deep, deep sleep," he whispered.

When I awoke, I was lying on my bed. Alone. No longer was I a young man of only twenty-one years. I was an ancient soul returned. Tibet's secrets were known to me, and I was ready to leave that ancient land of mystery.

The next day I bade the lamas farewell. I hugged Cyani, holding him a little tighter, for he was the teacher under whose care I had crossed over from student to adept, from knowledge to light. Lopsam, the taskmaster of my soul, gave a kiss, murmuring, "You are the treasure of my life, the reason for my existence."

Although I longed for a word from the Grand Lama, nothing came.

For the first time, I felt like a real man in fact as well as in law. Although all my past lives had not been revealed to me, there were enough shown to let me know for sure I was an old, old soul rather than a mere youth struggling into manhood. It was just short of staggering that what once had been a mere game with Yochanan was actually true.

I had led my people into the Promised Land long ago and turned it into a killing field, all in the name of God. Surely, I must be the one to remedy that deed. But how? Even the training I have had does not give me that, I thought at the time. My question was not answered.

But truly I was a changed man, full of information. Wisdom, however, was what I needed. If I did not get all my questions answered and did not have great wisdom after spending three years with two-hundred-year-old men, where would I get it?

Chapter 22

Laga

As was the custom in lamaseries, I walked out of the gates without a backward look. Map in hand, I looked toward the tiny dot that represented Laga, a small village five hundred miles away over the roughest route known to man. Only a few weeks before, the walk to Laga would have seemed impossible and getting to Isfahan in faraway Persia only a dream. Now it was just another ordeal one must encounter and overcome on the way to perfection.

Six months later I staggered into Laga and collapsed at the door of a Buddhist monastery, nearly dead. Climbing up and down the mountains had been so arduous I barely made two miles a day. I hardly knew where I was, or cared. The lamas took me in and restored my strength.

"The worst is over," they kept whispering in soft voices. Soon my mind took up the words. I sank deeply into a peaceful slumber. When I awakened, I was nourished and feeling wonderful. I raised my hand to my ear and felt something attached to the lobe. Trying to pull it off, I discovered it went clear through.

"Oh, no!" I shouted, as I realized it was a tiny gold earring.

"You must have it," an old lama insisted.

"Why?"

"To prove you have traversed the impossible."

"Winter came early," another said. "You should have died."

"We are in awe you made it," murmured another.

I fingered the earring hoping I could worry it off. What would my mother think? What would the people of Nazareth say? I knew what they would say. "Lunatic. Bereft of reason. Mad. Possessed of a devil." The Essenes would disown me. Yochanan would laugh me out of Palestine. But nothing worked. I had it on my ear and there it would remain.

"Not only is my nose too big for my face," I said helplessly, "but now I have a gold ring in my ear. It might as well be in my nose."

The lamas thought that funny. "It is good that neither man nor woman look at you with lust," said the head lama, "for in this part of the world men are raped as often as women. That must not happen to you. We have guaranteed it."

A more pleasant surprise was the horse the lamas furnished me for the remainder of the journey. It was a great white stallion, stamping with energy to burn. They gave me a map showing a route that led only through valleys.

"Guard the map carefully," they cautioned "for it is a secret map concealing our isolation. We would be in great danger if we were discovered. You will come near the Great Indian Desert after Hardwar. There are bandits, terrible and dangerous. You must be careful. They prey on lone travelers. If they demand this horse, give it to them and ask for an exchange; they will give it to you."

How surprising! Why would bandits give me anything?

Victor, the horse, was amazing. He flew like the wind down the trails and across the meadows. Nothing slowed that horse. We raced the clouds, the birds, the shadows. Everything came and went at such speeds that I knew Persia must be just ahead. Hardwar came and went. Even going around the twenty-five-thousand-foot Nanda Devi peak was easy compared to the slow, tortuous trip across the Himalayas.

The lamas had urged frequent rest stops. "So Victor can outrun the bandits who may come."

However, when one is young and on a prime horse, warnings scarcely register. The mind of such a one says, "It could never happen to me."

On we flew across the autumn haze of Indian plains. From Saharanpur to Ganganagar on the edge of the Great Indian Desert, man and horse became one, covering the vast distances effortlessly.

About fifty miles from Ganganagar, from out of nowhere, the bandits came. Swarthy, leering men, dusty from days of riding the desert, scarred and coarse from hard living—they would rape a camel as soon as a fair maiden or a wandering Jew. I longed for freezing temperatures, icy caves, even a bottomless pit.

I spoke many languages, yet I had no idea what the leader said to me. A sudden blow from him sent me flying off my horse and onto the ground at their feet. The men laughed as they saw I was not going to run. They fell upon me like river leeches tearing off my clothes. As my hood fell off my head, I heard one shout a single word. As quickly as they attacked, they ceased, backing off to leave me lying in the sand. The leader came over and picked up my bruised, half-clad body. Carefully, he pulled my hair back from the ear that had the ring in it. He showed the ear to all around as though I were a piece of goods for sale.

The men backed off even further, with "ahhhs" and "ohhhhhs." They were looking at me as men only look at other men who have committed an act of extreme courage. Each one came up to me as I stood there beside the leader, fingered the gold ring, made a strange sound, touched their foreheads and walked away murmuring strange words.

As the last one walked away, the leader slowly began dressing me. The other men were now on their horses with their backs to me. Helping me to remount my horse, the leader spoke in perfect Aramaic, "You are obviously a holy man protected by the god of the mountains, for you have survived where no man dares to travel. Forgive us for having touched you with unclean hands. I give you this stone with the sign of Khan. If anyone else comes near you, show it. They will touch you knowing their bloody days are over."

He touched his forehead, bowed gallantly, and with one leap straddled his horse, riding off as suddenly as he had appeared. His band rode hard behind him, making wailing, piercing, chilling cries. Then they were gone, like a dream, leaving me shaken, with sweat pouring off me.

Clutching that stone of Khan until my fingers cramped, I tried to tie it to my head so all could see it. A thousand ways flooded my mind to display that stone. But all I could do was grip it in my hand and pray not to lose it. When Victor finally trotted down the dirt path into Ganganagar, I was in a shambles. I wondered why I had been unable to use any of the powers I had learned when confronted with such danger. My mind was blank. I gratefully hauled myself into the waiting arms of the magus of Zoroaster on the edge of India. The magus seemed to know what had happened to me.

"Your earring saved your life, Issa," he said

"I know."

"Never look with shame on your salvation."

"A good lesson."

"Your powers are not for yourself."

My eyes opened wide. Of course I could not use my powers to save myself. It would be an abuse. Amen had made that clear, even in Egypt. "Initiates must not resist nor try to save themselves," he had taught at orientation. Yet, to save myself from freezing, I had used the powers.

"The elements are one thing; man is another," admonished the magus. "Divine will is still another. You must always be conscious of divine will. That is your ultimate guide, not one of us."

As my body relaxed and my nerves renewed themselves, I realized the experience was not for me alone. The bandits had a stake in it. They had a choice. They were children of God, too. Saving myself with magical powers would have awed them, but it would have taught them nothing. As a group, they had moved a little higher up the chain of being by letting me go. How far could it be from refusing harm to a protected one to refusing harm to anyone?

I saw the magus nodding. I flushed as I realized he was following my thoughts. "It is so good to be with a brother," I said. "All of learning is merely remembering, for 'before this time, we were,' to quote a famous Greek."

The magus urged me to spend time at the Indus River just ahead. "It is sacred to all holy ones and you will cross it several times before you reach the plains of Persia. There is something about washing and worshipping in a large river that purifies the soul." The magus worshipped God in spirit more so than any other I had met.

Life itself is a river flowing from the mind of God, so I supposed that a river of water related to that, somehow. As Victor and I sped away, I called out farewell and promised to spend time at the holy river. My eagerness to get to Isfahan began to mount. I felt the best had been saved for the last part of my travels.

Chapter 23

The School of Zoroaster

Just outside the tiny village of Bahawalnagar lay the first of the rivers that flow into the mighty Indus. Like the Nile, it flows through former deserts that were redeemed from wasteland. Victor rode into the water without slowing. We spent several hours there, moved on, and finally reached the main river, keeping the promise I made to the magus.

Sitting on the banks of the Indus, I contemplated my study in Persia. Before Omar, there seemed no good reason to go to Isfahan. It was not Sum or Persepolis, famed cities known all over the world. Persepolis was the city of Darius, who had once ruled the world. Although the Persian Empire was now in decline, the country had been the home of the Jews for many years and had a special meaning for me.

As days flowed into weeks, I finally crossed into Persia, sensing the glory that had enveloped it five hundred years before. Our holy writings described Persia firsthand.

The Persians were Aryans who for the first time overcame the Semites as a world power. They were the bridge between the East and the West. Darius had established schools, improved trade and communications throughout the world, and laid the path for the rise of Greece and Rome.

Darius was also the first ruler to embrace the teachings of Zoroaster. The tenets of that belief had restrained the Persians from slaughtering the vanquished. This was an elevation of consciousness superior to all prior ones. The Jews and Persians made such good "bedfellows" that the idea of returning to Palestine seemed to many of the Jews like leaving home for a foreign land. They refused to go.

At Kerman I turned northward toward Isfahan. It was just short of two years since I had walked away from the lamasery in the mountains of Tibet, and I was still nine hundred miles from Palestine. Traveling alone does much to a man. Nomadic tribes had been kind in allowing me to eat with them and even join celebrations at feast time. The men would greet me with a kiss on the cheek.

I sat around their campfires listening to their wonderful tales, I learned about their version of God. The tale of how Zoroaster made a convert of Vishtasp, thought by some to be Hystaspes, father of Darius, was a favorite among the nomads. God, whom they called Ahura Mazda, commanded the people not to use statues, temples, or altars in worship, nor to try to give God the aspect of a man. They sacrificed on mountaintops, calling the vault of heaven, God. Fire was their symbol for God, so every nomadic campfire represented God, and God burned in their midst.

These people of the land exuded an irresistible charm. Their vitality swept them along ahead of the winds blowing constantly across the plains. They taught their sons three things: to ride well, to shoot the bow and arrow straight, and always to tell the truth. The nomads celebrated their birthdates; they even celebrated mine with a feast. Their hospitality was limitless. Never a stranger, I was always treated like a brother. Zoroaster must have been a powerful master to be remembered so well more than a thousand years after his time.

As I worked my way across those plains, spending many nights alone under the stars, I appreciated the solitude. YHWH comes when I am alone, quiet, and accepting. Man does well to seek God, not in books or people or places, but alone with nothing standing in between.

Late in winter, and barely ahead of a howling snowstorm, Victor and I rode into Isfahan. Minutes later I stood knocking at the door of the house of Omar. As the snow began to swirl around me, the door opened and my burly friend cried out: "Jesu! Welcome! Come in my house before you freeze."

We fell upon each other as long-lost brothers. Our mutual love flowed back and forth. We laughed and cried and howled. We were a sight to behold, I am sure. Omar stood back to get a good look at me. "The boy has become a man."

He drew me into the circle of his family, sat me down on a carpeted cushion, and called each member by name. His children had beaming faces and his wife glowed with unconditional love. Light flowed through that family.

After we finished a lavish meal, we reclined on cushions, and I asked, "Tell me what has happened to you. I can wait no longer to hear."

"I located the Zoroastrians, as you directed," Omar began. "My life has not been the same since, nor that of my family. Baungha awaits you. He has been expecting you for weeks. The magi are truly magic. They have been charting your progress ever since you left Tibet. Their inner sight even informed them of your encounter with bandits.

"They use their wisdom in such wondrous ways, never to hurt nor even to pressure. It is just there, like a river from which one may drink, or not. Truly it is divine, and they share it with all who come. They saw me coming for days before I finally arrived and were opening their door welcoming me even as I knocked. Who could fail to believe in God with such souls pointing the way?"

Omar opened a heavy calfskin and said it was part of the Avesta, written by Zoroaster himself.

> *One Spirit is good, the other bad:*
> *And of those two, the right will choose aright,*
> *The unwise choose not thus–and go astray.*

"Ahura Mazda means 'God the Eternal Light,' just as you said of YHWH, so I realized it is the same God that you told me about. Here it says 'God created all creatures for progress;' and here it says, 'He who heals with the Holy Word, this man is best. He will drive away sickness from the body of the one of faith.'"

Omar's excitement with the teachings in this book was magnificent to behold. I noticed these writings were much like those of the Essenes that I had copied so many times at Mt. Carmel.

"Here it says," cried the excited man, "'The dead shall rise. Life shall return to their bodies, and they shall breathe again.' Resurrection; it is talking about resurrection."

Omar's excitement was contagious. It increased my own. "Do the Zoroastrians give everyone such a wonderful book?" I asked.

"Oh, no. Baungha allowed me this one to share with you. It is sacred and seldom allowed outside the house of the magi. Everyone in my family had to pass an examination by Baungha before he concluded the sacred Avesta was safe in my hands."

I marveled at the similarities of the Avesta and the Essene Book of Life. Perhaps Zoroaster had studied in Egypt at the same time as Moses? Or maybe he had been a contemporary of Ezra, the Hebrew prophet who was also an Essene. The possibilities were many, but the result was the same. Enlightenment is everywhere. Man has only to open his mind and look.

Omar had found his mission. In fact, his family was part of that mission. Drinking from the fountain that flows from the mind of God, this family spread its waters to all who thirsted. Of people such as these is the kingdom of heaven made.

"Tomorrow," declared Omar, "I must take you to Baungha. He allowed me this first night alone with you, but wrung from me a promise of not waiting one more day. I have taken the liberty of sharing you with our nearest and dearest friend, who is coming soon. He is a healer. He has healing in his hands. More than that, he is a seeker and together we study the Avesta at the house of Baungha, where all the books are."

A knock at the door heralded the man of whom Omar spoke. One of the children ran to open it. Standing in the doorway was a young man shimmering in light. The white lights were full of tiny hooks that sparkled all around him: the sign of an adept. His robe was a deep sky blue and his cloak was a dark blue. His eyes were so blue they looked like a sky with no clouds. Love poured from those eyes–warm, kind, accepting love such as I had seldom seen. His face was firm and strong and handsome. He looked as young as I. I loved him right away.

"Luke!" Omar's boy cried, as he threw his arms about the man. "We are awaiting you. The holy man has come."

Luke moved into the room with grace. When he spoke his voice was like that of flowing waters. He clasped my hand in both of his and kissed me on the cheek in greeting. What a warm way to seal a brother's love! It is so like the Essene way.

Our discussions went on far into the night. Hamaya, Omar's wife, sat with us as an equal, making no move to assist the servants or the children.

Hamaya contributed to our discussions in a most effective way. At last, another Judith. A female magus would be unique in this world dominated by men. After all, the God we sat discussing was no respecter of gender. All souls are the same to God. Everyone who sought YHWH would be received, filled, and sent out again, for that is how the kingdom of God grows. No man has the right to trim even the most fragile of twigs from the tree of life. God alone is the gardener.

We all agreed that the subjugation of women had crippled the world. Denying women the right to serve God in every capacity prevented the spread of God consciousness. God had commanded man to subdue the Earth, not woman. How far men had strayed from the mind of God! What would it take to reconcile the mind of man with the mind of God?

In the early hours of the morning the four of us agreed the atonement of God and man must take place.

"I will work on it in Isfahan," said Hamaya.

"I will take it on my travels," said Omar.

"I will work with it wherever I go," declared Luke.

"And I, too, in Palestine," I said.

"We four form the base of the pyramid," observed Luke.

Exhaustion was overcoming me, even with the conversation taking such a dramatic turn. We all headed for sleep. There are many kinds of dreaming, but occasionally a dream comes from one's higher consciousness. That night I had one of those.

King David appeared, saying, "Halls of fame and power and wealth set in palaces of gold–that is how the kingdom of man appears." King Solomon appeared, saying, "The peaceful kingdom built on wisdom alone falls short of the glory of YHWH." Moses appeared, saying, "The kingdom of laws will fail, for man makes the laws to suit himself, and changes them from day to day."

When I awoke, the day was almost gone and long shadows lay across the land. I pondered my dream, then laid it aside for the future. I knew I would never forget it.

Realizing that I had completely forgotten about my horse, I jumped up quickly, threw a robe about me, and raced out into the main room.

"My horse," I cried.

Hamaya laughed. It was a melodious laugh that tinkled like a bell high on a distant hill. "My eldest son tended to your horse last night, honored guest. Surely you do not think we would mistreat the animal that brought such a treasured one to us from so far away."

I was embarrassed and a bit shamed. "I was so glad to arrive I thought not at all about my wonderful companion. It was a grievous fault, not yours to attend."

Hamaya laughed again, saying, "We take care of every detail for our guests. You can count on it. We want your stay to be one of pleasure, not worry. Come now, you must be hungry. Your mighty horse has eaten three times already."

Allowing that gracious lady to lead me to a banquet table laden with the finest foods, I decided I must still be dreaming. Sitting by my side, she would urge me to eat more. Her servant washed my feet (still clean from the night before) and seemed happy to do so. All the servants seemed overjoyed to serve. It was apparent that in this house everyone was full of love, and service was the way it manifested.

Hamaya sat by my side engaging me in conversation throughout the breakfast. She regaled me with stories of Isfahan, the servants, close friends, even the magi. She would take a plum from a silver bowl and plop it in my mouth without pausing in her story. Momentarily, I wondered about Omar and the children, and Hamaya slipped an explanation of their absence deftly between her stories. She read minds, I realized.

I thanked YHWH for my training in keeping my thoughts pure, especially for keeping away those ugly thoughts just outside the mind always seeking entry.

Hamaya smiled, even at that thought. What would the world be like when everyone achieves the natural gift of reading minds? It is coming–the evidence is at hand.

Already the selfless can do it. These are the ones who accept everything as a simple gift.

The meal concluded and I was led to a room of steaming rocks and bubbling pools. I was bathed, soaked, scrubbed, perfumed, and finally draped in glorious robes fit for a ruler. My hair was brushed until it was alive then combed gently with an ivory comb. My beard was trimmed to frame my face. My finger- and toenails were scrubbed, clipped, and primed with oil. Calluses disappeared from my feet as the servant filed them away. Such attention to my body I had not received since the School of the Open Mind in Ahmadabad. But this time, the attention was to make my body feel good rather than like a painfully peeled onion.

Feel good, I did. I smelled good and even looked good. I looked at myself in a mirror. My dark reddish brown hair surprised me, since it had been a kind of orange gold the last time I had seen it, which was when Ishfani accompanied me on the way to Ahmadabad.

My nose did not seem too large for my face anymore, a definite improvement.

One cannot help but look carefully at oneself after being groomed for hours. When the servant braided my hair, I knew this was an effort to improve my looks, not just clean me up. In my mind I was still a young boy in spite of having seen images of my many lifetimes, but now I could see I was a full-grown man, a lot like other men.

"Ah, Jesu, now you look civilized," boomed Omar as he came striding through the door. "I can deliver you to the house of Baungha without feeling like my first teacher is but a sack of rags."

We laughed. He was so anxious that Baungha think me wonderful that he quite forgot that such a thing comes from the inside. Omar was the consummate merchant, always packaging goods to sell. But YHWH looks only on the heart, and that is what man must learn to do.

"As much as it grieves me to lose you so soon, we must go," said Omar.

"Will I not be in Isfahan for at least a year?" I inquired.

"It is I who am leaving," declared Omar.

"Why? Where are you going?"

"Off on my rounds of selling and telling of the universal God," he explained.

"So soon?"

"Yes, now is the time. Tomorrow is not assured to anyone. Luke and I travel together, and he has a patient to see south of here. He likes to travel with a companion of like mind. Our territory stretches from Azerbaijan, the reputed birthplace of Zoroaster, to Susa. It goes from Persepolis to the Indus River and all the villages in between. We have many miles to travel and yesterday is not soon enough to have started."

"I almost missed seeing you leave."

"Not so. We waited for you. Luke plans to extend his territory all the way to Palestine someday. He says his mission is intertwined with yours."

"I must talk to him before he leaves," I exclaimed.

Omar laughed and assured me I would get to see Luke once more.

"My second son is having his thread ceremony in an hour. It is our custom to honor the ritual with our finest clothes and best friends. You must come. It is an ancient ritual."

"Thank you for including me. I shall be happy to share so important a time with you."

We walked to the house of the magi. It was no longer snowing, but the village lay covered with snow. The light of the moon turned the snow into a vision of diamonds sparkling like a million stars. The cold air was invigorating after the steamy bath.

Baungha was an absolute replica of the Elder of Carmel and of Azata of India. His hair was silvery white and cascaded onto white vestments. His eyes were clear and sparkling. It would be natural for men to think YHWH must look like Baungha, for the ancient writings declared man was created in the image of God. Baungha was as if God were manifest. This is a difficult concept that is not explained well anywhere from the places I studied or traveled. The essence of a man as the image of YHWH is hard to grasp.

The ceremony was solemn and impressive. Baungha tied a girdle around the boy's waist and handed him the thread of life. This signified the boy was now prepared to take up the duties, beliefs, and blessings of Zoroaster. There were several young girls also receiving their threads; the boys and girls were treated exactly alike.

The priest raised his hands in blessing and stated in a loud voice: "Long ago our master teacher, Zoroaster, caught a glimpse of God. He stood before the throne of the King of Kings, but could see only the reflection of God's light, for it was too bright even for the master to gaze fully upon it. What Zoroaster saw was like a fire flaming in the dark, flickering on the walls of night. He was given a name that he might call and that name is Ahura Mazda, God of the Eternal Light.

"Hear now, the name of your God is Ahura Mazda."

The evening closed with merrymaking. Luke was there, surrounded by admiring friends and patients. Soon he disappeared. To my chagrin, I realized there would be no opportunity to discuss our mutual missions. It made me regard the night we had talked, sharing our mutual dreams and passions, as even more precious.

Zoroaster was the subject of my first few days with Baungha and my teachers. It is always enlightening to learn about the life of a master teacher, how he rises from "sleep" into full consciousness.

"Zoroaster was a farmer and revered life," Baungha began, addressing the class of five students. "Fasting and self-denial will not help a garden flourish, so Zoroaster treated himself at least as well as his garden, tilling his soul, feeding his body, and harvesting many good fruits.

"Although his father, Porushaspa Spitama, was a camel merchant, Zoroaster was a dreamer. He dreamed about God as a young boy, even as I did. He wondered which god of the many he heard about was the real one, which one was the greatest, and which priest of God was telling the truth. They all claimed to tell the truth.

"Because his father was a rich merchant, Zoroaster was able to study with the best teachers in all of Persia, yet all seemed unable to answer his questions. After ten years of study, he departed the schools and traveled widely. Upon reaching the age of thirty, he declared he had found the truth and began to teach. So powerful were his teachings that he was able to sway many people from a belief in many gods to belief in the one God.

"He would build a fire for men to see. He would tell them 'See that flame? It is a tiny light compared to the great light of Ahura Mazda. When you see the flame of your campfires, know that you see only a tiny reflection of the flame of the spirit that burns in the body of man. That spirit is merely a reflection of the flame of God, the Eternal Light.'

"Zoroaster used candles and campfires so often to teach the people that his disciples came to be called fire worshippers. Nothing could be further from the truth. Simple things are needed to teach simple people.

"Nevertheless, the flame became sacred to the simple folk just as the river is to the Hindu and the holy of holies is to the Jews."

Baungha led us to a room that housed the original Gathas written by Zoroaster; the hymns were written on calfskins and bound with rings of gold. The book Omar had shown us was only a part of the many books that make up the great book called the Avesta. It would take a caravan of camels to carry them all, he said. The Avesta was written in an early form of Aramaic, so studying it was no problem for me after a little instruction. I spent weeks reading and studying the prose that covered many areas of the life of man. The Gathas were much like the Psalms.

Its story of creation reminded me of the ancient writings we had spent so much time copying at the Mt. Carmel scriptorium. According to Zoroaster, the world was created in six days by Ahura Mazda. Ahura Mazda created a man named Mashye and a woman named Mashyane and placed them in a garden called Paradise; then he drove them out for disobedience.

"Evil exists not, only the past. The past is past; the present is a moment; the future is all." This is how the book summed up the struggle between the kingdom of darkness and the kingdom of light as envisioned by Zoroaster.

The master predicted the complete destruction of the kingdom of darkness of Ahriman as well as the triumph of the kingdom of light of Ahura Mazda.

"A tree is the law itself," declared the ancient Avesta, meaning that a tree is in complete harmony with the forces and laws of nature. It furnishes the best kind of food for man. Without trees, man could not exist, for trees maintain the perfect precondition for life as they cleanse the air.

"A man is good only when he is willing not to do to another whatever is not good for himself. God is the giver of all good and perfect things," wrote Zoroaster. He said that whosoever believed his words would not perish but have everlasting life. "Eternal life" occupied a whole section of the Avesta.

"When did Zoroaster live?" asked one student in our class.

"We believe there were three different Zoroasters, or that two men took upon themselves the task of articulating what the first Zoroaster taught," said Baungha, "The first Zoroaster was probably a Sumerian philosopher who lived five thousand years ago. We have discovered his teachings to be that old. The second man was a

Persian who compiled an encyclopedia of all those traditions that survived the earlier Sumerian civilization. The third one was a Median priest, who lived somewhat less than a thousand years ago, who revived the half-forgotten teachings of his predecessor."

"Which one wrote the parts of the Avesta we ascribe to Zoroaster?" asked another student.

"Zoroaster! What does it matter which one?"

"Did one of them or perhaps all three ever study in Egypt?" I asked.

"Perhaps," smiled Baungha.

Our questions ranged on and on until finally Baungha sighed and remarked, "The questions you need to ask are not forthcoming and the questions you do ask are not relevant. Therefore, this class is closed so that you can study and contemplate the message of the master."

There was so much that the Zoroastrians taught that was like that of the Essenes that I felt I was repeating my Carmel studies. It was interesting to me to see so much similarity, but at twenty-two years I finally wanted to cease my studies of other religions, other people, and other times. The here and now began to have an urgency for me.

Although I had not spent as much time in Persia as I had in my other schools, I knew that the laws were the same. The Jew and the Persian are brothers in the soul.

It was not long after that a message arrived from Palestine. Yosef was sick unto death. Hurriedly, I packed up my belongings and loaded them on Victor. Baungha assured me that Yosef would live until I arrived, but his time was closing quickly. "Do not use your powers to keep him on this plane," urged Baungha.

"Why not?" I asked.

"He is ready to go."

"How can I know when it is one's time and when it is not?"

"He will tell you if you listen."

"You have talked to Yosef?"

"You are not listening, even to me," Baungha said.

That drew me up short. He was right. For some reason I had thought Yosef would live forever. I suppose that is how one always views his parents, who seem immortal and omnipotent to a child.

"Why does Yosef want to die?" I asked, ready to listen.

"He has grown old and weary and wants not to be a burden to your mother, who is still young. He does not want her to see him slowly lose his sight or his hearing, but most of all his masculinity. He has earned the right to decide. And it is a test for you."

"For me? How is that?"

"I am not permitted to tell you any more."

Off we rode down the trail out of Isfahan, racing with the winds that swept across the plains.

As we galloped through the valley, heading for the Zagros Mountains, the phrase "Once long ago, the Grand Lama of Lhasa was called the high priest of Pon," flashed through my mind. It was Cyani's answer to my query about the beginnings of Hinduism. "We have always been mystics of God. As times change, we change the names, that is all. Progress sometimes requires it. The Buddha came along and we adopted his teachings as our own. Now, we are Buddhists. But someday we will be something else."

At Susa I tarried only a few hours. I saw the ruins of the palace built by Xerxes. He had inscribed here in three languages almost the identical words he had used at Persepolis. They were the words of Darius: they praised Ahura Mazda and said, "May Ahura Mazda protect me and my rule, may Ahura Mazda protect that which I have built, and that which my father has built." Material kingdoms seem not to survive, no matter how great and powerful they are at the time.

The empire of the Greeks replaced the Persians, and that was followed by Rome, but Rome will be no different. It was a fitting climax to my years of traveling and studying to walk around Babylon. This is all that was left of the Babylonian empire that had enslaved my people, Israel.

A caravan was leaving Babylon, the crossroads of ancient trade routes, and I was tempted to join it. I love caravans. They are like huge parties. What happens to one person, happens to everyone. Even the sounds are exciting: the tiny bells on the animals, the weird cries of the camels, the shouts of the drivers, the chatter of the merchants, the cursing of the caravan master.

The lush valley of the Tigris and Euphrates Rivers was a welcome sight after all the plains and deserts I had crossed in the past few years. I dared not cross the desert on my own, where many lone travelers had met terrible fates, or so I thought.

"A shortcut to death"–was how the merchants described the great desert that lies between the lush valley and my home in Galilee. I drank in the lushness as I rode along, marveling at the faith that had led Abraham out of Ur to a land he did not know. That is the kind of obedience all men must have to enter the spiritual kingdom. I had resisted the idea of joining the caravan. Time was short and caravans slow. My fears proved unfounded.

"Obedience, obedience, obedience," I whispered in Victor's ear as we rode along the fertile rim of those two great rivers.

Long gone from my mind were the dire words of the Grand Lama. I was no longer burdened with that dark mantle of sorrow. My heart was once more full of joy, and I looked forward to seeing my beloved family once more. Even Yosef's impending death failed to throw a pall across my soul. I knew it was all part of a divine plan, somehow, one I could not see clearly. Yet I realized even then that it was in place and I must obey the will of the Divine in my life.

Chapter 24

Nazareth

A month to the day, I rode into Capernaum late in the afternoon. Victor's tongue lolled out of his mouth, but I was certain he was as happy to see that city by the sea as I was. We went directly to Yosef's house. It was quiet, and I could not find anyone about, not even the servants.

"Anyone here?" I called out.

A neighbor heard me and came across the way. "The family of Yosef is in Nazareth," the man said. "Yosef is near to death and wished to die in his cottage in the hills."

I thanked the man, and he returned to his home. For a while I sat in the garden by the house enjoying the familiar feelings of "home." It felt so good, even with the sadness that surrounded the place. It was growing dark and Nazareth was sixteen miles away. I decided Victor and I had traveled enough for one day and that tomorrow would be soon enough to set out on the final leg of my trip to bid my father farewell.

As I stood there in the half-light, I heard a sound. Turning, I saw my oldest brother coming up the hill. "Y'cov," I cried as I ran to meet him.

Although I had not seen him in ten years, I recognized the stiff way Y'cov held his head and the angular gait of his walk. Had I been able to see only his face, I might not have recognized him, but his essence was dearly familiar.

"It's Yeshua!" I cried as I tried to hug him. I felt his body stiffen. Then it relaxed a little. He burst into tears and sobbed into my shoulder, releasing years of tension.

"Oh, Yeshua," he moaned, "I am so glad to see you. Father is dying. Every day a little more life flows out of him. I cannot bear it."

I held my brother tightly and let him spend his emotions. At seventeen he was more man than child, but there is a point when all men dissolve into children again. I knew Y'cov had maintained the position of man of the house for our mother and the younger children. It was a relief for him to turn that job over to me, and I was glad to relieve his burden.

"It is Yosef's choice to go," I whispered into that sobbing soul, thinking it would comfort him.

"How do you know?" he snuffled, pulling back from me in amazement.

"Ah, Y'cov," I tried to soothe him, "we all choose our destinies, whether to come or go. The soul never dies. Yosef is useless in his eyes if his body is failing him. He can take on another."

"That is just a story," Y'cov declared, refusing to be comforted. "It is all over when we die, and we have nothing to do with it. No one wants to die."

"Y'cov," I feigned amazement, "you have been listening to the Sadducees."

"They are right!" he sullenly insisted.

"How truly dismal, if they are," I replied, not wishing to argue theology with him in his despair. "Are you on your way to Nazareth?"

He dried his eyes and said, "No, I must tend to some things here at the house, and I have come from the shop. I am much too tired to drag one foot behind the other tonight. I am going at first light."

"Good," I agreed. "I, too, am tired."

We went into the empty house, both sad that this house that Yosef built stick by stone over the years would never again be home to him. It was with heavy hearts that we prepared a light supper and turned in early for sleep. I could feel my brother struggling with my words. As I moved off to my old room, he asked the question.

"Why?"

"He does not wish to slowly deteriorate before our mother," I said.

"Ohhhhhh!" his mouth formed a circle as he nodded his head. He seemed to understand that men are often humiliated to have their bodies fail them when their minds are clear and their spirits willing. Tender loving husband as Yosef was, he preferred to say goodbye when life was full and before pity became apparent.

There would be some who would think Yosef a selfish man for choosing to go rather than suffer the years of degeneration. However, when a man has so lived his life that he has a choice given by the angels, who can say his choice is wrong, or selfish? Surely judgment must be left to YHWH. I smiled at my inner dialogue, as I drifted off to sleep.

As the cock heralded dawn, Y'cov and I were up getting ready to ride to Nazareth. We rode down the path just as the sun appeared over the Sea of Galilee. The miles between Capernaum and Nazareth had always been my favorite stretch of land. Sea to the east, the hills to the west, the valley winding its way south–somehow it brought me peace.

Y'cov was silent as we rode. The overly talkative boy I had left ten years before was now a brooding young man struggling for maturity. As I studied him, I noticed his long face seemed even longer with this sadness about it. His drooping eyes and thin brows accentuated the sensitivity of his face. Y'cov the righteous one: this is my brother. He would always choose the right path, think the right thought, give the right advice, follow the call of duty forsaking all pleasures. What better kind of man could our father entrust with the safekeeping of the family and the business? I longed to lighten his sorrow and burden. But Y'cov did not want to talk.

Finally he asked the burning question, "Will you remain with us now?"

Although I knew it was coming, it startled me. "I cannot stay," I whispered in an effort to soften the blow.

Y'cov's spirits sank into a deeper gloom. What could I say that would turn this sorrowing soul into a joyous one? At this moment there was nothing. When did Y'cov stop believing YHWH?

We reached Nazareth, nestled in the hills of Galilee, as the sun reached its zenith. Riding into the village, we headed up the high hill to the synagogue that dominated the village. Yosef's summer cottage was nearby. Memories flooded back in me of the summer Yochanan and I spent there with Y'cov, who constantly insisted we take him on our forays into the hills. Once in a while we would take him, but more often than not we left him behind with the admonition that he was too young. Boys of thirteen can be unintentionally cruel to boys of three or four years old.

I remember believing ourselves "men" because of our recent bar mitzvahs. We thought anyone as young as Y'cov would be without feelings or memories, so often we treated him as we would a buzzing gnat that interrupted our discussions. How thoughtless we had been.

I could see my brother, too, was remembering those days. I wanted to apologize, but that would have added insult to his injury to acknowledge I knew he still was in pain from our callous neglect. How could I convince him now that I was sorry we had been thoughtless?

We rode up the hill in silence. I tried to spread balm on his wounds with my mind, but the block between us was powerful. I perceived the fear rising in him: he who had once been too young was now about to be given the full load of a grieving family and a demanding business on his youthful shoulders. I could not overcome that, for it was true. If I followed the will of YHWH, I would leave the day after Yosef's entombment for Egypt to complete my studies as an initiate. Following the will of God for my life is simple when no other demands are made of me, but now there was much to consider.

My mother, Miryam, was the first to greet us as we came through the door of the cottage. "Yeshua," she cried, "I am so glad you have come. Yosef will not die now that you are here. Please save him for me, for all of us."

Her eyes were tearful and her voice full of pain. Tears ran down my face as I held her closely in my arms. How could I tell her that I could not interfere with my father's wishes?

My mother sobbed as I raised my eyes to my sister, Ruth, now fourteen years old. She was the very image of our mother—the way she held her head, those clear steady eyes so full of light. Ruth was in charge of the household, giving our mother time to grieve. "Welcome home, dear brother," she whispered as she took mother into her arms. "Yosef awaits you, but just barely. He is in there."

I hurried to the room of my father. Yosef lay upon his pallet covered with a heavy blanket. He was ashen. The gray cast of death was all about him. In the shuttered room a single candle glowed, flickering as did the life of my father. I took his hand in mine and called softly, "Father."

His old eyes slowly filled with recognition. "Yeshua," he breathed. "Now I can go in peace."

His eyes closed again, and I thought surely he was gone. But in a few moments he struggled back to life. "My son," he whispered hoarsely, "I waited for you to come."

"Yes, Father, I know. I came as quickly as I could," I said as I held tightly the hand that had once been firm and strong, guiding me toward manhood. As I gripped that hand, it became a thread of life and he seemed to grow stronger. I knew it was only temporary, and so did he.

"I knew of your mission before you were born," he began. "I was chosen by the elders at Mt. Carmel to take Miryam for my wife as we prepared for your advent. It was my deepest pleasure not only to be chosen, but to live my life with such a woman. From a young girl, purity of soul and purpose has been her essence, I give her to you now, to hold and keep until that day when we will all be together in heaven."

Again Yosef closed his eyes, seeming to sink into another plane. I leaned closer to see if he were gone, but he tightened the grip on my hand and opened his eyes slowly. "I have carefully prepared Y'cov to administer the business and provide for the family and also your needs as you do God's will. He is a good and righteous young man who will do a fine job, for work and duty are his calling. His spiritual life is lacking. I leave that to you.

"Your brother, Joses, is also good at business even at fifteen years. Unlike Y'cov, Joses is able to see all sides of every question. He is a believer and the perfect one to assist Y'cov. His strengths match the weaknesses in his brother.

"Simon is a joy to my soul. He will work long hours and he will play just as long and hard. He never complains, regardless of what it is. It is all the same to him. My three sons can handle the work and provide handsomely for your mother, your sister, and you. In their hands the business will prosper.

"My precious daughter, Ruth–already she is much like her blessed mother. She takes charge of the house and runs it as well as my sons run my business. There is a young Roman, Philoas, that she wants to marry. Y'cov will have none of it. He is a good man, but not of our faith. It grieves Y'cov. He holds Rome to blame for everything and lets his wrath fall on Philoas. Keep these things in mind and do as you see best. I am not learned."

Again Yosef closed his eyes and his breathing grew harsh, then so faint I could not tell if he breathed at all. Still his hand clung to mine. Slowly, his eyes half opened.

"Jude is the child of my old age. The joy of my life. He has kept me young just to keep up with his quick mind. At four years he is much like you. He will follow you. He cares not at all for business. He seeks the stars and the fireflies."

I took my father into my arms and held him close, whispering over and over my love for him. Slowly he slipped away and was gone.

When I pulled aside the curtain to Yosef's room and my anxious family saw my face, they knew Yosef was gone. They did not enter, but began to prepare for the burial ceremony. Even little Jude, sitting alone, wiped away his tears and joined in. We gathered in the main room of the cottage to break the bread of life and drink the wine of remembrance. We took bitter herbs to signify the sorrow of our separation.

As the news traveled around Nazareth that Yosef was gone, friends and neighbors began to arrive with gifts of food and flowers, friendship and love, which are the best forms of sympathy.

Among Essenes, death is celebrated as a part of life. We believe it is a passing from one phase of life to another. How then can one remain sad for long? The only sadness is the moment of parting. We know that we shall all follow one day.

So we washed our faces and hands, put on clean garments, and received our guests with smiles. Only Y'cov refused to smile. Yosef was laid to rest in a cave above our house that he had discovered long ago and claimed for his own. "Where I can keep an eye on you," he would say with his wonderful smile of love and mystery.

Y'cov spoke to no one. He sank into a deep brooding and stood apart. After the ritual of entombment, I sought him out. We stood silently for a while as I attuned my mind to his thoughts. He was torn with accusing me for failing to save our father and fear that he would fail when I left them. His self-torment would surely kill him. The anger he was using to overcome his fear was a killing passion.

I saw that in a few years he could die of this fear and all its negative companions, resentment, hate, hostility. How could I reach such a heart? Sadly, I knew I could not. I would have to leave my brother to YHWH, who heals all souls.

"I must leave," I said.

"Go!" he muttered through clenched teeth.

My heart sank. A thousand reasons for staying flooded my mind. Surely a loving God would not want me to leave. Surely the situation was such that I was required in Galilee for a few years. Surely a merciful God could see that abandoning my fatherless family would not be fair, even thoughtless. I considered every aspect of my role as oldest son and heir, and could not come up with a good reason for adhering to the traditions of our people. As I struggled with the choices presented to me, the voice of Yosef broke through my indecision, "O my son, I have carefully prepared Y'cov and his brothers for this time."

This declaration cleared my mind. I realized we all have our missions in life. I must follow my own, rather than take up Y'cov's or that of my other brothers. I could not follow his path, nor could he follow mine. Strange that I should confront this struggle again after having dealt with it with Yochanan, years before.

Joses and Simon were almost joyous. They made jokes and spoke lightly of their brother–me–who loved the land of the Pharaohs so much he kept returning to it.

"Yeshua loves the pyramids better than the Temple of YHWH," stated Joses solemnly. "They fit his idea of God better than the synagogues."

"Yes, yes, that is so," agreed Simon. "I hear the pyramids tower above everything on stark and barren plains and they are free of ornaments. Perhaps Yeshua worships the pyramids?"

"Simon," exclaimed Ruth, "You blaspheme!"

"How so, fair sister? By telling the truth? Ask him."

The three turned to me. What had started out in jest became very serious. "The Great Pyramid is ancient and has stood despite every disaster. You are right. That does fit my idea of YHWH better than the more recent buildings of man.

"The pinnacle of the pyramid catches the first rays of the rising sun and casts that light all around. It is like a beacon seen for miles.

There is mystery about how it was built and who did the mighty task. Many create stories about it. There are many, lesser pyramids nearby that try to achieve the greatness of the great one. That is how I see it.

"No man knows exactly why the Great Pyramid is there, but standing near it, I receive a lot of energy that is strange and unusual. It attracts me more than anything I have seen on this Earth. Yet man has constantly tried to tear it down, rather than preserve it and add to its beauty.

"The pyramid stands in the geographic center of the lands of the earth, as though all life emanates from it. It is as though the landmass flows from it. You are right. It fits my idea of God better than the temple."

They stood there thinking that over. I turned to Ruth and declared, "The only way one blasphemes God is to deny the Holy Spirit."

"What do you mean?" Simon wanted to know.

"Another way to put it is to call the work of the Holy Spirit the work of evil rather than the work of good."

"That is a tough one, Yeshua. I do not understand it at all," cried Joses. "Are you saying that if I see something happen and think it evil instead of good, I have blasphemed the Holy Spirit of God? What if I just make a mistake?"

"Do not fret yourself. God looks upon the heart. No one can accidentally blaspheme God. It is a matter of intent."

They all breathed a sigh of relief. "You are already a rabbi, Yeshua, teaching us," Ruth declared.

"I have much to learn before I am ready to teach, my little lamb," I murmured. "Five more years of study in Egypt at least stretch out before me. And there is the problem of leaving you.

"Do not worry, Yeshua, I will take care of everyone," said Ruth. "We are not babies. Our mother was married and had you at my age."

"Yeshua," chided Joses, "do not let Y'cov tear you away from the will of YHWH. He tries to tell us all what we should do and what we should not do. When that does not work, he intimidates us with guilt and threats. We know he means well."

"He will be the head of your household when I leave," I remarked. "You must now give him all the respect you gave our father." That startled them all.

"What?" cried Joses. "He is only two years older than I. How can I give him the respect of the wisest man who ever lived–my father?"

"You must learn to," I said.

"He will not let me marry Philoas," cried Ruth, wringing her hands, tears rolling down her face.

"You must persuade him with love," I persisted.

"Ohhhh, Yeshua, you have been gone too long. Nothing persuades Y'cov," said Simon.

"It is impossible for this family to survive and the business to prosper if you fail to give Y'cov your love and support. If you love him, you will keep his commands, whether you agree or not," I urged. "Mother will help you. When it seems beyond bearing, go to her."

I saw Y'cov standing in the shadows listening intently. I hoped his well of bitterness would turn to a spring of joy with love surrounding him from such a blessed family. He caught me looking at him and stepped away, quickly. Hugging each one, I searched for my mother.

She was such a joy. How could this woman be my mother? She seemed more like a sister, a companion. Leaving her pained me. "Shall I stay?" I asked.

"The path is yours alone to travel, as is making the choice," she said softly.

"How can I tell what is God's will for my life when desiring that seems selfish in the eyes of others?"

"You have spent all your years so that your will and that of Adonai are the same. Now the urgings of men will test you constantly. You rescued me from my selfish desire to keep Yosef here with me when he wanted to die. You wanted him to remain here as much as I, but you chose rightly."

"Thank you, dear mother," I replied, wondering how she had moved into this truth so quickly.

"Your purpose in life must determine your choices. It is a clear path once you accept that universal law," she added.

Again I went to my brother Y'cov. Nothing had changed, except he realized his opportunity to vent his rage was about to pass.

"How can you do this to our mother?" he pled, realizing guilt might work better than anger.

"She wants me to go," I replied, a little startled he brought our mother into this subject.

"You think what you want to think. You care nothing for us. What about my life and my wishes? I, too, might want to be a rabbi and travel the countryside rather than toiling in a dirty shop all day and watching over children," he bellowed.

"Why, Y'cov. Come with me. You would make a wonderful Raab."

"What? Abandon mother? Abandon my brothers and sister? Abandon the business that Yosef so diligently built? Abandon all of that for my own selfish desires? Is that what you will teach men, to abandon all responsibilities?"

His accusing daggers plunged clear into my soul. His raging had become so loud that Ruth, Mother, Joses, Simon, Jude, and the servants were gathered around us, listening, but fearing to interfere lest Y'cov's wrath fall on them.

"You choose rightly, my brother," I whispered, "for you. It is my earnest prayer and deepest conviction that I, too, have chosen rightly for me."

With that, I left them. Jude ran to the edge of the hill calling out to me, "God go with you, dear wonderful brother. We love you." I knew which child's love would eventually undo Y'cov's anger and fear.

I traveled the length of the valley past Mt. Moreh, and longed to turn west to the mountains of Carmel and see my beloved teachers once more. Judith and the Elder surely could restore my grieving soul, replenish my resolve, and send me refreshed on my way. But I resisted, for I knew I could stop only for a short while. Passing through the hills and valleys of Samaria, I debated whether to stop at Qumran to see Yochanan. I knew it would be difficult to go so far out of my way then fail to stop at the home of Lazarus and Martha. The desire to see Mina was overwhelming, but I resisted that too. The voice urging me to detour from my path might be the one that weakened my resolve to continue on at all. Still . . .

Yochanan, fully grown now, must be even more striking than he had been at fourteen. How I longed to see him. Would he urge me to stay? Would he come with me now? Ah, that was a thought full of joy. Amen had said Yochanan would return to Egypt some day.

Would he come now? As that thought flashed through my mind, I turned Victor east for Khirbet Qumran. Located on the eastern shore of the Sea of Salt were the caves of the Essenes. It was late evening when I arrived and they were parading into their central meeting house below the caves. This was their second and last meal of the day, so I was glad I had arrived in time.

As I swung down from Victor and looked about, I could not see Yochanan anywhere. Would I recognize him? Perhaps he was out in the desert raiding bees' nests or catching locusts for his evening meal. Standing by a fresh spring watering Victor, I saw a familiar figure coming up the path. Stopping in his tracks, he stared for a moment then shouted wildly, "Yeshua!"

"Yochanan," I called out, and losing all poise, I flung myself headlong into his open arms.

We laughed and cried and hugged and danced around in a frenzy. The Essenes coming in from the gardens watched us, not able to recall ever having seen Yochanan carry on like this. They did not recognize me at all until one of them declared: "It is Yeshua ben Yosef of Nazareth."

With that they crowded around us, hugging and renewing acquaintances. We moved indoors and broke the rule of silence. What ordinarily would have been a solemn meal of communion with God became a festival. We ate and drank far into the night, until I finally pled exhaustion and urged sleep. Even so, Yochanan and I talked until dawn.

"I'll give Egypt another try," he finally consented, "if you will give me a few days to wind up affairs here. I cannot leave on such short notice."

How could I refuse such a happy compromise? "Of course, Yochanan. Anything you ask I would do for your companionship. How I have longed for you the past ten years."

"I have missed you, too," he returned. "I want to hear about everything, and I know going with you to Egypt is the only way."

It was not surprising to learn that Yochanan was now the leader of the Essenes. Better than anyone, he knew the ways of the desert. Like all born leaders, he was not constrained by man-made rules. He had helped his fellow Essenes locate hidden springs that fed pools of delicious water; he found caves perfect for storage of their precious scrolls. Yet he shunned their simple comforts, preferring the wilderness. He often went there for days. They believed him holy despite the fact that he was a son of Aaron, an ordained priest of Moses.

The community lamented his leaving and fretted over losing his counsel. The women presented us with white garments for our trip. Yochanan reluctantly exchanged his usual garb of camel's hair and put on the robe. He smiled broadly at this last gesture of the women to clothe him in the manner of Essenes and joked, "Since I am going to an alien land, I guess I must wear alien clothes." They cheered. They adored him.

Several days later we departed Qumran for Egypt. As we rode, we recalled the time ten years before when we had walked this route. We tried to remember places we had stopped to eat or sleep. Yochanan was far more mellow than he had been as a boy. It gave me great hope he might remain with me for a few years.

He listened intently as I told him of my travels, experiences, studies, and powers. "The things I do, Yochanan, you can do also. They are not supernatural. In fact, they are very natural. Everyone could do them if they were willing to discipline themselves, purify their thoughts, and be rid of all thoughts of self."

"Show me a trick, O Magus of the East," he twitted. But he did so tenderly and I was not offended.

As we settled in for a night's rest, Yochanan exclaimed, "Yeshua, now is the time to produce a soft bed, a table of fine fare, and perhaps some entertainment, maybe a dancing girl or two."

We giggled at that. "Listen to the Lion of the Desert roar for things he rejects whenever they are available," I retorted with mirth.

We stretched out on our bedrolls and looked up at the stars. "These special things I have learned to do are like breathing and hearing. There when needed, but not things to brag about or produce for show. They come slowly as a part of growth, like getting wiser. They are not done for oneself, rather to manifest the love of God. The need calls forth the act."

"Hmmmmmmmm," Yochanan murmured.

"Take reading minds," I sought to further explain. "I don't read every mind I meet nor any mind all the time. Only when I need to know what someone is thinking, or when what they say does not seem to be what they think or mean. Then I go into that mind and see what is there."

Yochanan slapped his hand slowly across his forehead in mock apprehension, declaring, "I am hiding from you what I think, Star of Bethlehem."

It was comforting, hearing again the name he had always used to tease me, and to experience again his teasing manner even in the face of most serious discussions. I loved Yochanan even more as a man than I had as a boy. Yochanan and I felt a closeness that is often difficult between men. It was as though the years had fallen away and we were boys again, racing over the hills playing Romans and zealots. Ten years of separation disappeared as if they had never been. Yochanan had paternal feelings for me, and I felt safe with him. The wild eyes of his youth were even wilder now, but there was wisdom in them.

I could have traveled the world with Yochanan. For now we found ourselves trotting down a dusty track in Heliopolis, home of pharaohs, pyramids, and mysteries.

Chapter 25

Gods in the Making

As we rode into the ancient city of On, I asked Yochanan if he had heard of Yosef's passing. I was not prepared for his reaction. He paled noticeably, then howled as wildly as any animal. I knew he had loved Yosef and considered him his father, but I did not expect such grief. As his tears flowed unashamedly, Yochanan said, "May I now weep for the loss of my own father and mother?"

Then I understood. He had shed not one tear nor even commented when his mother died. Neither of us were old enough to understand the event when his father was murdered by the Temple priests. Lamenting the loss of those whom he had chosen before he was born was something only now he was willing to permit himself. It was with admiration that I beheld the lamentations of this great soul. Had he announced he was the Mashiyah, the Christed One, I would have fallen down before him and never questioned it.

The villagers stared at the unusual sight: two white-clad Jews riding stallions down the dusty trail of an Egyptian village, one of them weeping wildly. We stopped at the well to water our horses. As they were drinking, Yochanan quieted and spoke in a voice I had never heard before, "The scales that covered my eyes are now washed away, and I begin to see. The pent-up emotion of my soul has been released, and I am swept clean. My mind, long ironclad, is now unfettered and I am open to learn. Teach me, Yeshua. Teach me."

Breathing a sigh of relief, I perceived my cousin would stay with me for a while. He had become the seeker of truth and knowledge we must all become to find our way.

We headed for the temple of Osiris and registered in the school as Jeshua and John. No longer affected by a house dedicated to a pagan god, he no longer winced at studying with pagan priests. He even greeted Amen with open arms. "Ha, the beloved teacher of my beloved cousin. How grateful I am to be in your country and in your presence."

Amen was glad to see us both. "You brought him with you once more. I am happy he stayed long enough this time for me to meet him." He embraced Yochanan, and hugged me like a returning son.

I was overjoyed Yochanan would remain so we could explore the pyramids, the Nile, the desert, the Great Library, the delta, and all the other places I had left for the end of my studies. My happiness spilled over onto Amen and Yochanan as we talked on and on. It was one of those rare moments when men feel that God is in Heaven and all is right with the world.

After receiving instructions concerning our first classes, Yochanan and I headed for the synagogue. Here we would live with my longtime friend and mentor, Micah. With great relish I re-introduced the little rabbi to Yochanan, for I knew that he would now appreciate my rotund friend.

"Micah says, 'Do not do as I do; do as I say to do.' Fasting is not in Micah's vocabulary. Like you, Yochanan, he is an Essene who answers only to God."

"He must be a truly great man," Yochanan solemnly observed.

"He subscribes to his namesake in our ancient writings:

> *What does God require of thee, O man?*
> *To do justly, to love mercy, and*
> *to walk humbly with thy God.*

"That sums up Micah."

"He is a man after my own heart," agreed Yochanan.

"He is no slave to tradition. He would rather create it than follow it."

"Truly sublime," murmured Yochanan.

"The world would be at peace," I laughed "if everyone were more like Micah."

We found him at the camel driver's station where he went daily to greet strangers and welcome them to Egypt. The amiable man was talking to a dusky camel driver who I realized was my childhood friend, Asmy. The reunion was a repeat of all the enthusiasm of other reunions I had in Galilee, Judea, and Egypt. Micah took to Yochanan at once. Kindred rebels, they knew each other from many prior lifetimes, I could see. Micah drew Yochanan into his family circle. Micah cooed about how much he had heard of the Lion of the Desert. I heaved a sigh. My fears disappeared.

"Come, Asmy," he invited my old friend. "Tonight we feast at my house."

Reaching the synagogue, we smelled the rich aromas of baking bread. Micah had prospered. He now had four apprentices to tend the ovens. He had added new rooms for his living quarters and no longer slept in a corner of the same building in which he taught, worshipped, held weddings, and sold bread.

Nevertheless, Micah said, "This poor rabbi will have to scrape the bin for enough food for so many mouths. He'll have to bake a few extra loaves from bartered flour."

Yochanan, unused to Micah's sense of humor, offered to pay. Micah drew back in mock outrage. "You insult me! Does the son pay the father for his food? Not so. I will manage . . . just barely." He grinned as he pulled baskets of food, wine, and bread from his stocks. He had enough to feed all of Heliopolis.

"My poor feast does not match the banquets of India, I am sure," Micah continued, "but it will have to do." He roasted lamb, sliced cheeses, and even served up a platter of carob fruits for Yochanan. Micah, of course, was the only one who ate in banquet quantities. "I must eat to keep up my weight," he chuckled.

Asmy was no longer a starving child as when I was young. He ate a man's lot. He too had obviously prospered. No longer did he hide food in his sleeves for his hungry brothers and sisters at home.

While Micah and Asmy consumed the heady wines, Yochanan and I enjoyed goat's milk.

"Asmy keeps me informed as to who is arriving and who is leaving," Micah said. It was apparent that Asmy was no stranger at Micah's table.

"Micah's God blesses better than the gods of Egypt," said Asmy.

Yochanan's ears perked up, recognizing a potential convert. My evangelistic cousin wasted no time. "Adonai blesses those who ask," he said to Asmy.

Asmy nodded his head in agreement failing to pick up the bait. Yochanan was not put off. Yochanan began talking about the transmigration of souls. "Since I seem to feel such a closeness with Elijah, our prophet, who was fed by ravens, my question is: Was I Elijah in a past life, or the ravens?" he smiled broadly.

"Souls do not transmigrate," insisted Micah hotly.

"Not you, of course, honored host, but we lesser lights, well, I am not so sure. Maybe we do."

Asmy's eyes widened as Yochanan went on with tales of that remarkable prophet, Elijah. I added bits about my own fancied past lives. Micah guessed the direction Yochanan was going and joined in the exploration. Asmy asked the question that has hooked men for centuries. "Do you think I might have once been a pharaoh?" he asked, scarcely daring to breathe for fear he was and for fear he was not.

I wondered what Yochanan would say. I sat still and hardly moved. Yochanan closed his eyes in deep concentration. Then as he slowly opened them, he told the truth. "You and you alone are the only one who can know the answer to your question for sure, for God reveals the truth to those who seek it."

"How can I f-find the answer?" stammered my now-converted friend.

"By seeking first to know Adonai, the God of the Universe," replied Yochanan. "God is truth and truth is God. It is all the same."

My ears picked up. Was this Yochanan, the Yochanan who had never left Palestine, now speaking like a Hindu? Had he learned in the desert isolation of Judea all I had learned traveling across the world? But of course it must be. The source of truth is the same wherever you may walk.

That night marked the beginning of Asmy's earnest search for God. I, too, learned from my cousin. I watched him use the simple truths he had learned. He realized that each soul must be accepted for where he is before he can be led forward an inch. I could tell Yochanan had a disciple, and I was grateful to YHWH, who, stone by stone, built a house of reasons for Yochanan to remain with me in Egypt.

It was the first of many evenings around Micah's plentiful table. His moaning that the three of us would eat him out of house and synagogue was his merry cover for letting us know we delighted him. Yochanan was able to retain his Essene qualities in the face of Initiates from every faith by living with Micah.

Because of Micah the priests of Osiris were no longer a threat to Yochanan's view of God. His flaming spirit grew brighter by the day.

As before, we had several weeks to explore the surrounding area before our classes began. We met in the library every morning for orientation, where a priest named Zar described the sites, events, and feasts. Each morning he provided details about the history of sites along the Nile. "Free passage is available for you to take a vessel on the Nile. You are free to visit these places I have told you about. Surely you should visit them. Let us know when you are going so we will know where you are and when to expect you back," directed Zar.

"Let's take the next felucca," whispered Yochanan.

"Agreed," I responded.

The upper Nile rises hundreds of miles to the south of Heliopolis and flows north into the Great Sea. Our felucca had sails and oarsmen, for we were sailing against the flow of the river on our way to Memphis. The oarsmen pulled hard against the rushing current.

"See the Sphinx," I shouted as we pulled into the main river.

"Look at that!" exclaimed Yochanan as he viewed the Great Pyramid for the first time.

The oarsmen lifted the sails, allowing the north wind that blows continuously from the Great Sea to easily carry our felucca south, against the current of the river.

"We will explore those ancient monuments to the ingenuity of man on our way back," I suggested.

"Right," agreed Yochanan. "Save the best for last."

Of all the peoples on Earth, the Egyptians are surely the most blessed with natural gifts. Protected from invaders from the west by the Great Desert, to the south by the myriad cataracts at Aswan that prevent armies moving by boat, and to the north by the fan-shaped delta that invites large ships to move into them from the Great Sea only to become marooned in marshy shallows far from targets, Egypt was protected against aggressors. When Egypt was seriously threatened by invaders, it moved its capitol from Heliopolis to Memphis to Saqqara, then back again.

The Nile floods at the driest time of the year, unlike the Tigris and Euphrates Rivers that flood when the delta is already soaked by winter rains. Flooding, the Nile feeds the thirsty earth and lays fertile, rich soil over the valley. Drop a seed and grow a tree: effortlessly harvest food from the rich ground. The Nile is everything to its people–a highway of commerce, a farmer's salvation, village food basket, and nation's defense.

We spent days wandering through the temples of Hathor at Dendera, and of Hashepsowe at Deir-el-Bahri. The Colossi of Memnon staggered us. "No wonder Asmy would like to have been a pharaoh in his past," mused Yochanan, as we stood before the thirty-six-foot-high statues of Amenhotep III and Queen Tiye.

"This figure of a child at their feet is their son, Akhenaten, who lived about the time of Moses," I explained.

"Who said?" he asked.

"Amen," I replied.

"How does he know?"

"I am not sure, Yochanan, but he seems to know a lot of things, as you will see."

Yochanan seemed more concerned about Moses being a part of Egyptian royalty than anything else. Our ancient writings described Moses as a child of Jewish parents, but Amen indicated otherwise. I wondered if I should tell Yochanan.

"Moses was Egyptian," I carefully remarked.

"What?" screamed Yochanan.

I jumped back at his alarm. I thought I had surely misspoken that time and Yochanan would set sail for Palestine immediately from that very spot.

"The name, Yochanan, the name is thought to be Egyptian," I soothed. "Do not get so excited. You do not have to agree with everything said in Egypt, or anything. They have a lot of stories. Some are designed only to make one think."

But Yochanan was not fooled. "Do you think Moses was an Egyptian?"

"It is probably a story the Egyptians tell," I countered.

"Probably?" he thundered. "You casually drop a thunderbolt on my head and back off as though it were nothing?"

"Well," I searched wildly for an acceptable explanation, "Amen wants us to use our heads rather than passively absorb everything like a sponge."

"He does this by twisting our most sacred beliefs?"

"Are they so sacred they cannot withstand challenge?"

He cooled off and thought about it. Finally he laughed. "You are right, Yeshua. You had me going there for a moment. What do I care if these Egyptians want to claim our lawgiver as one of their own?"

Relief knows no limits such as I felt at Yochanan's decision to ignore the incident and go along with the teachings of the ancients. Although I had not actually said Moses was part of the royal family of Amenhotep, Yochanan had "heard" me suggest it. He knew I was considering the possibility. He had functioned with my thoughts rather than my actual words. I realized I would have to watch out. Yochanan's mind was open and he would notice every fleeting idea of mine, including those strange to his own thoughts.

Although many of the monuments in the Valley of the Kings were no longer intact, they still embodied the grandeur built into them by Egypt's only female pharaoh, Hashepsowe. Senmut, the queen's chief minister, was an artist who knew how to juxtapose the creations of man against those of God, in this case, the magnificent cliffs, fashioned by time and the river. Yochanan and I walked up the sweeping ramps, marveling at the symmetrical colonnades that seemed part of the rugged cliffs rising above. The ochre color of the cliffs seemed as if painted by an ancient painter who loved golden earth tones.

Anything created by God can never be completely destroyed by man—to realize this is the beginning of the miracle of wisdom. We saw this in the sandstones of Egypt made fifteen hundred years before we were born; I learned more about the Egyptians from those monuments than from anything else. It humbled me to see how God writes truth in the land itself for man to read if he will only clear his mind of preconceived ideas.

"Our holy writings say, 'I shall call my son out of Egypt,'" I remarked to Yochanan. "What do you think of that?"

He grinned at me, and I knew a jibe was coming. "Must have been miswritten," he rose to my expectations.

"Ahhh, Yochanan," I urged. "Come on. Let us discuss this ancient land and its possibilities. After all, it was highly developed when the children of Israel were just a gaggle foundering in the desert, a band of homeless wanderers."

"What is your fascination with all of this?" he cried. "Do you believe you were a pharaoh, like Asmy?"

"No, of course not," I assured him without mentioning that I had been privileged to see my past lives in Tibet, "But how can anyone be sure who fails to seek the truth in all possibilities?"

"You think my mind is still closed a little?" he asked.

"You do refuse to entertain the possibility that Moses might have been an Egyptian."

"Don't you believe our holy scriptures?" he asked.

"I believe in YHWH," I said, whispering the sacred letters. "That is all I have to believe."

"Don't you believe our scriptures are the inspired word of God?" he asked in alarm.

"Yochanan, I believe God. Isn't that enough for you?"

"I am sorry," he murmured. "Of course it is enough for me. Who am I to demand anything of you? The Pharisees are the literalists. We must be continually enlightened by God or sink into the ruts they travel, stagnating into a dead religion. I guess I just see you growing far beyond my ability to understand, and it frightens me."

I held him close. "Fear not, for all that YHWH gives me, I will gladly share with you."

He sighed as we pulled apart. "I know I do not understand where you are headed, but I am content to travel with you."

Concluding our exploration of the river and its ancient peoples, we headed for our home away from home, bypassing the Giza pyramids for now. We were too full of wonders to add another. Perfumes wafted across our path as we walked toward Micah's place. The sacred gemmeiz trees lined the path in complement with the prolific palms. How abundant life is along the river and its many fingers when just a few yards away nothing grows for lack of water.

Like the river, YHWH always gives life to whomever cares to drink. Like the river, YHWH must never be blamed for the tragedies that occur when one refuses to drink and wanders away.

We spent that evening feasting, telling Micah and Asmy about our travels and impressions of the ancient world. Yochanan was content to let me rattle on while he nodded, grunted, and generally resisted the urge to twit me in my enthusiasm as I recounted people long dead and crumbling structures, which is how he viewed it. He was tolerating me more than anything else.

Yochanan whispered to Asmy once, "You were probably Menes, whose ka has returned to see what happened to the united kingdom."

Asmy rose to the challenge and solemnly announced he would study the life of Narmer to see if it could be true. We noticed he refused to use the Greek name for the Egyptian ruler and that he did not know that ka meant soul.

Classes began the next day. I was especially anxious, fearing that it might be the one and only class for Yochanan. As I looked at his wonderfully craggy face, his resolute mouth, and wild hair, I resolved that if Amen could not hold him, there was nothing I could do. Yochanan was as God had created him, and that was perfect. I would accept whatever happened rather than continue to press for something more.

As we entered the room of Hor Akhet, I noted some familiar faces. I was not the only one who had returned from faraway travels. Not one of them had been to the Tibetan lamasery, however, and only one had gone to Persia. It was evident most of them believed everything of importance could be learned here at the School of Mysteries.

While we sat talking, a black man entered the room. "An Ethiopian," I whispered to Yochanan.

"Perhaps a cousin?" opined Yochanan, recalling the Ethiopians considered themselves a lost tribe of Israel, their kings descendants of the union between King Solomon and the Queen of Sheba.

His name was Ugri. His skin glistened like polished ebony and was drawn tightly against the blue white of his eyeballs, which were punctuated by deep black pearls. He was boldly handsome. Surely he was a prince, but he claimed to be a eunuch in search of God.

Suddenly, the room quieted. Amen entered. It was the custom to greet a teacher with the respectful silence of a relaxed body, for it signified the arrival of a friend. Certainly anyone who teaches is a friend. Amen stood, looking at the circle of Initiates, then took a seat amidst us and began.

"For the next few years we will be studying and testing you. Those of you who continue to persevere may someday be added to our list of great Initiates. It is not a particularly long list, but it is a very illustrious one. Those great ones are an ideal for you to measure yourselves against. Everything that you will study, they studied.

What I am about to tell you was told to all of them. It is an open secret available to all who can hear. It is a great mystery–few understand it. Some are so frightened by it, their minds reject it instantly. Some twist it to their own purposes. Others are mystified.

Having whetted our appetites, Amen again surveyed the room. Every eye was on him, every ear intent.

Yochanan was leaning so far forward I thought surely he would fall on his face. The cool stone floor threw up a musty odor that I became aware of as I waited expectantly. The silence grew, enveloping the room.

"You are all gods in the making." Amen's words stunned us.

Everyone gasped. Eyes sprang open. Even I was surprised that the "secret" was one of the ancient Hebrew writings in the Psalms. Yochanan looked at me. He loved the Psalms as much as I and knew them well. Neither of us had ever considered that verse a secret, nor had we given much thought to its meaning. Amen was right: most people skipped over it, including us, even though Hillel had taught it to us as a truth, those glorious days so long ago. I had resolved to teach it to everyone; nevertheless, it was startling to hear it from Amen here in Egypt as a secret.

Amen allowed a little time for contemplation of his open secret. Then he said this method of teaching was the Socratic method, named after one of the Initiates who had given his life for truth. The question-and-answer method of reaching a conclusion seemed reasonable to me.

Amen continued. "You are all gods in the making."

Class was dismissed. We looked at each other in surprise. Was that it? All we knew was that Amen would meet with us again the following morning. Yochanan and I headed for the great library. We ardently searched the manuscripts for information on gods. We planned to be as prepared as possible for tomorrow's discussion. Neither of us wanted to be short on questions or information.

"Consider Apollo," Amen began the next morning. "The Greeks call him a god. Yet once he was an initiate, just as you are. He sat where you now sit. He was one of our finest students as well as the most beautiful. He had a perfect body that matched his brilliant mind. He studied hard and purified himself. He learned to perform great feats of mind and strength far beyond the average man. He even tried to lift his people and teach them to do the things he did. He concentrated on building beautiful bodies rather than a universal consciousness.

"Those who followed soon discovered that if they called Apollo a 'god,' they would have a reliable excuse for failing to do the great feats that Apollo could do. It is a mistake made over and over. The Greeks created families of gods and goddesses while losing sight of what Apollo tried to teach them.

"Apollo established a temple to God at Delphi and placed a female there as priestess to teach that God is no respecter of gender. That message failed. The oracle is a woman, but the priests are men who use her to manipulate the people.

"It is important that you consider the mistakes of Apollo, who above all was well intentioned. We live in a time when people readily make gods out of mortals. There is only one true God. Man can make gods of no one."

Again he closed the class abruptly, and again we were mystified. Yochanan and I walked and talked with the other students about the pros and cons of the godhood of Apollo and how we could became gods, if in fact we were gods in the making. The question was whether Apollo succeeded or failed.

Weeks passed this way. Amen talked about an ancient mythical god, then sent us on our way. We gathered around a certain fountain each day to continue the discussion, arguing, debating, wondering.

The morning that Amen talked about Moses was the day I almost lost Yochanan again. Amen claimed that Moses was an Egyptian prince who led slaves out of Egypt to establish a kingdom of priests. He hinted that Moses might have been a pharaoh whose name and reign had carefully been stricken from all records and monuments by priests of Osiris. Yochanan could not abide such desecration of the ancient writings of the Hebrews. He jumped up in the middle of Amen's lecture and shouted: "That is not true! Moses was Hebrew. Moses was never of the same blood as pagans. Moses was pure and holy and dedicated to YHWH from the moment of his birth."

"What is pure?" Amen quietly asked, not offended with Yochanan's outburst.

We were stunned. Yochanan shook his head to clear his thoughts. "P-pure is free of all contamination," he stuttered.

"Is it one's race that contaminates the soul?" Amen wanted to know.

"Well, no, I guess not, no, no, n-not usually," he stammered.

No longer could I sit idly by and let Yochanan drown in his devotion to his beliefs. Arising, I offered, "God is purity and purifies all things."

"Yes, that is right," agreed Yochanan. "God is pure and holy and the truth."

Amen slowly looked around the room. Then he spoke quietly, "I can see that our two Hebrews are gods in the making. They are the only ones in all the weeks I have stood before you who chose to challenge a word I have said. You have learned your first law.

"Gods in the making are not sponges who accept every word, every act, every event, every teaching as if set in stone. Gods in the making are creators who are constantly standing in the image of the Creator, creating new thoughts, new ideas, new worlds."

From that moment everything changed. The discussions arose quickly, the challenges were mighty, and the learning great. It was an intoxicating time that created razor-sharp minds from previously only bright ones. Clearly, "argument" is a teaching tool designed to reach consensus, not separation.

Yochanan became convinced that Amen's remarks about Moses were for debating purposes only. It was a happy day when I realized that YHWH would keep Yochanan in Egypt as long as it pleased YHWH–not one day less nor one day longer, nor could it be determined by any of us.

"Clearly," I said to Yochanan, "if our God is also our Father in Heaven, then we must be godlings already. How can it not be so? And, if we are godlings, then we have to grow up to be gods. Mature, that is. It just takes many lifetimes of studying, living, practicing to mature into a god. Don't you think so, Yochanan?"

"I will wait for the Promised One who is yet to come to explain it all to me, Yeshua," he responded. "Surely if God created us in his own image, we must be children of God, and children do tend to grow up to be just like their parents, more often than not."

"Truly, it is a mystery," I sighed. I wondered about myself as a godling, a son of YHWH. Have there been others before me who have made it? Narrow is the way and few are there who find it, but I must make it easier, somehow. A world full of gods? Would YHWH be the head god? Or would all gods be equal?

Chapter 26

The School of Mysteries

It seemed every day in Egypt was more beautiful than the last. The sky was often swept clean of clouds and was as starkly blue as the western desert was pale yellow. Sahara, they called this desert. Pour a little water on it, and it blooms. Life is just beneath the surface awaiting the call. According to the records of the lands, long ago the Nile crossed the Sahara and emptied into the Great Western Sea. In those days the Great Sea was dry land, and one could ride a horse straight across the "Sea" from Alexandria to Rome without ever going "overland" through Palestine.

This intrigued me, but it bored Yochanan. "I want to explore the desert, not read about it," he complained. He was a man of action and longed to walk for miles out into the Sahara and chance never finding his way back. He gave feet to the dreams of the Essenes. No wonder they loved him.

At home with Micah things took a different turn. We cleaned the heavy ovens, swept out the synagogue, and sold bread when Micah was away. On the Sabbath, Micah would insist that either Yochanan or I lead the discussion and reading of the Scriptures.

"You should learn something practical while you are in school," he would say, winking at us.

One evening Yochanan told Micah about Amen's story of Moses. It was evident Yochanan expected Micah to reaffirm the truth of the story as told in the ancient writings of the Hebrews. We were unprepared for Micah's discussion. Micah was aware of what Yochanan wanted to hear, and it took him a while to say anything. He sat silently sipping date wine while Yochanan fidgeted. Then he began a most marvelous dissertation:

"We Jews of the Diaspora do not see YHWH exactly like you who live in Palestine. Nor do we see the plan of YHWH like the priests of Jerusalem see it. To us the Temple has been destroyed many times and probably will be again. We will never see this one in any case, nor even the Promised Land. Therefore, the things that matter greatly to Palestinian Jews are not so important to us.

"We do not attach God to a building, even if it is the temple. We do not attach God to a place, even if it is the Promised Land. And we do not attach God to a person, not even to Moses. God is a spirit and as such is everywhere and in everyone. Whether Moses was a Jew, and the son of slaves, or an Egyptian, and the son of kings, is of no importance to us. It is not important who one's parents are. God can raise up descendants of Abraham from the very stones of the Earth and does so in Palestine or Egypt, Persia or Tibet. So what does it matter in the cycle of births who one's father was in one incarnation?

"Moses made a great nation out of ragged slaves. He was a 'prince' to do so, whether in fact he was the son of a slave or a king. Does it matter? Is God diminished because of the one through whom the great plans are worked? There is only one God. Decide everything from that belief.

"I tell you truly, all of this will pass away, but not one word of God will pass away. The important thing for you here and now is to release your mind from its fetters and allow it to build a perfect soul for perfect companionship with your perfect God.

"How can you expect God to be a companion to those with closed minds or those entangled in material concepts? It will never happen.

"Do you think Lamech died in sin because Moses was not yet born? Do not believe it. God has never left the created ones without a messenger to point the way, whether the messenger was named Moses, Buddha, Zoroaster, or Osiris. The way has always been the same. The message never changes, just the messengers.

"Even the priests of Jerusalem could reach out to God and be saved," Amen finished his speech with a smile and a wink at Yochanan.

Yochanan bowed his head and sighed, "You are right, great master. How could I be so blind?"

My heart jumped with joy. Yochanan's mind was opening as surely as night turns into day. He did not say much the rest of the evening, but Micah and I could feel him turning those thoughts over in his mind, lingering over the most startling idea: "God can raise up descendants of Abraham from the very stones of the Earth."

The next morning as Yochanan and I struggled out of our pallets before first light and walked to the river to greet the dawn, Essene fashion, we were silent. We stood there with arms outstretched, waiting to welcome the warm rays of the sun. As the first fingers of light appeared in the eastern sky, we chanted a mantra to the sun, acknowledging how it brought and sustained life to all the Earth, and thanking God for having created it all.

The ritual prepared us for Zar's class; Zar was the teacher of ideals. He was older than most of the priests of Osiris, but unlike the others his head was shaven like the Tibetan lamas. His robe was linen, seamless and unbleached. Bright of eye and firm of step, he could have been fifty, or even eighty years old. We could not tell. Occasionally, his voice cracked from his intensity. A long, jagged scar ran down his face from his eyes across the bridge of his nose and across his right cheek into his square jawline. It could have rendered him grotesque, but it did not. Rather, it gave his features a look of rugged handsomeness.

"Ideals!" Zar said in his opening statement, "These are the basis of all teachings. One must set an ideal, or even a group of ideals, for one's life and constantly measure oneself against them.

"Be not concerned with the ideals of others, for they have nothing to do with you. It is your own ideals against which you will be tested, and found true or lacking."

I glanced at Yochanan. He seemed puzzled, as was I. How often had we been led to believe that there was only one measuring stick and that one was set for us by the high priest, a rabbi, a parent, or someone else. What a revelation to hear that we must set our own ideals, then be measured by the ones we set. I knew I was hearing a truth, for I had a sudden case of chilblains.

It made sense that Yochanan, a boy of the desert, could not be held to the same measure as I, who had just completed world travels and studied in the greatest schools. Who could measure me without knowing all that I had done? Or whom could I measure? Judge not is the same. I had copied it many times at Carmel. Now I finally understood it.

"Be alert," cautioned Zar. "Whatsoever you measure another with, you also shall be measured. Do not think you can set standards for another that you yourself can then avoid.

"Ideals . . . " Zar mused, as though looking far away. "We will teach you a perfect set of ideals from which you may pattern your own. Those who achieve this set of ideals will become fit companions for God and able to fulfill the ancient secret: 'You are gods in the making.' Perfect patterns make perfect persons. Follow your pattern closely. If you set your ideals too low, you cheat yourself."

Zar set forth a set of ideals that seemed to be the synthesis of all teachings of all time. The first one sent us all scrambling for definitions.

The poor in spirits
Will achieve the Kingdom of Heaven.

"Are you bodies? Are you spirits? What are you? Who are you? Think on these things," commanded Zar, dismissing the class.

"What is this?" muttered Yochanan. "Questions are dropped on our heads with no answers, then class is dismissed."

"I think the idea is for us to search out the answers," I suggested.

"We could do that in Palestine," he argued. "We did not have to come to Egypt for questions we could not answer."

"But that is part of it," I insisted. "Zar is saying the answers are within us. We are not asked questions in Palestine. We are told answers and that those are the only ones. Judith was the only one who ever suggested we might already know anything. She was the only one who ever discussed bodies versus spirits."

"She said we are spirits. So do we have any answers for Zar?"

"I confess I don't have it, either, but that is what we are here for, so let us talk about it."

"All right," Yochanan reluctantly agreed. "What does Zar mean by poor, spirits, and getting poor in spirits? You tell me."

"Wellllll . . ." I drew it out as long as I could before I took a wild guess. "Look at you. You are single-spirited. You look only to God for guidance. You deny there are any other spirits around."

"That is right. There are no other spirits except the spirit of YHWH," Yochanan declared, hotly.

"If we each are a spirit, then there must be others around, other spirits, don't you think?"

Yochanan thought that one over. "I guess the spirits of my mother and father could be about, but they are good spirits. And your father, Yosef, his spirit could be about."

"True."

"There must be other spirits, but I never think about them nor contact them for guidance. Only YHWH."

"Perhaps that is being poor in spirits," I offered.

"Yes," he agreed, "We don't go about seeking information from a group of spirits, some of which may be even more misinformed than, well, than say some priests in Jerusalem or even this sect."

I now understand "Poor in spirits" means one does not seek nor enlist the help of spirits from the Other Side. One focuses on the spiritual nature of God, the Presence. We all had a problem dealing with the unseen, as do most people. We argue furiously to maintain what we know, when instead we could open our eyes to what we do not know, cannot see, and thus fear may be false. I tried to help Yochanan get past this tightness in his belief system, which also helped my own..

We laughed. Yochanan never let it rest about the priests in Jerusalem. He lumped them all together as the blind leading the blind. Meanwhile, we thought we had come up with an explanation that anyone could grasp.

The next day was surprising. Arguments erupted among the Initiates. Many claimed we were only bodies, that there are no spirits of any kind. Others claimed the spirits of those who had gone ahead of us in death are much wiser than we are and we should listen to them. Some equated "poor spirits" with poverty of material circumstances.

Both Yochanan and I were amazed at how differently each one had heard Zar's single statement. We were amazed also with how each student filtered that statement through his experiences, arriving at explanations far from the meaning of Zar's statement, in our estimation.

"If I follow a life of complete poverty, I will inherit the kingdom of God," one claimed, "and so become a god."

"If I forsake all riches and become poor, then I will get rich again," another said, "then I shall be like a god."

Few heard the "s" at the end of "spirit" and even fewer thought about it. Zar seemed to enjoy the debating. Then one morning he warned us: "Once you find the solution to a mystery, the urge will be to share it. However, you must be very careful about that."

"Why so, Great Master?" asked Yochanan, who always questioned now.

"Who will believe you? People will think you mad and be afraid. A people full of fear seek to kill, first thing."

"I am willing to die for what I believe," declared Yochanan.

"But are you willing to die just to share what you believe with dogs?"

He thought about that for a while. I gave a lot of thought to that one, too.

"Will you cast your pearls before swine?" continued Zar.

Yochanan and I walked about the delta, considering the teachings of Zar. His admonition had stumped us. "Who would have thought I would learn new things in this alien land?" questioned Yochanan. "I had to mature before I could even walk into one of their temples, or see their gods, or understand their search as one for the one true God, rather than seeing it as a blasphemy against my view of God. I was selfish, was I not, Yeshua?"

"A closed mind is not ready to drink from deep fountains," I said. "We all wake up at different times of the day. Do not be too hard on yourself. You are awake now."

"But I have been as bad as those whom I criticized," he persisted.

"We can see only the faults we possess," I hastened to point out.

"Well, I suppose a faultless person would see absolutely no faults in anyone else?"

"Perhaps," I agreed. "How can we see faults we know nothing about? On the other hand, if someone points out the faults of another, then, perhaps, we can see that. It requires clear eyes, I am sure. It is a knotty problem."

I wanted to get Yochanan's mind off castigating himself lest he fall into a depression and more negativity, so I urged a swim in the Nile. "To cool our overworked brains."

Instantly we were in the water splashing around, floating, and talking. "Our own scriptures warn us to beware of fortune tellers, soothsayers, and spirit mediums. Is that what Zar is talking about?" asked Yochanan.

"Surely, it must be," I agreed. "Most of these truths are probably found in our own writings. After all, they came from Egypt."
"What?" he exclaimed. "Came from Egypt? Came from Egypt?" he bellowed. "You are in love with Egypt. How can you say such a thing?"

"Did not we just agree that Zar's teachings are scattered throughout our scriptures?"

"Yes, but that does not–"

"And did not Moses come out of Egypt?"

"Yes," he agreed.

"Was not Moses an initiate here, like us?"

"But," he persisted.

"Are not our writings called the books of Moses?"

"Moses got his teachings from YHWH," he protested.

"All things come from God." I replied.

"But," struggled Yochanan, "our scriptures say they were handed down from God to Moses on tablets of stone on top of a mountain in the desert of Sinai."

"That is what they say," I agreed.

"Don't you believe it?" he whispered.

"Do you believe Moses studied in this school and learned nothing?"

"Are you saying Egypt is the cradle of Judaism?"

"Our people were here for four hundred years. They were not a nation before that period. It is here they were tempered by trials of fire."

After that, Zar's teachings seemed to take on new life for Yochanan, as well as the lessons of all our other teachers. These teachings inspired me to ask more questions.

"Who taught these truths to the Egyptians?" I asked one morning. "Are we gaining or losing as we go? Were men once wiser than now?"

"The mysteries exist to purify your souls," declared Amen. "So that you may see God for yourselves."

"The answers to all questions are within you," declared Zar.

The weeks that followed were full of all the teachings from all over the world. The passage to the Great Hall of Records was trod by all of us who wished to know about the past. There I learned of a mysterious race of superbeings who could fly through the air in machines, warm everything with crystals, and power all things from a single source.

These beings were from the land known as Atlantis. They were powerful beings who struggled with darkness. The struggle became so intense their land sank beneath the sea. Some fled here to Egypt; others traveled to a far-distant land over the Great Western Sea. Here, they built the Great Pyramid. Their minds were so powerful their thoughts alone lifted great blocks of stone to great heights, setting each perfectly against another to complete the pyramid.

The class on human emotions was taught by a gentle soul named Zebediah. He was so kind-hearted that he allowed mosquitoes to feed on him lest he accidentally kill one by slapping at it. His daily walk with God was an inspiration. He was the epitome of his own teachings. He was the only teacher I dared ask why Egyptians continued to worship many gods when the priests knew there was only one.

"The great masses of people are simple beings," he explained. "Their lives are mostly a bare existence. It would only confuse them to expect them to worship a god they could not see, nor touch, nor hold. We give them a god for everything and statues so they will know what it looks like and so they can see what they are worshipping. We think our one God wants it that way."

His broad smile was so kind that I was charmed. Still, I pursued the question. "But there are not many gods. There is only one. The statues are not how God looks. If God is spirit and truth, those teachings are neither the truth nor spiritual."

I caught my breath at such forwardness with my teacher. He patted me on the head and said, "Good, Yeshua. You are so serious all the time and so very young, much like your own Moses when he was here. Take it from me, our way is more practical. Take the many gods away from the people and you will learn what real trouble is. Look at what happened to Akhenaten. He tore Egypt apart, lost his throne, and was cast out. No, no, dear young man, our way is best. The secrets are not for the masses of people. Look at the Hebrews. They are slaves in their own land."

Ordinarily Zebediah never presumed to be an authority on his subject. He often insisted he could be wrong. But on this point he was adamant. So I turned away from him on that subject, quite forgetting there must be a reason for so gentle a teacher to become so defiant so suddenly.

Orion, who taught us astrology, talked about the stars as though he had been to each one and knew intimately everything about them. He talked about the influence of the stars on one's destiny as though there were no question about it at all. How could I question it with a star playing such a part in my own life?

Orion had devices to measure the light of the stars, to figure the extent of cycles, and to chart each one's life course. He claimed each life was planned like the path of the stars. He taught the zodiac and its influence on kingdoms and men and how it helped one to see into the future. "Know your astrological chart and you will know your life, your destiny," he said.

Orion was tall and thin and anything but gentle. His shaggy eyebrows overhung his squinting eyes (from gazing at the stars too long, Yochanan claimed). He had the stance of a man of authority. He paced as he spoke and carried a long pointer that he used to locate distant stars on his sky maps, and to rap smartly on the table to get our attention when it wandered. "You are here to learn, not dream." The second rap was on the student's head.

"You are not fully grown until you are fifty," he declared.

The Hebrews have that same ideal, and I could see from whence it came.

"I was born out of time," Yochanan snorted, "and I care not what the stars have to say."

Even so, we spent a lot of time looking through the great glass at the stars. Yochanan had studied the stars in the desert of Judea all his life, and knew things about them that neither Orion nor I knew.

"I have charted my course. I know my path. I do not need an old one like Orion telling me about the path I must trod. He is only guessing, anyhow. My guess is as good as his," argued Yochanan, when we were alone.

The months flew by; Yochanan stayed at the school for two years. One day a message came from Qumran reporting trouble. "I must go," he said. And somehow, I knew he must.

As we walked out into the Sahara for the last time, we clung to each other. Standing together near the pyramids, we talked of many things. Our parting was one of happiness and sadness.

The two years we had dwelled together as brothers had been close and satisfying. Yochanan's mind was open now, his mission in his grasp. He had taken studies apart from mine in fields that interested him most. We were separate, yet one in spirit. My mission was separate, yet intertwined with his, much like two strands, when tied together, make a rope five times stronger than a single strand.

"You are a gifted rabbi," he said, "Everything becomes clear when you speak. I have learned far more from you than I have from Zebediah, Zar, and even Amen, from whom I have learned much."

I wallowed in the kindness of Yochanan's words. We both wanted to achieve the full power of our soul, and we bolstered each other in that desire. "I look forward to returning to the land of our fathers," I replied, "and basking in the warmth of your great soul."

"I will wait for you in the desert between Bethany and Qumran near the Sea of Salt," he said. "Look for me there."

"Yes, yes, I will," I promised.

"I must make straight the path of the Mashiyah so he can come," declared Yochanan. "My mission is clear."

"That is a wonderful mission," I breathed. "You are blessed indeed. With you making a way, how could he not come?"

"He will come," said Yochanan. "The Essenes have been preparing the way for nearly two hundred years. The time is ripe. I saw it in the stars."

I gasped, "You did not tell me you looked to the stars for messages."

"No, I did not. I wanted to surprise you that I could get messages from the stars. I get better ones than old Orion," he whispered.

I had never heard Yochanan boast about himself. It sounded odd. From him I knew it was more a display of devotion to his calling than an exhibition of power.

"When is he coming?"

"Soon, very soon. Three or four years at the most."

"How will you know it is he?"

"I had a vision. I will see the spirit of YHWH pouring out of the heavens down upon him," Yochanan described.

"Where will he come?"

"Where I will be baptizing."

"You are going to be baptizing?" I asked in astonishment.

"Yes, at the River Jordan. I will be giving the Essene baptism to any and all who come to the river and want to help make way for the Mashiyah. I will proclaim the Day of the Lord is near."

I was awed. "Will the Essenes get upset?"

"Why should they? They are the 'expectant ones' who have prepared the way. They will understand the time is soon. They will be the first disciples of the Mashiyah. After spending all these years making a way for him to come why should they rebuff the final act of passage?"

"Surely you are right," I exclaimed. "Those old ancients love you so. They will believe and follow you. This is so exciting. The Mashiyah is coming soon! I can hardly wait."

Yochanan laughed at my excitement, but he was excited, too. "You may even be the one to escort him to the river, Yeshua," he declared.

"Oh, how I hope so," I said in eager anticipation.

Yochanan left early the next morning. It was a quiet parting, not as painful as one might think, for we had set a time three years hence and a place to meet again.

I did not realize it was a test for me. Leaving my grieving family in Nazareth had been a test. We never know when we are being tested until after it is all over. We must make our choices, then discover whether we passed or failed, sometimes years later. My desire to go with Yochanan to Palestine and be handy in case God needed me to help was strong. There were good reasons for going. No one was urging me to stay in Egypt. Yet, when I told Zar how much I had wanted to go with Yochanan, he laughed and said he was glad I passed the test of selfish desire one more time.

Recalling how Rabat had failed his test of grief, I shuddered. How could anyone pass that test? Yet, sooner or later, one must pass to be worthy of companionship with God. Selfishness in any form is a canker on the Godhead, and not permitted anyone on this path of "gods in the making."

How fortunate we have many lifetimes to correct our errors of the heart. What a loving God we have. My desire to become one with God increased over the following years. The passions of my youth fell away, and I prayed daily to know the will of YHWH for my life. Often I fasted. Often I went into the desert or climbed atop the

Great Pyramid to attune my spirit with that of God. The Infinite Will and my will slowly became one as I became aware of my mission: there must be no mysteries between God and man.

Chapter 27

The Final Rite of Passage

My journal had finally brought me to the present. I no longer cared who read my writings or what they might think about them. I was tired. I looked around the small cell that had been my home the past year, and noted the row of urns filled with scrolls bearing my words. I was glad they would be stored in a vault somewhere within the deepest recesses of the Hall of Records, never again to be seen by human eyes. I have done my best, as God knows. It is all that is required of me.

I stood for a moment to stretch my legs and arms. As I walked out of the cell for the last time, I gloried in the warm Egyptian sunshine and desert air. I wanted to fall down on my knees and thank my Lord, God of the Universe, that I was finished. Finished? That is a great word. I trembled at what the high priest of Osiris would think when he read my words. What will be will be, and I am too weary to care.

"I have completed my task of writing," I told my faithful servant who had stood by my door all this time. "I am through. My journal is ready for the high priest."

My silent servant immediately went into the cell to collect the urns and take them to the high priest of Osiris. He called on others to help him, for there were many. But he kept a watchful eye on them, lest one be left behind or get lost on the path to the high priest's lodging. He looked proud, as he carried them to the chamber of the priest, where they were to be read then sealed forever. I had already heard that most, if not all, of my teachers had already declared they knew me well and had no need to read anything I might write. They had whispered, one by one, that they approved of me, knew my travels and training, and were without exception ready to bestow upon me the mantle of graduation without any further examination. I was awed by such devotion. Perception, if nothing else, had been the great mark of all my teachers. Nevertheless, I was humbled. Examination is a time when good students, even sometimes the best, can fail.

"The high priest is old and soon to meet the dead," whispered one teacher. "He will look at your writings of these many months, perhaps look at only the first page, determine it will be too much for him to read it all, and put them away. We have given him our stamp of approval; he will not weary himself for nothing, although his approval is required as the final one. Already he is giving away his duties to others. Do not fear. Your secrets are safe."

That gave me a start. Had they already read of my discussions with Hillel? With Judith? Did they already know I had chosen my mission years ago? Did they approve? Or what? I relaxed. It is forbidden for anyone to read my journal before the high priest does. He has the right to decide if anyone else could even see them, much less read them. I almost hoped they were right, and he would not read my messy scrawls.

That idea made me laugh. I could see the face of the high priest as my servant and his helpers brought in the urns full of scrolls scribbled in hen scratchings. I could hear him saying, "Set them over in the corner. It will take me forever to read all of that. I shall let them rest there for a bit. Put my stamp on them, seal them, and retire them into oblivion."

Surely it happened, for my servant let it slip later that I could have left every scroll blank for all the high priest would ever know. They had been accepted, stamped, sealed and already were in the vault of the Hall of Records. The teachers had laughed and clapped at predicting so accurately the way of their high priest. Even I was happy about it. I had passed. I had passed! And now I could take the final rite of passage.

The silent priest, who had stood by my door all these months, kept smiling at me, so I believed he was happy with my journal being accepted. But, no, there was more. As I tuned in to his mind, I perceived he had read some of my writings and agreed with my decision. The School of Mysteries was about to be mysterious no more. What had been held in deep secrecy for thousands of years was about to become common knowledge. Even the slaves would know all the mysteries. The silent priest had rubbed the urns as if they were magic balls, such was his eager anticipation.

I might have known. This silent priest was my shadow for months. Of course he could not resist a peek while I slept or took nourishment. Had he passed the word along? How many of my teachers agreed with me? I backed off on finding out this information. I did not want to know, even as heartwarming as it was to learn that at least one old priest agreed, and a priest of Osiris at that.

I saw fear clutch at the soul of the priest. He must think that I would be killed on the spot if the high priest had chosen to read my journal. But then a laugh assured me that it was merely another passing idea, fleeing as quickly as it came.

"Why are you laughing?" I asked him. "Did you read my awful scrawls?"

It was a hard question, I knew. He would not want to lie to me, but it was forbidden for him to do such a thing, so I waited for his reply with anticipation.

"I am laughing at our high priest," he finally said. "He is such a funny old man, clad in his purple robes, pretending to be on top of things, yet fading fast. I giggled at his pretense and he called me 'old in the mind.' I could not help but ask under my breath, 'Which of us is senile?'" The normally silent one laughed and laughed, and I had to laugh with him, for he certainly got out of that one. I did not press it, either.

He left me and I clearly heard him breathe a sigh of relief. He was one of only two sons of Israel at the school. He was there as a scholar in our beliefs, history, and people. Although few Jews ever found their way to the school, it had been decided long ago that some or even one might come so the school leaders must already know how to deal with such a one.

We agreed that the children of Israel were in deep trouble with YHWH. Hiding away the great truths from any of his people was surely a sin. Separation from God is a death-dealing sin. Who truly can live without the great All? Yet, my people of Israel have fallen far and live in darkness. "Hear ye, O Israel, the Lord God is one." Such a powerful cry, but it is a mystery to men. It must not remain so. I knew my faithful servant agreed. How could he not? Truly he loved God, as well as me.

So I presented myself to the master examiner for the final examination. I realized I had been tested all along in ways I could never be sure of. Some of it had been almost deadly. I must have passed. I was here. Alive. Ready to take the final examination. Hoping I would pass, but not knowing.

I felt cleansed from pouring out my life on scrolls of papyrus. Cleansed more than I ever did from the scrubbings in India, the bracing cold from the Tibetan snows, or from the trials of traveling alone. I became conscious of a well of spiritual ideas slowly filling in the vacant spaces in my soul. Could I have achieved these feelings with simple prayer and meditation and fasting?

"Ah, Jeshua, you are ready to begin your final days here," declared the master examiner.

"Yes, Master, I am," I gladly responded, drawing my cloak around me and doing my best to look taller.

"Good. That is good. Everything is good. I am happy to inform you that your teachers have unanimously exempted you from any further examination and pass you to graduation. The high priest concurs."

Whereas I had heard this occasionally happens, I had attributed it more to wishful thinking on the part of an initiate. Or to rumor, designed to encourage one to keep going, but never really happening. I was jolted. Zebediah had said it was rare and probably occurred only to one who had traveled long and far to dangerous places and survived under the most harrowing circumstances.

The master examiner continued: "You have performed well. You have emptied yourself of all selfish things, desires, wishes, thoughts, everything. You shall now go into solitude once more and determine whether to accept this exemption, or not. It is yours to decide whether to take the final rite of passage or not."

"I already know," I whispered. "I do. I truly do. It is what I have spent years preparing myself to do. I need no more time to decide."

But he continued as though he heard me not. "You can take several weeks to make this important decision. This is the most dangerous rite of all. You can graduate as a master without it."

"Can I be Christed without it?" I pursued.

"Probably not. But that is unimportant. Christing has not happened in at least five hundred years, if ever. Most of us believe it has never happened. Or, if it has, it has not been for thousands of years. Perhaps even before the time of this great pyramid. We do not know."

Clearly he wanted to dissuade me from the rite. Just as clearly, I would not be dissuaded. I had looked forward to it with anticipation. I felt I had been born for it, although I could not be sure, considering all the mysteries and rituals I had encountered. I must know the difference between religion and spirituality. I believed I already knew. But this last rite could surely show me. I must do it.

"I have made the decision already," I urged. "Please do not keep this rite from me. I am ready. I want it. I must do it. I will not fail."

The master examiner gasped aloud. "Such arrogance, Jeshua. Know you not that such assertion of ego goes before a master fails? Perhaps I should fail you now on that alone?"

"No, no," I cried out with fear that he might be able to fail me without so much as my trying. "I meant no such display. I am washed clean. I have spent my life preparing. I only meant that I do not plan to fail the rite. But, surely if I do, I want everyone to know I begged for it without any qualms or blame on anyone else at all."

He smiled sadly. He knew he did not have the right to refuse me, and he knew that I knew it, too. He gave up with "Such a soul just might pass." Maybe. Might. Perhaps. I saw those emotions sweep across his face and knew I was accepted for the greatest rite of all.

"As you wish, my son," replied the master examiner. "You have passed each and every examination ever given you. Your life has been perfected. You fully understand obedience. The final choice is yours alone and you have made it. You have the best chance of anyone to survive it since Moses over fifteen hundred years ago. We think he may have been so tested, but we are not sure. He was our prince and became the Lawgiver for your people by choice. All things must be done by choice to merit passage."

"Thank you," I replied. "Thank you." I wanted to thank him over and over, but I feared he might change his mind. Although he had relented, things have a way of changing in the blink of an eye.

"Present yourself to the priest of passage two weeks from now," he said walking away. He seemed sorrowing, his shoulders hunched, his feet dragging.

I called one more "thank you" after him and went my way. It was only a little while until everyone was in an uproar. It was alarming to me to hear people say the final rite of passage was dangerous unto death, urging me not to go through it. My teachers urged me to graduate without it. I wondered if these dire warnings might be tests themselves. I reasoned that Micah would know, and sought him out. As I proceeded wearily to the Synagogue of Refuge, I hoped that nourishment of a more material kind would be waiting. And it was.

Micah was waiting when I arrived. I supposed he had already heard the news. Word travels fast in small villages and he threw himself into my arms as I greeted him at the door of the synagogue. He managed a wan smile.

"I am so proud of you, Yeshua," whispered the little rabbi.

"The weariness of ages has settled in my bones. Why am I so tired?" I asked my dearest rabbi.

"It is normal," soothed Micah. "You have written and written for over a year, believing that what you wrote might undo you in the eyes of your teachers, or at least the high priest. Yet you insisted on writing the truth, for there is no untruth in you."

"You know that?" I asked, a little surprised.

"Anyone who knows you at all knows that much about you," smiled Micah. "You have no guile whatsoever."

"I guess not," I responded looking down at my hands and spreading my long fingers widely. These could only write the truth, regardless of what it was. I could not so much as force myself even to color it a little to save my scrawny neck, much less my life. "If I cannot live with the truth, at least I know I cannot live without it."

"You probably were not even tempted," Micah mumbled.

"In the beginning I was. The thought passed through my mind, but like birds of the air, I could not stop them from flying over my head, but I could prevent them from building a nest in my hair."

He laughed aloud. "Always joking, Yeshua. You are always joking. You will probably laugh on your way to your death, even if it's to hang from a tree."

We both laughed at that. It was true. I had no fear of death. Another journey. Another time, perhaps. But not now.

"One must always count the cost of whatever the choice may be. My task is simple, to tell the plain, unadulterated truth, as I know it to be. I cannot tell someone else's truth. Only mine. I gave some thought to the consequences of total truth, of course, but then I thought of the consequences of lying, harming not only myself, but also others. I could not bring myself to do it, even if it kills me not to do so. I am happy I passed. I admit that I am surprised. I thought my writings would upset the high priest of Osiris, at least, but then I have never met him at all. I do not know him."

"He never read it," declared Micah, "that lazy old fake."

"So I was informed," I said. "But it probably only delays my trial to later on. I believe my decision for my life will cause much consternation in high places."

"For now you have passed. That is what is important. When is the graduation ceremony?" he asked.

"Immediately after the final rite of passage, I am told."

"Yeshua! You are not going to do that," he exclaimed.

"I thought that you already knew it," I said in surprise.

"No, no. I just had heard all about your finishing the journal, how it was accepted, and all of that. I had no idea you decided to go through the final rite. You must not. Nobody survives it. Not even you," he fairly shouted at me.

"I will," I said. "It is mine to do."

"No, no," he urged. "You cannot. It is all myth and rumor. No one has ever passed it. It is used to get rid of egomaniacs, not good men like you. You are the one we have waited for for over a thousand years. You cannot die before you begin. You must not."

"I must." I tried to soothe his fears.

"You can graduate without it," he insisted.

"I cannot be Christed without it," I explained. "Someone must have passed it at least during ancient times, else why is it there?"

"It is a nasty rumor," insisted Micah, "designed by senile men to rid themselves of challenging young Initiates. It was designed to encourage them into death. A sacrifice to gods they no longer believe in."

"Micah," I laughed, "I am surprised at you. Not once have I ever heard you disparage the priests of Osiris, much less the high priest. You are sounding like Yochanan."

Although my friend laughed, too, it had a hollow ring. He was frightened. Anguish was written all over his face. He twisted the rope around his waist, nervously. "I should have known," he half said to himself. "What can I do to dissuade you?"

"Nothing. Nothing at all," I said.

I hugged the little round man and begged for time to sleep. Off I went to my room and sank immediately into a deep sleep for the first time in over a year. Micah paced the floor in deep worry and concentration the rest of the day and far into the night. It was nearly dawn before he went to bed realizing he could do nothing to dissuade me. It was out of his hands. I had established earlier that I was a man who made my own decisions. Not that I never asked for advice, but always in the final throes of decision making, I alone made them. Micah knew that YHWH was in charge of my life. It was Micah's test, as all men are tested, to allow me this life-threatening decision, even though it was breaking his dear old heart.

The next two weeks were pleasantly spent. No more discussions with Micah or anyone else on the impending rite of passage. I did not have to fret or worry or argue or even wrestle with making a decision. Mine was made.

Occasionally I would catch Micah staring at me lovingly and sadly. When I turned to catch his eyes, he would turn away quickly. As the real world came back into focus for me, I realized it had been deep fatigue that had sent me to Micah in the first place for consultation on my path. He had been a mentor to me since I was a babe. In my weariness I sought him out, worried him, not even asking him whether he approved or not. He could not give any more than he already had given.

Henceforth, I would never mention to anyone what was truly between God and me. I had no right to put such a burden on anyone, least of all a friend or relative or anyone else at all. Only I can know God's will for my life. I am never alone, for God is with me. Only YHWH, my most holy Father in Heaven. The great All of the Universe.

Yet, when I presented myself to the priest of passage, the elderly priest whispered in my ear, "My son, you do not have to do this final initiation. You have been exempted. You are free of it."

"Yes, I know," I replied. "But I would never be free if I did not."

It was as if he did not hear me. He kept pleading, "Turn back now, for I have never known of anyone to come back alive from this final ritual. It is a test, never to be taken seriously, you see. It is only for the uninitiated. It is for those who believe they cannot fail because they live a charmed life, rather than a pure one. Draw back," he urged.

"There must have been some who came back."

"There are records that claim so, but let me tell you, I do not believe it. And neither does the high priest. Nor anyone else I have ever known. Your teachers and the high priest have asked me to dissuade you of this terrible thing you want to do. I am to tell you that you passed this test, also. It is not meant to be taken actually, but only as a means to discover if you are willing. That is all," he said, with tears streaming down his face.

I was never so deeply moved as this. But still, I recall the Elder of Carmel telling me that I must meet this challenge and overcome it. I had no choice.

"Why are you telling me this? Do you really want me to turn back?" I questioned him closely.

"I have grown to love you above all who have ever passed this way, Jeshua. We all have. You can do many great things without this deadly ritual. You can be a master without it. No one will fault you."

"But to be Christed, I must do this final initiation, is it not so?"

The old priest hung his head. When asked, he was ordered to tell the truth. "It is so."

"Then, that is reason enough. I have been called to do the will of my God, and it is the will of my Father in Heaven that I show myself approved in all things," I explained to him.

"But if you die, it will be all over. All the years your people have waited will be for naught. All your travels and training will end unfinished." He wrung his gnarled hands, shedding tears, and wiping his withered face with the sleeve of his robe.

"If I cannot overcome death, it was all for nothing anyhow," I soothed the old man. "I will not be fit to be Christed."

"Ohhhhhh, ohhhhhh, ohhhhhhh," moaned the priest. "I am undone."

"Have faith in me, good father," I urged. "I shall overcome death. My time is not yet to die. I would know it if it were so, would I not?"

He stared at me, a mix of confusion and despair. He had no idea what I was saying. It was all beyond him and he confessed he no longer knew his right hand from his left.

We walked slowly to the entrance of the Great Pyramid. I stopped at the entryway and removed my outer robe. Standing only in my light cotton shift, I also removed my sandals. It felt good with the day growing hotter as the chill of early morning melted away. The cool red granite of the entryway felt good to my feet, sandy and hot from the walk.

I handed my robe to the ancient one, speaking words of comfort, "This is truly the beginning, not the end. Believe in me."

As I disappeared into the passageway, the old priest raised his hand in farewell. It was clear he never expected to see me alive again. Reluctantly, he turned away to put my clothes in other hands.

As I entered deeper into the Great Pyramid, I remembered to breathe deeply and exhale from my mouth. I loved the openness of the mountains, the desert, and the sea so much, that the very thought of this tunnel gave me a feeling of tightness I could not fathom.

I had to stoop after a while to progress and discovered that I had to remain stooped in order to move forward at all. Accustomed to standing tall, I already had found a trial in the tunnel, much like a difficult birth. As I moved along, it seemed to me I was having to stoop even more to keep from bumping my head. I felt my way along carefully lest I suddenly knock myself out. The light from the entry was soon completely gone and the darkness enveloped me.

It was not the darkness I minded so much. Even if the moon were shining and a billion stars lit my way under the vastness of blue black skies, this closeness was nonetheless chill and forbidding. I might have listened more closely to my masters, especially Micah. I was tempted to turn back. I argued with myself that I could teach and heal and raise others from the dead. I did not need this experience to be effective, or did I?

A voice within me seemed to say, "My people Israel need it."

I had the culmination of centuries of knowledge in my grasp. No one could take it from me, but there were wise men all over the world. I knew, for I had studied with some of them. I had been in every center and studied every master's teaching. I had been tested and found true at every level. No one would fault me. I crouched lower and moved onward. I would fault myself. I had to overcome death. I could not refuse so close to my goal just because of a little tightness in my throat and an empty feeling in my belly. The warnings were taking their toll on me.

The idea that all before me had died suddenly rose in my mind. Did they lose their way and die of starvation? No one had said. Were they killed by some unknown beast crouching just ahead in the darkness waiting to devour some silly initiate who thought he could do what nobody else had ever done? I lost the last bit of my ego right then and there, and most of my breakfast. You are so sensitive, Yochanan had always said to me.

This was crazy. I could easily scare myself to death. I sat down and began to meditate, calming my whirling mind, relaxing my being, and chanting a prayer to God. In a few moments I saw the entire structure of the Great Pyramid: from the well shafts to the Pale pit, from the Grand Gallery to the Queen's chamber. I knew where I was and how to get where I was going. Oh happy day when I learned this! I arose and climbed quickly to the center of the Great Pyramid. My head was clear and my resolve firm once more.

There was a torch shining brightly just above a sarcophagus of pure red granite in the great room. The chamber was lined with giant blocks of polished stone, including the ceiling. In the corner of the chamber an open coffin stood: an invitation? Studying the room, I realized what I was supposed to do. This was it. This was where an Initiate shook hands with death, never to live again or to return to life victorious.

Without hesitation I climbed into the coffin, lay down on its icy bottom, and closed the lid. Cold took on a new meaning. Cold colder than the snows of Tibet. I closed my eyes and slowly sank into oblivion, willing myself to rendezvous with death, which would come as soon as I used up all the air in the granite box.

I felt myself leaving the room, although I could see my body in the sarcophagus, very still as in death. I was floating free and could see eternity. I felt as though I were thousands of miles above the Earth. I saw it as a round ball, hanging in space, with a thin blue envelope of light around it. A great light loomed ahead of me and I felt the Great Presence that had always seemed to be with me stronger than ever before. It was the Divine Essence men call God, YHWH, Buddha, Mahatma, Ahura Mazda, the All. The unknown, yet the knowable.

Like pictures passing before me, I saw all my past lifetimes since my creation. I was Adam, the first man: the soul that was spirit and became flesh. I also saw all the mistakes I had made from the beginning. The pictures horrified me. I killed my own son, over and over and over. From murder to wars, it was always I who killed, for I was first and from me all men and women have come.

Again I realized what a blessing it is not to remember. What soul could continue life with so much blood and blame filling it to the brim? Then, I saw that I had been created before the foundation of the world, as a thought in the mind of God. I saw the greed for power that had thrust me out of my perfection and glory into the body of man with all its limitations. Adam. I had limited myself. It was always me. I chose the material over the divine. And I persuaded all others to follow me.

But that was not all. Following my many lifetimes, I began to see that I seemed to be improving and urging others to do so, too. Then I saw myself as Joshua, leading my people into battle for the Promised Land. I could have chosen peace and persuaded the inhabitants to follow the God I had only lately sworn to uphold, but I refused to see them as my own. Children of my children. How could I have been so near to God, and fallen again?

When the people demanded a king, I was there, pleading with God for them to have what they desired. Saul first, then David. Building the Temple with Solomon. Always thinking that what was best for man in man's opinion was also what God wanted. The Temple was glorious. But I failed, for God had said his people were to become a kingdom of priests, bringing the Earth back to the peace and harmony it had in its beginning. Created out of chaos, it had been a picture of peace. I had failed to see. I had eyes, but chose not to see. Ears, but failed to listen.

Then everything faded and I saw Mina, the beautiful Egyptian orphan I had sent to Bethany years before. She was a young girl, living in Magdala and had taken the name of Mary. She would later become my first disciple, teaching women who would follow me. I saw all those who would follow me from the very first and those who would come later. I saw that it would take three hundred years for my teachings to spread and grow into a religion separate from what is now my own. How could that be? It is not what I came to do. Separation is not my mission. Then I saw the cross. Hanging on the tree only a few years hence. My followers blaming my people. My people claiming I am a false prophet. Even my disciples abandoning me, leaving only women standing silent vigil at the foot of the cross, my mother and Mary Magdalene.

Then I saw the ultimate. My rejection, not even so much as a lowly messenger from God. My kingdom that was to be spiritual becoming a kingdom of men. My teachings twisted from those simple ones into kingly ones and myself crowned king of it all. How can I change that future? It is not God's will, nor even mine. Then I saw my teachers in Egypt mourning my loss. Fighting among themselves. The high priest refusing me. My lonely vigil walking home. The cross becoming a flaming torch. The glory of God settling on my shoulders as Yochanan, who would be known as John the Baptist, baptizing me in the River Jordan. The divine words claiming me as God's son, His messenger, His Christ.

In the far-distant future, I saw man at the crossroads of choice: my teachings will finally overcome the world and there will be thousands of years of peace; or man will choose war, money, and evil. Then this will destroy most of the Earth and most of the inhabitants. Some who love peace will survive and only then will there be thousands of years of peace, for man will no longer have any heart for war. In either case, we shall have peace on earth.

My spirit melded with God's. My consciousness became God's. I could only be Christed by YHWH, the creator of all consciousness. Christ is consciousness.

In the distance like a low, rolling thunder before a sudden rain, I heard the voice of God saying, "Yeshua, you are my beloved son in whom I am well pleased. Be not afraid, for I am with you always. Time is not, for I am all there is. Your glory is yet to come when all the world chooses peace. You are only halfway there."

Angels encircled me with music and singing and balm. The warmth and love that surrounded me wooed me, and again I entered into the Presence. Thoughts flooded me, offering a choice. I could remain in the Presence forever or return to my present life. I had won my crown if I remained with the angels, but agony and a second death would await should I return to my body. This was my choice, except for me there was none. I must save the people I had caused to move away from God. Until I brought each one home to paradise, I could not be at peace with myself.

The moment I held this thought, I could hear the Presence saying, "Thy will is mine." Then, I could feel the cold of the sarcophagus, heard voices, and realized I was back in my body.

"Is he still dead?" asked one leaning over the coffin. Another held a mirror to my nose.

"Yes, quite dead, as he has been the past three days and nights."

"Is it time to remove his body?" asked the other anxiously.

"No. He has another hour to raise himself from death."

"Oh, oh, he will never make it. No one ever has before. If our blessed one cannot, nobody ever can. I knew it. I knew it. Why did he want to do it? Why did we allow it? The rite must be abolished from this day forward. I will tell the high priest and work to remove him if he refuses," wailed the sorrowing priest. I recognized him as my faithful silent one who had stood by my door, always waiting.

"Everyone advised him not to do it. We all urged him. Even the high priest instructed the doorkeeper to inform him it was just a myth used to discourage initiates, written on the very walls and steles to confuse, rather than instruct. But he refused to take our warnings. We must not blame ourselves. Yet you are right. Teaching cannot be misleading. It is a fatal flaw to think false statements can teach anything useful. I will help you with the abolition of this hateful rite."

"Aghhhh. Now we have lost the only truly pure and perfect initiate ever to grace our halls of learning. We did it to ourselves with a big lie. Madness. We have been engaged in madness, not education."

They were holding their lamp over my face, peering so closely at me that I could smell the garlic on their breath. Not wishing to frighten my teachers, I slowly opened my eyes and stared into theirs. At first they jumped back, then one exclaimed, "It is normal. Put the coins back on his eyelids to keep them closed. We left them off too long."

I quickly opened and closed my eyes several times, first one and the other, and coughed.

"He's alive," shouted the silent one. "He lives. Oh, this precious boy of ours still lives." He was weeping and laughing at the same time, jumping with joy, even as was the other priest.

Quickly, they raised me up, rubbing my arms and legs vigorously, then wrapped me in a heavy woolen cloak "lest you catch your death of cold and really die," they explained.

"You are truly the first," they kept saying as they laughed and cried at the same time. "You are the first one in all our recorded histories who survived the final rite of passage. You truly are a god."

Chapter 28

The Declaration

In my twenty-ninth year I came before all my teachers in the Hall of Initiates. It was customary to do so for the presentation of the doctor of laws degree for the master teacher signification. Also, I was to be Christed, a never-before-performed ceremony. Having raised myself from the dead, as required for Christing, I was no longer subject to any man's power over me. I was now free to decide what to do with my life, my body, and my own powers.

As was the usual procedure, I would be presented a special mantle for master teacher. It was so special that I would henceforth be known wherever I went as one who was well traveled, educated in the most advanced schools and in many disciplines. Thus, master teachers wore the special mantle whenever they left their houses. It was the key to open the doors of kings and high priests and all halls of power. I could always count on not only being welcome, but also revered, without question. Thus, it was precious and never bestowed lightly.

The mantle was white with red and blue piping and stripes that gave it the appearance of purple, the color of royalty reserved for persons of royal blood only. The red indicated kingship kin, while the blue indicated spirituality. Woven from the finest linen and without seams, it draped around one's shoulders and hung in folds to the ground. It had the insignia of the School of Mysteries embossed at one end in gold and the sign of deity at the other.

To be Christed was another matter. It was unique–no one knew quite what kind of ceremony to have, nor what would signify the honor. The priests had searched through in the Great Hall of

Records, but nothing had been found about such an event occurring, much less details for a ceremony to honor it. So they decided to create a special ceremony for it.

It was also customary for the graduating Initiate to tell all those gathered what the chosen mission would be and how he would accomplish it. This was always done just prior to mantling and was as exciting to the master teachers as it was to the graduate. The many requests from all over the world that flowed into the school gave many grand and glorious opportunities for its graduates, and mission usually was the fulfillment of such a request. The graduating initiate usually kept his selection a secret so that there was suspense, mystery, and surprise for everyone. This added to the specialness of the ceremony.

Only a few days before, the emperor of Rome had sent a request for the finest Initiate graduating this year. Even the high priest was excited. It was always an honor to have one of their graduates advising a ruler, even more so the emperor. Amen was especially excited. Having been at my birth, he knew a special mission for me had been decreed by the stars before I was born. Perhaps the emperor would turn his empire over to me, he dreamed, as he informed me of the request. Amen continued, "I am so proud of you, Yeshua. When it was reported that you had lifted yourself up from the clutches of death, I took a deep breath and realized that here indeed was the savior of mankind, the long awaited Promised One of the Jews. I don't mind, Yeshua, that you are Jewish. You are truly universal, a sainted soul."

His dreams carried him onward. "Yes, the emperor of Rome would surely turn the reigns of power over to you, once he realizes you can now turn the world into a paradise in which everyone will soon be free of pain and death and other frightful things."

I smiled at his daydream. Now a devoted worshipper of Ra, Amen had no problem with switching gods for songs of praise. He seemed so happy that I did not yet tell him of my decision, of my need to follow my own path laid before me by my Holy Father, YHWH.

The ceremony would include my being carried into the Great Hall in an elegant chair by four of my peers. I had resisted mightily to no avail. "Shush," the priest of ceremonies had insisted, "the ceremony must be different from all others. This is the best we could come up with on short notice."

While I waited in the garden outside the doorway, I heard the others whispering about me. They were in awe that I had taken the final rite, much less passed it. "What manner of man is this?" they asked. It was a question I would hear often.

The gatekeeper called out, "It is time for the ceremonies to begin."

The four chosen ones put me on the chair and lifted it up for the trip into the Great Hall of Initiates. It took only a few minutes. They set the chair down in the midst of the illustrious gathering and backed away, leaving me alone under a great shining light. All I could see was the high priest of Osiris, smiling. He was sitting on a throne and was wrapped in gold cloth. The hall was ablaze with light from a thousand candles and torches of all sizes and shapes. The very walls had been polished to a high luster, reflecting the flickering lights a thousand times over. All were dressed in their finest robes of white with their mantles all aglow allowing me to see flashes of color within the light.

Solemnly, Amen arose. He walked over to me. Standing to my side, he began the presentation. "With this mantle I am about to place upon your head, O Son of the Great God of the Universe, I will ordain you a master teacher with all the rights and privileges of the sacred order of the mysteries. Your name shall be added to our list of greatest Initiates. In recognition of your successful accomplishment of the final rite of passage, you shall be placed at the head of the list, signifying you have been Christed and henceforth shall be called 'the Christ' by all nations."

The priest Orion stood and intoned, "Before this great gathering and before conferring the mantle of masterhood, we beg of you, O Great Teacher, tell us of your chosen mission. What great mission has the Christed One chosen?"

Here it was. The moment when I rose or fell in the eyes of my teachers, the eyes of the high priest, the eyes of the world. I could not help but be apprehensive. I cleared my throat, but my carefully prepared speech failed me. I could only whisper what I must do to save the world, especially my own people, Israel.

Once more clearing my throat, I heard myself croak, "My

chosen mission is to make known to all men all mysteries now separating them from God."

Silence enveloped the gathering. As my words began to sink in and the high priest realized I would not be going to Rome and understood what my words really meant, he fell forward and died instantly. A gasp went up from the room. Amen fainted dead away, and Orion, trembling, shouted, "No! It cannot be so."

Rage consumed the masters. Zar confronted me. "There is a vow of secrecy you cannot violate!" he shouted.

The gentle Zebediah tried to reason with me. "Yeshua, know you not that you will destroy our school, our brotherhood, our very being? You cannot be so cruel to all of us who have loved you so all these years, nurtured you, taught you everything, even to the death. Surely it is not so. You are testing us."

"We will order you put to death," declared the new high priest of Osiris, automatically established with the death of his predecessor.

I remained still while they raged about me.

Amen regained consciousness and struggled to his feet. I saw the anger on every face, twisted in rage. Amen was my sponsor and I knew he felt obligated to stop me at any cost.

He shouted at me: "You cannot do this, Yeshua. We will fight you every step of the way. You will die a horrible death and be completely discredited. Men will despise you and spit upon you, especially your own people, Israel. All of your work and study and travels will be for nothing, for dogs eat their own vomit. Have we taught you nothing?"

I felt the tears running down my face, yet I was not crying. Whereas I had known they would not understand, I had not expected so much hatred from those who only a few hours before had proclaimed such undying love for me. I was sorely grieved. I said nothing; my path was set and I must never look back.

When the new high priest saw that I would not relent, he rose and pointed a long finger at me. "We take from you the mantle we were to so gladly give you this day. You have failed all your examinations we will say to all who ask. We will strike your name forever from all our records. From this day forward, no Jew will ever be admitted to our halls of learning. This is what you have done for your people, Israel.

"Furthermore, your people will become a despised people because of you, because you have taken willingly all we had to give and broken faith with us. The whole world will seek you out, you and your people, Israel, and persecute you all. We shall urge all nations to drive you out of their lands and leave you with nowhere to go and no one to care about you. Israel will curse your very name. We shall see to that, you vile dog."

I was speechless at the intensity of their raging. It was so intense that anything I could have said would have been useless. My silence seemed to increase their hatred so much that I walked out and into the shadows of the Egyptian desert, heading for home. As the moon slowly rose, I pondered what had happened. I should have felt a great loss, but I did not. I was finally going home to my people, home to Yochanan, whom I knew would be waiting with soothing words, eager for us to begin the new day with the good news. No longer would our people look to corrupt priests for intercession with YHWH. No longer would they be forced to haggle for sacrifice. No longer would the Temple be a place filled with robbers. It would become a house of prayer, as intended.

I took heart. I was even happy not to be loaded down with a master's mantle. I was free and young and full of vitality. Although I had left all my belongings, I was filled with glorious fullness. I began to run. Soon, I sought to reach the sea and cover my tracks, for I was sure they could come after me as soon as they realized I had left. One did not have to be a seer to understand the stoning of the prophets before me. The greater the truth, the more eager the killers.

I envisioned the Great Hall of Initiates full of turmoil. I could hear the conflict among them as they planned how to stop me. Although it was the custom for an initiate to argue the right for a chosen mission, I had said nothing, for I knew they would never relent, and neither would I. I had broken that tradition.

A long time before me, Gautama the Buddha had argued furiously for his right to give the secrets to his own countrymen. He had failed and renounced his high birth and princely surroundings to spend the remainder of his life among the people. His refusal to obey them was what had prompted the priests to devise an oath of secrecy and force all Initiates to swear to it.

Moses had already tried giving the great secrets to the people, taking those who would follow him out of Egypt into the desert of

Sinai to teach them. He appointed Levites to be priests until all could be educated in the ways of YHWH. "I shall make you all a kingdom of priests," he told them. But once the Levites realized the power of priesthood, all was lost. They had taken the mysteries and twisted them into unrecognizable rites and defeated the purpose of their journey out of Egypt into a promised land of peace and harmony and prosperity. I took comfort from these men who had tried and failed before me.

The Israelites were not a nation of priests and never had been. They were a nation carried off into other lands in bondage. Even now they were slaves in their own land. A heretic had built their Temple. Their priesthood pandered to Rome. The people wallowed in misery and fear and intrigue.

It dawned on me that I had never taken the oath of secrecy at the school.

Amen had not required it of me because we Essenes refuse to take oaths. Thus I was not in violation of their rules. Still, using this as an excuse would probably cause great suffering to Amen. They would accuse him of allowing Yochanan and I into the school to do this great harm to it. Always blaming others for harm done. Never accepting that the entire system was corrupt from its very inception, built on hiding the truth.

They knew they could not have me killed, for I had overcome death and was not afraid. But they would try to keep me running, using every method they could devise to thwart my message. They would send messengers to Caiaphas, our own high priest, warning him about my coming. Insisting I failed all things. Declaring me unfit to teach dogs. I would be denied teaching in the Temple, but I cared not. The sea would be better for me, anyhow. I love sitting on a hillside breathing fresh air, receiving a fresh message from YHWH, or walking by a lake with good news pouring from my lips.

They had done me a favor. Only now do I see it. How glad I am that I have not been caught up in their trappings. I again tuned in to the arguing I knew was going on among those priests of Egypt.

"What if Jeshua is truly the Mashiyah, the Promised One for whom they waited so long? He passed the rite of passage we all believed was impossible," argued the always-tentative Zebediah. "Will we not be the ones cursed for working against God? Will our own guilt not be multiplied for turning against this one put into our trust for training and safekeeping?"

"We have the benefit of centuries of records," responded the new high priest, anxious to display his power. "Every time a great one goes forth and shows the mysteries to the people, they stop worshipping God. Instead they worship the teacher, and soon they say he is God. Look at Gautama. Look at Moses. Look at Zoroaster, and all the others before them, Apollo, Zeus. A myriad."

"The Jews do not worship Moses," argued Zebediah.

"Give them time," sneered the high priest of Osiris, as he settled back in his chair and drew his purple-lined robes about him.

Zebediah persisted: "Jeshua has overcome death. He is our greatest Initiate. Why are we not willing to give him a chance to save the world his way? Why not trust Jeshua to find a way we can all follow?"

Amen sighed with a deep sorrow. He wanted to heed Zebediah, believe him, and above all believe in Yeshua. Yet, he said Yeshua had failed to indulge in persuasion (at which he is very good), so how can he be trusted? There were balances to be met. One could not fling tradition to the winds and hope everything worked out. Besides, Yeshua had left without even telling his old teacher goodbye. He had walked out without so much as a backward glance, never to return.

Lest tears begin to flow like the river Nile, Amen encouraged righteous rage to pervade his body, shouting so everyone could hear: "We must stop this criminal! That ungrateful Jew has taken our pearls and is about to cast them before swine. Send a messenger at once to Jerusalem. Tell him to say that Yeshua has great powers with which he will poison the people and turn them against the priesthood, even their Sanhedrin. Say he will cause trouble between Israel and Rome. Say he seeks to establish a new kingdom and it will not include the priesthood of Israel. Yes, that is it. Tell the high priest of the Sanhedrin that Yeshua is out to destroy them. They will take care of him for us."

Everyone stared at Amen incredulously. "Did he really say all of that? When did he say that?"

Amen muttered, "He did not have to say that. It is the natural outcome of removing the veil of mysteries. There will be no need for priests once man understands he can approach God directly."

The argument was over. None of the priests were willing to lose their livelihood to this young upstart. They agreed to send a messenger to Jerusalem. The high priest swore them all to work for enmity between Egypt and Israel. "Claim that it is all the fault of Yeshua, who broke faith with us all. We cannot trust this renegade, for he may succeed where all others have failed. He truly has no lust in his soul for power. He does not want to be worshipped. He cares not for worldly things. He is on a mission from God. He truly is divine."

It gave the others pause for thought. How could the high priest believe Yeshua to be divine and seek to destroy him?

In answer to their question he said, simply, "We are not destroying him. The Jews will do it for us. But it will take them at least two thousand years."

One more time Zebediah tried to reason with his fellow priests. "Would it be so bad if the teachings of our own initiate were believed and brought the whole world into peace and prosperity? Would that not be better? Would not Yeshua's love be better for humanity than war and mystery, as we have now?"

Zar pointed out, "True, Yeshua is a gentle man and we all came to love him, but he will not live forever. Men are evil. They will twist his teachings into weapons of war. We all know they will. It will just be a matter of time. They will say that Yeshua was God and therefore no other man can be God, so why even try? They will go on their evil ways."

"I have cast among the stars for answers," declared Orion. "It is already written that the Jews will reject him and continue looking for the Mashiyah to come. Soon most will stop even that. A few will follow him, but even they will be rejected. It will cause a separation between the body of Israel and those who claim Yeshua is Christ. It will take hundreds of years for his teachings to make any difference at all, and–"

"What?" they all exclaimed in unison.

"The Jews will hang him on a cross, their most vicious way of killing thieves. Even their own scriptures say, 'Cursed is the one that is hanged on a tree.'" Orion danced around at his pronouncement. "Let him go. Send our rumors to the high priests in Jerusalem. Nothing is going to change. We are safe."

I had heard enough. I suppose knowing their plans should have given me great courage, but somehow it did not. My master teachers are still men like all other men. They mislead, they hide, they engage in subterfuge and call it expedient. How can I change this, even with my powers? How can I reveal the mysteries, even with God and all his angels? How to show them eternal life is real?

In a death followed by resurrection, I shall be in the best position to teach eternal life as a fact, far better than as a supposition only, one that no man can actually prove. After all, any teacher wants his pupils to be strong in their faith in the teachings, and to have the teachings heard by as many people as possible. So I must try, for my path is now clear. I shall wait for the best possible moment to announce my message, to tell them I have been sent by God to his people, Israel. I shall wait until after my crucifixion to raise myself from the grave, again, and announce to mankind:

"Behold, it is I, the Christ."

About the Author

Dolores Pevehouse is an artist and owner of a co-op art gallery in Monte Rio, California. A lifelong advocate of peace and peace initiatives, she has walked many paths in her life including mother, teacher, philanthropist, and publisher. *I, the Christ* came upon Dolores in a burst of inspiration in the mid-1980s. She had never written a book before. Nonetheless, she trusted her inspiration, wrote the book, and then waited fifteen years for it to be published and find its readers. "I have always walked with God, especially in my darkest moments," she confides, "but I do not even pretend to be a saint or anything near to that."